RUSE

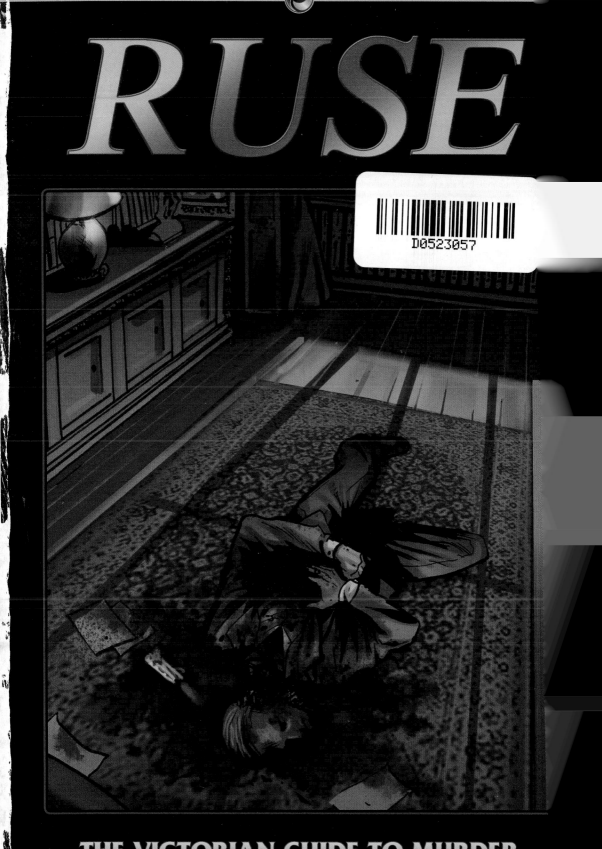

THE VICTORIAN GUIDE TO MURDER

D0523057

RUSE

THE VICTORIAN GUIDE TO MURDER

Well and Wittily Written by
MARK WAID

Artfully Illustrated by
**MIRCO PIERFEDERICI
& MINCK OOSTERVEER** (#3)

Carefully Colored by
**MIRCO PIERFEDERICI
& ANTONIO FABELA** (#3)

Legibly Lettered by
ROB STEEN

Covers Crafted by
**BUTCH GUICE, MIKE PERKINS
& LAURA MARTIN**

Assistant Editor
ELLIE PYLE

Senior Editor
STEPHEN WACKER

Executive Editor
TOM BREVOORT

COLLECTION EDITOR: JENNIFER GRÜNWALD • EDITORIAL ASSISTANTS: JAMES EMMETT & JOE HOCHSTEIN
ASSISTANT EDITORS: ALEX STARBUCK & NELSON RIBEIRO • EDITOR, SPECIAL PROJECTS: MARK D. BEAZLEY
SENIOR EDITOR, SPECIAL PROJECTS: JEFF YOUNGQUIST • SENIOR VICE PRESIDENT OF SALES: DAVID GABRIEL
SENIOR VICE PRESIDENT OF BRAND PLANNING & COMMUNICATIONS: MICHAEL PASCIULLO
COVER DESIGN: PATRICK MCGRATH • SENIOR VICE PRESIDENT OF CREATIVE: TOM MARVELLI

EDITOR IN CHIEF: AXEL ALONSO • CHIEF CREATIVE OFFICER: JOE QUESADA
PUBLISHER: DAN BUCKLEY • EXECUTIVE PRODUCER: ALAN FINE

RUSE: THE VICTORIAN GUIDE TO MURDER. Contains material originally published in magazine form as RUSE #1-4. First printing 2011. ISBN# 978-0-7851-5586-7. Published by MARVEL WORLDWIDE, INC., a subsidiary of MARVEL ENTERTAINMENT, LLC. OFFICE OF PUBLICATION: 135 West 50th Street, New York, NY 10020. Copyright © 2011 Disney Enterprises, Inc. All rights reserved. $14.99 per copy in the U.S. and $16.99 in Canada (GST #R127032852); Canadian Agreement #40668537. All characters featured in this issue and the distinctive names and likenesses thereof, and all related indicia are trademarks of Disney Enterprises, Inc. No similarity between any of the names, characters, persons, and/or institutions in this magazine with those of any living or dead person or institution is intended, and any such similarity which may exist is purely coincidental. Marvel and its logos are TM & © Marvel Characters, Inc. Printed in the U.S.A. ALAN FINE, EVP - Office of the President, Marvel Worldwide, Inc. and EVP & CMO Marvel Characters B.V.; DAN BUCKLEY, Publisher & President - Print, Animation & Digital Divisions; JOE QUESADA, Chief Creative Officer; JIM SOKOLOWSKI, Chief Operating Officer; DAVID BOGART, SVP of Business Affairs & Talent Management; TOM BREVOORT, SVP of Publishing; C.B. CEBULSKI, SVP of Creator & Content Development; DAVID GABRIEL, SVP of Publishing Sales & Circulation; MICHAEL PASCIULLO, SVP of Brand Planning & Communications; JIM O'KEEFE, VP of Operations & Logistics; DAN CARR, Executive Director of Publishing Technology; SUSAN CRESPI, Editorial Operations Manager; ALEX MORALES, Publishing Operations Manager; STAN LEE, Chairman Emeritus. For information regarding advertising in Marvel Comics or on Marvel.com, please contact John Dokes, SVP Integrated Sales and Marketing, at jdokes@marvel.com. For Marvel subscription inquiries, please call 800-217-9158. Manufactured between 8/18/2011 and 9/6/2011 by QUAD/GRAPHICS, DUBUQUE, IA, USA.

10 9 8 7 6 5 4 3 2 1

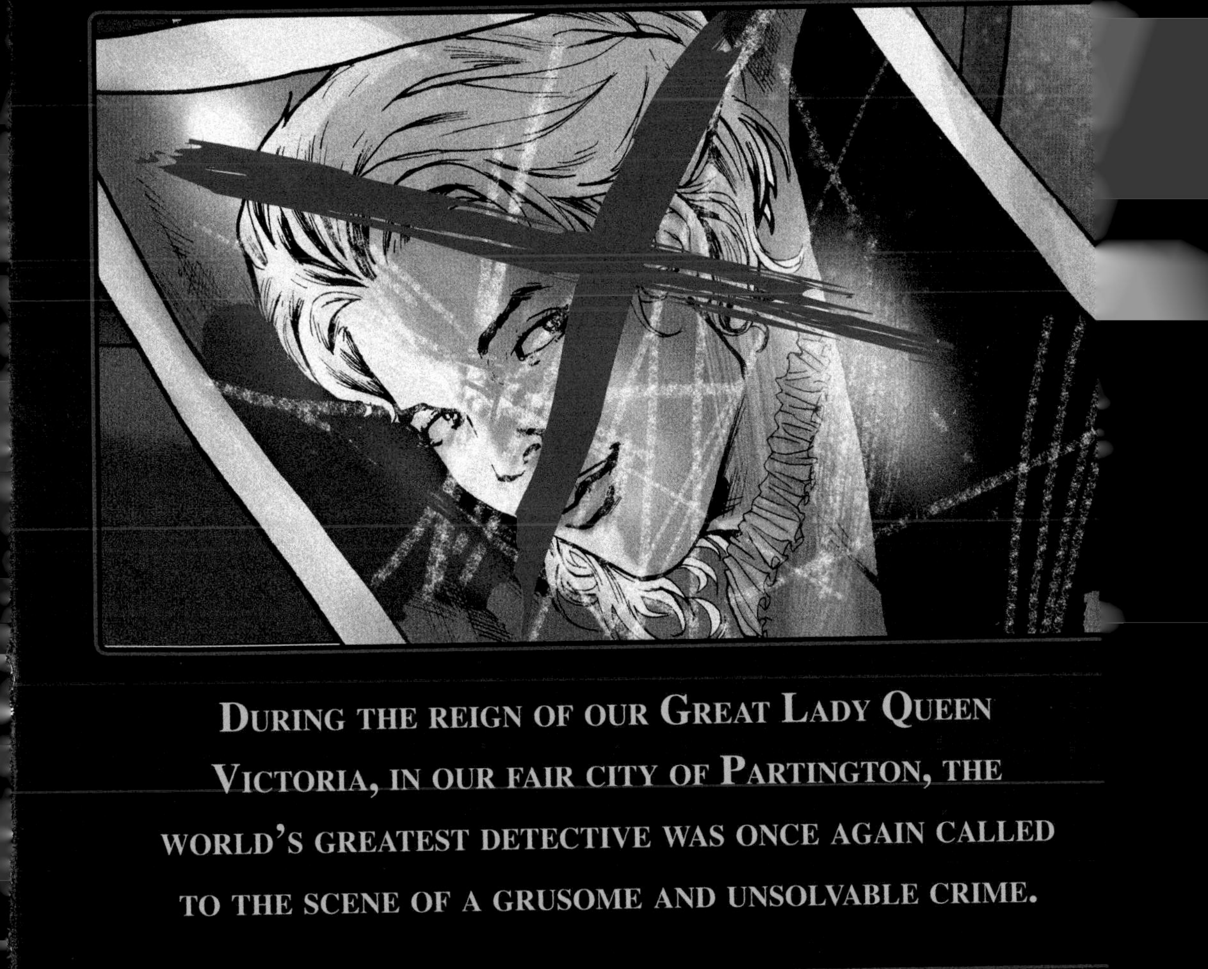

DURING THE REIGN OF OUR GREAT LADY QUEEN VICTORIA, IN OUR FAIR CITY OF PARTINGTON, THE WORLD'S GREATEST DETECTIVE WAS ONCE AGAIN CALLED TO THE SCENE OF A GRUSOME AND UNSOLVABLE CRIME.

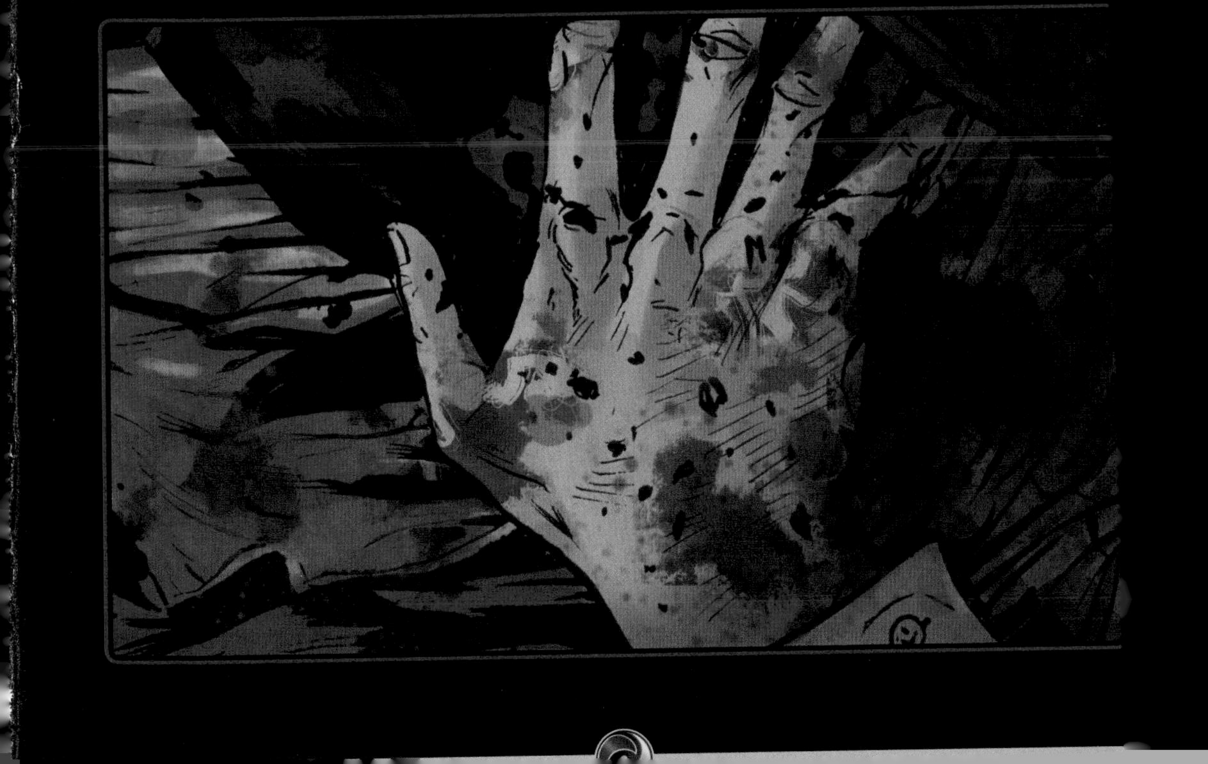

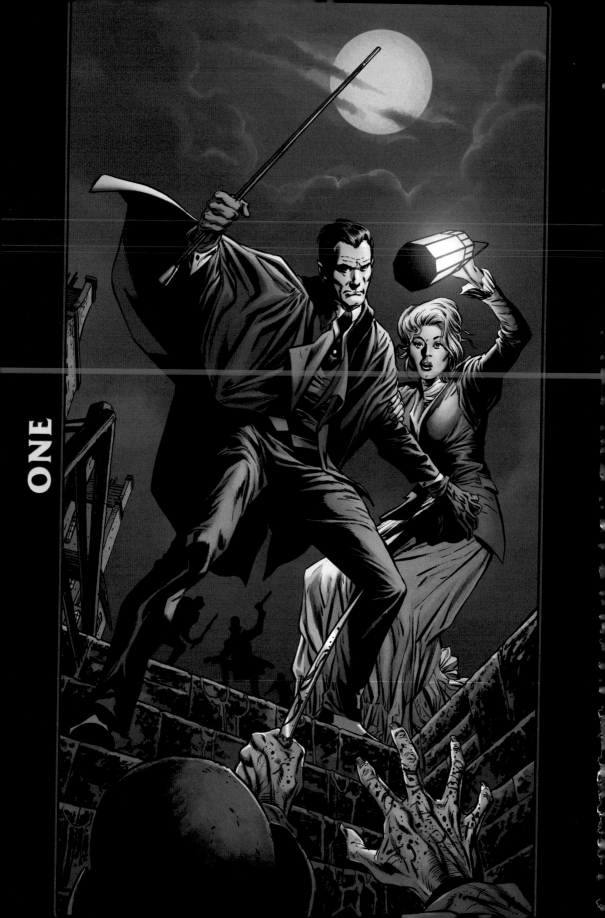

ONE

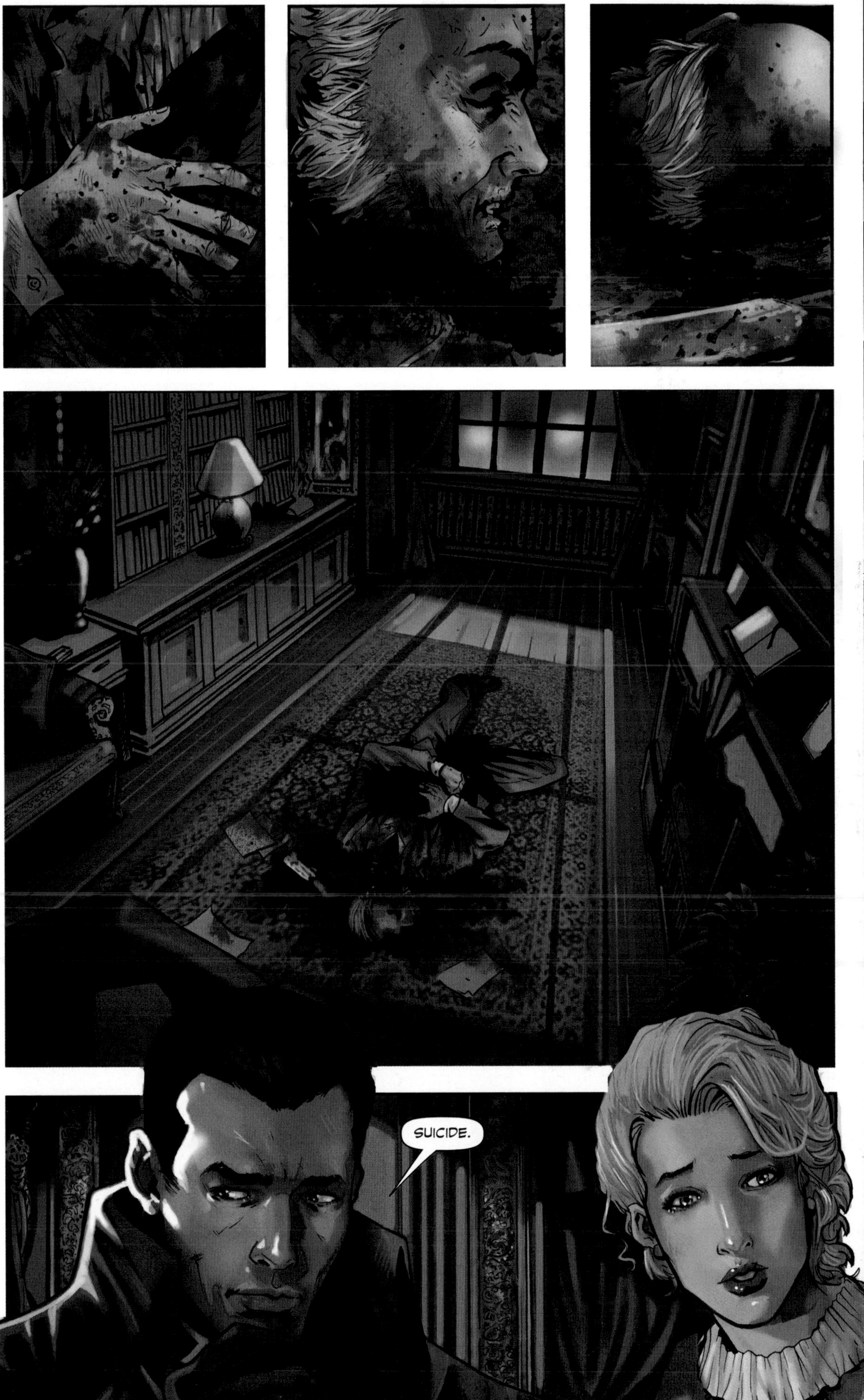
SUICIDE.

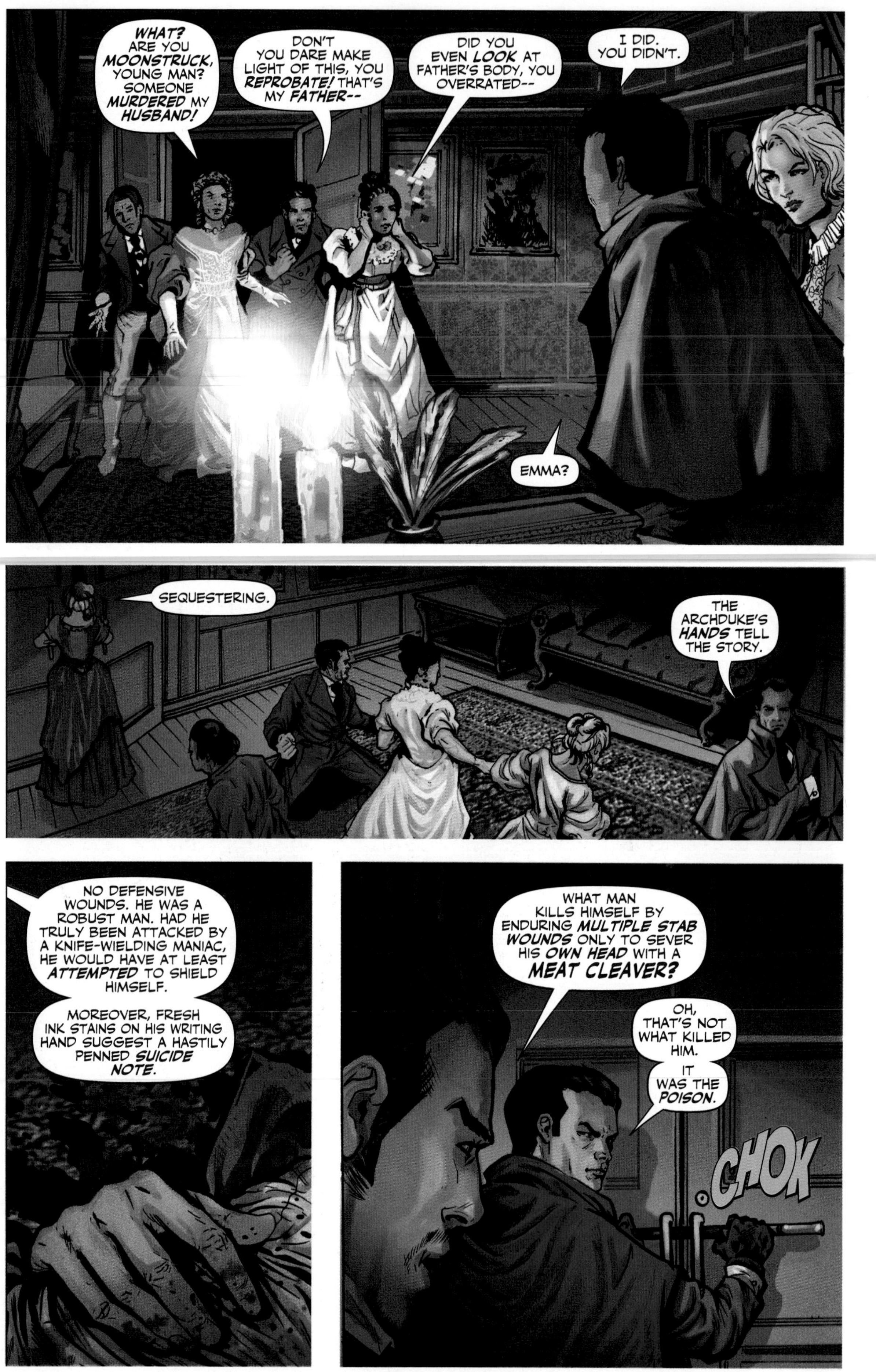
WHAT? ARE YOU MOONSTRUCK, YOUNG MAN? SOMEONE MURDERED MY HUSBAND!
DON'T YOU DARE MAKE LIGHT OF THIS, YOU REPROBATE! THAT'S MY FATHER--
DID YOU EVEN LOOK AT FATHER'S BODY, YOU OVERRATED--
I DID. YOU DIDN'T.
EMMA?
SEQUESTERING.
THE ARCHDUKE'S HANDS TELL THE STORY.
NO DEFENSIVE WOUNDS. HE WAS A ROBUST MAN. HAD HE TRULY BEEN ATTACKED BY A KNIFE-WIELDING MANIAC, HE WOULD HAVE AT LEAST ATTEMPTED TO SHIELD HIMSELF.
MOREOVER, FRESH INK STAINS ON HIS WRITING HAND SUGGEST A HASTILY PENNED SUICIDE NOTE.
WHAT MAN KILLS HIMSELF BY ENDURING MULTIPLE STAB WOUNDS ONLY TO SEVER HIS OWN HEAD WITH A MEAT CLEAVER?
OH, THAT'S NOT WHAT KILLED HIM.
IT WAS THE POISON.
CHOK

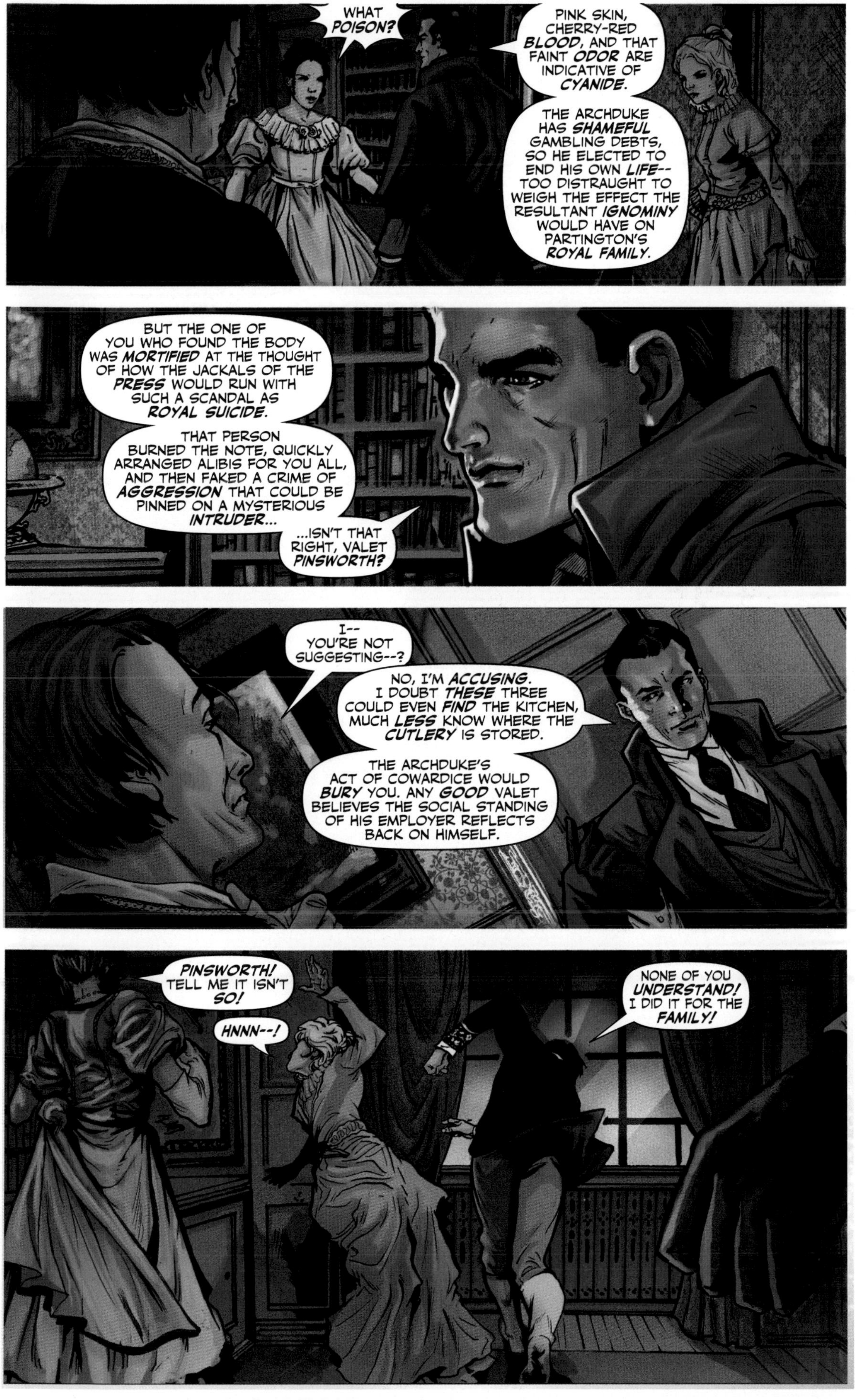
WHAT POISON?
PINK SKIN, CHERRY-RED BLOOD, AND THAT FAINT ODOR ARE INDICATIVE OF CYANIDE.
THE ARCHDUKE HAS SHAMEFUL GAMBLING DEBTS, SO HE ELECTED TO END HIS OWN LIFE-- TOO DISTRAUGHT TO WEIGH THE EFFECT THE RESULTANT IGNOMINY WOULD HAVE ON PARTINGTON'S ROYAL FAMILY.
BUT THE ONE OF YOU WHO FOUND THE BODY WAS MORTIFIED AT THE THOUGHT OF HOW THE JACKALS OF THE PRESS WOULD RUN WITH SUCH A SCANDAL AS ROYAL SUICIDE.
THAT PERSON BURNED THE NOTE, QUICKLY ARRANGED ALIBIS FOR YOU ALL, AND THEN FAKED A CRIME OF AGGRESSION THAT COULD BE PINNED ON A MYSTERIOUS INTRUDER...
...ISN'T THAT RIGHT, VALET PINSWORTH?
I-- YOU'RE NOT SUGGESTING--?
NO, I'M ACCUSING. I DOUBT THESE THREE COULD EVEN FIND THE KITCHEN, MUCH LESS KNOW WHERE THE CUTLERY IS STORED.
THE ARCHDUKE'S ACT OF COWARDICE WOULD BURY YOU. ANY GOOD VALET BELIEVES THE SOCIAL STANDING OF HIS EMPLOYER REFLECTS BACK ON HIMSELF.
PINSWORTH! TELL ME IT ISN'T SO!
HNNN--!
NONE OF YOU UNDERSTAND! I DID IT FOR THE FAMILY!

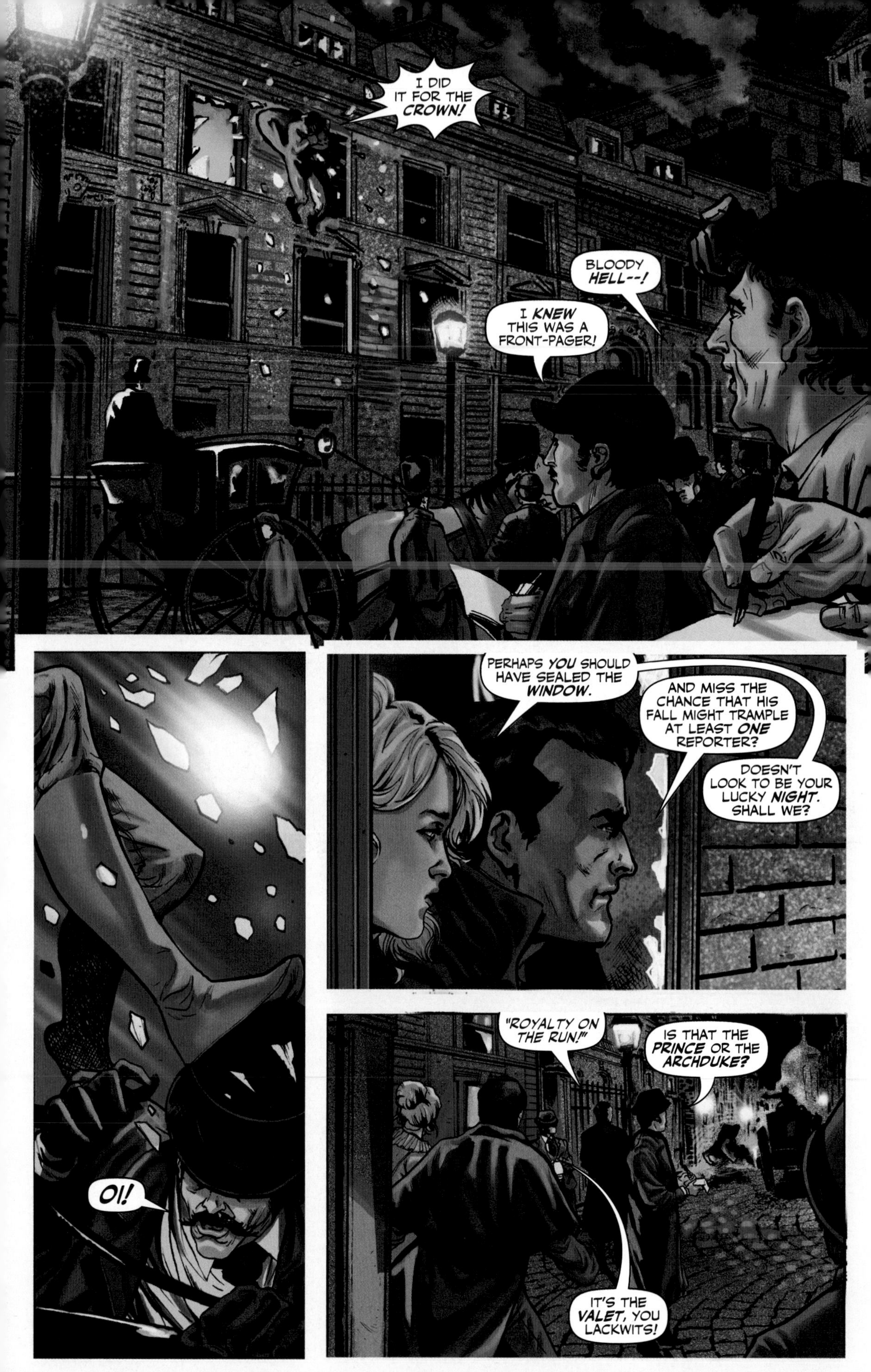
I DID IT FOR THE CROWN!
BLOODY HELL--!
I KNEW THIS WAS A FRONT-PAGER!
OI!
PERHAPS YOU SHOULD HAVE SEALED THE WINDOW.
AND MISS THE CHANCE THAT HIS FALL MIGHT TRAMPLE AT LEAST ONE REPORTER?
DOESN'T LOOK TO BE YOUR LUCKY NIGHT. SHALL WE?
"ROYALTY ON THE RUN!"
IS THAT THE PRINCE OR THE ARCHDUKE?
IT'S THE VALET, YOU LACKWITS!

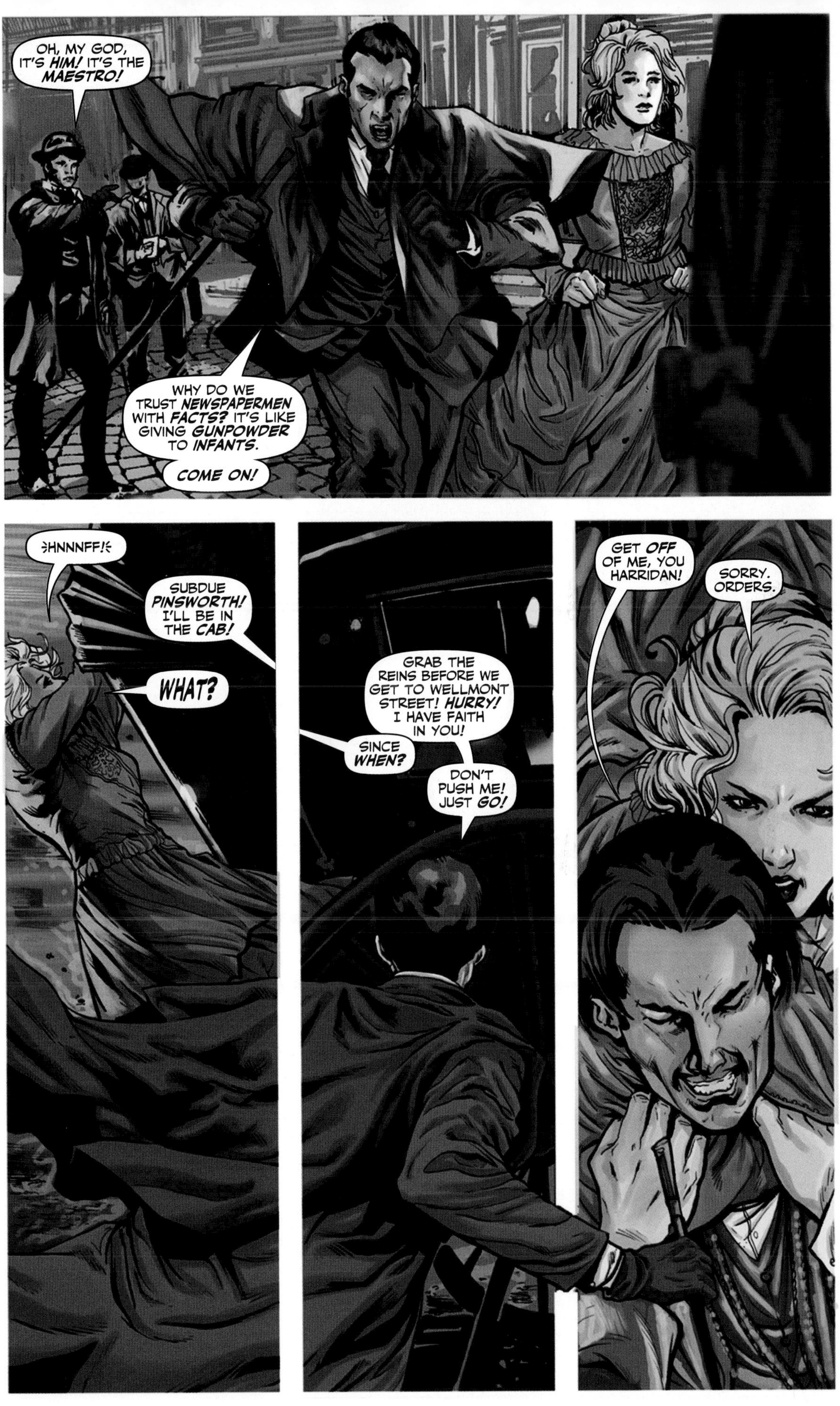
OH, MY GOD, IT'S HIM! IT'S THE MAESTRO!
WHY DO WE TRUST NEWSPAPERMEN WITH FACTS? IT'S LIKE GIVING GUNPOWDER TO INFANTS.
COME ON!
HNNNFF!
SUBDUE PINSWORTH! I'LL BE IN THE CAB!
WHAT?
GRAB THE REINS BEFORE WE GET TO WELLMONT STREET! HURRY! I HAVE FAITH IN YOU!
SINCE WHEN?
DON'T PUSH ME! JUST GO!
GET OFF OF ME, YOU HARRIDAN!
SORRY. ORDERS.

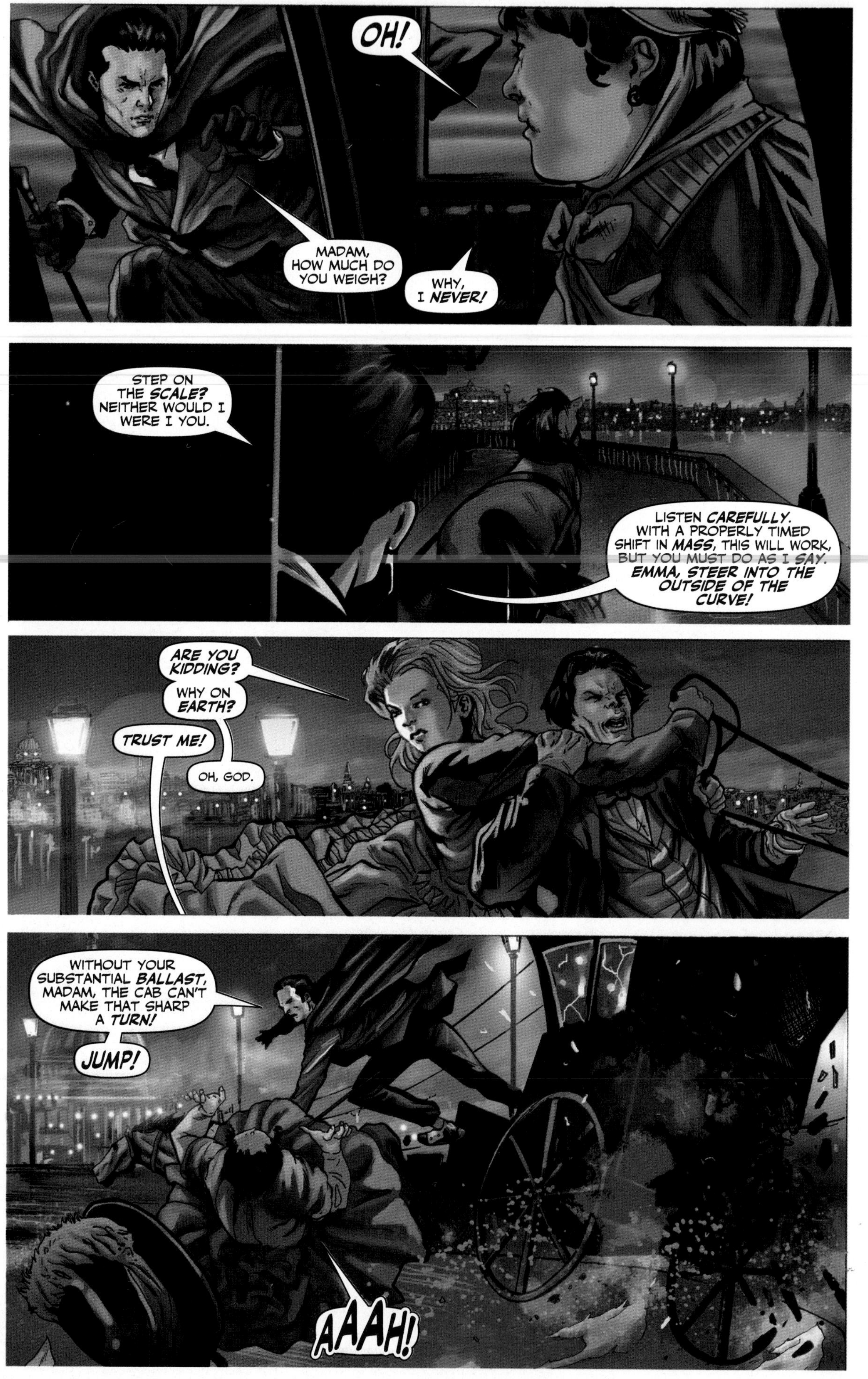
OH!
MADAM, HOW MUCH DO YOU WEIGH?
WHY, I NEVER!
STEP ON THE SCALE? NEITHER WOULD I WERE I YOU.
LISTEN CAREFULLY. WITH A PROPERLY TIMED SHIFT IN MASS, THIS WILL WORK, BUT YOU MUST DO AS I SAY. EMMA, STEER INTO THE OUTSIDE OF THE CURVE!
ARE YOU KIDDING?
WHY ON EARTH?
TRUST ME!
OH, GOD.
WITHOUT YOUR SUBSTANTIAL BALLAST, MADAM, THE CAB CAN'T MAKE THAT SHARP A TURN!
JUMP!
AAAH!

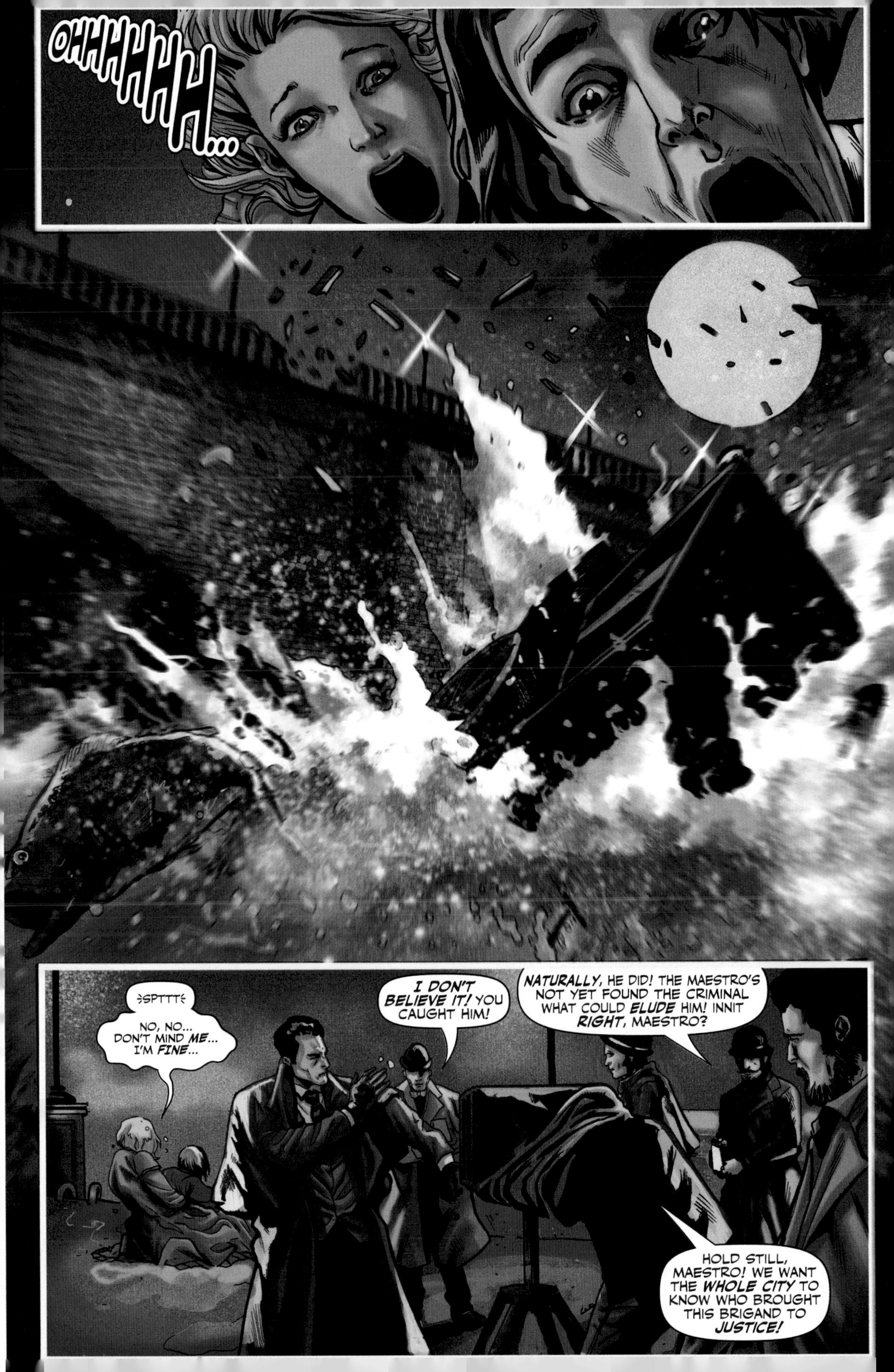
OHHHHHH...
SPTTT
NO, NO... DON'T MIND ME... I'M FINE...
I DON'T BELIEVE IT! YOU CAUGHT HIM!
NATURALLY, HE DID! THE MAESTRO'S NOT YET FOUND THE CRIMINAL WHAT COULD ELUDE HIM! INNIT RIGHT, MAESTRO?
HOLD STILL, MAESTRO! WE WANT THE WHOLE CITY TO KNOW WHO BROUGHT THIS BRIGAND TO JUSTICE!

The PENNY ARCADIAN

Copiously Illustrated   Afternoon Edition, Price One Penny

SIMON ARCHARD NABS BODY-BUTCHER

ROYAL FAMILY SHAMED BY FALLOUT

DETECTIVE ARCHARD AND ASSISTANT

SPIRITUALIST
PEERS INTO
AFTERLIFE
Page Two

FISTICUFFS
SETTLE VITAL
TAVERN MATTER
Page Four

Once again, the fabled sleuth Simon Archard has exposed a shameful bamboozlement perpetrated upon the fine citizens of the city of Partington.

Last night, called to the scene of an alleged murder at the home of Archduke Ehrlich, the detective effortlessly exposed the true criminal, the Archduke himself, who had taken his own life. Subsequent investigations undertaken by this newspaper into the Archduke's financial affairs reveal the royal family to be teetering on the edge of bankruptcy.

Risking his own life, the great hero Archard courageously brought to justice the Archduke's valet, who obfuscated the details of the suicide in a misguided attempt to salvage his late employer's good name. Eyewitnesses claim that the confrontation between Archard and his target involved a spectacular show of horsemanship that brought thundering applause from passersby. Once more, this city remains indebted to Archard for his selfless valor.

A blonde woman was also somehow involved.

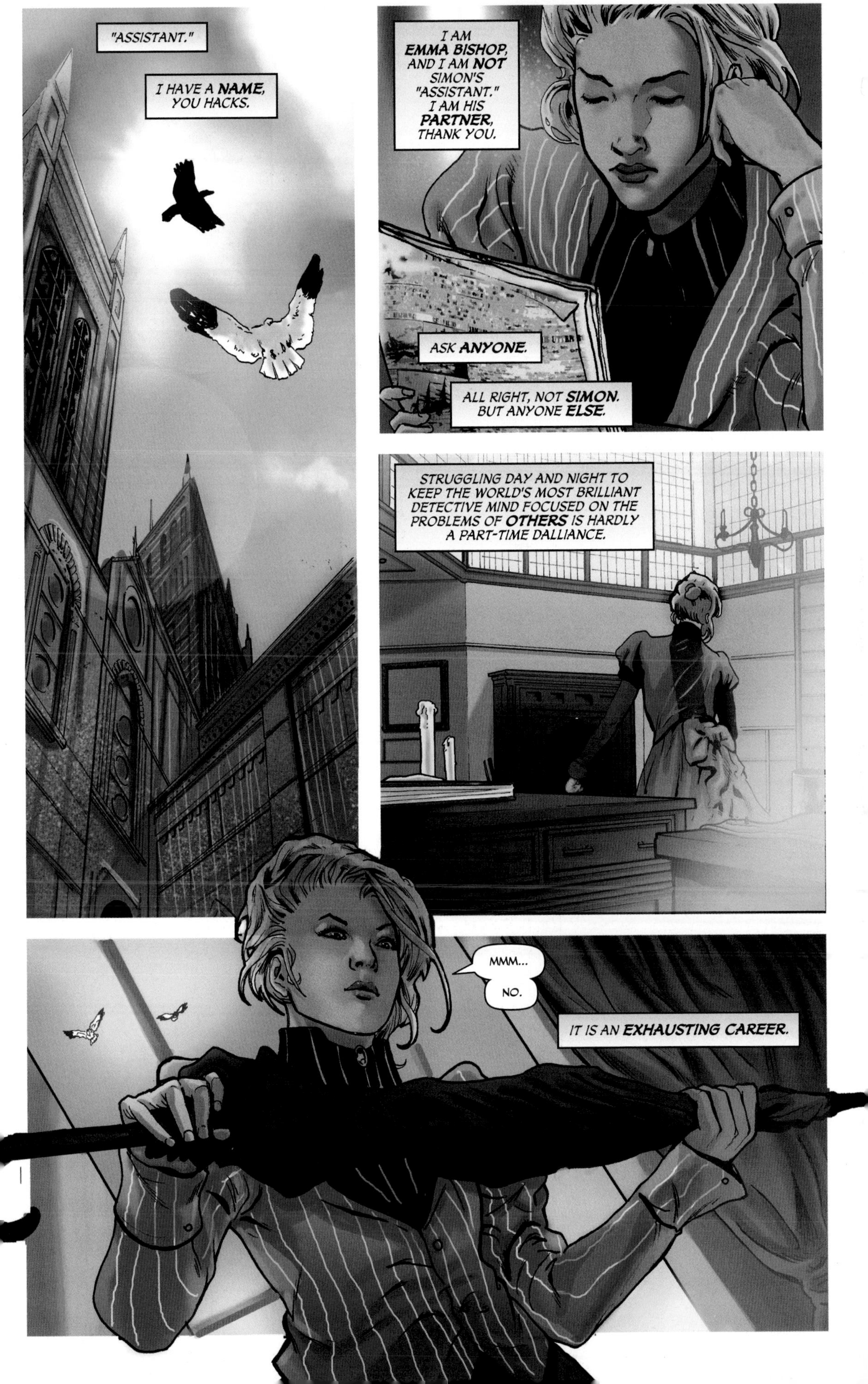
"ASSISTANT."
I HAVE A NAME, YOU HACKS.
I AM EMMA BISHOP, AND I AM NOT SIMON'S "ASSISTANT." I AM HIS PARTNER, THANK YOU.
ASK ANYONE.
ALL RIGHT, NOT SIMON. BUT ANYONE ELSE.
STRUGGLING DAY AND NIGHT TO KEEP THE WORLD'S MOST BRILLIANT DETECTIVE MIND FOCUSED ON THE PROBLEMS OF OTHERS IS HARDLY A PART-TIME DALLIANCE.
MMM...
NO.
IT IS AN EXHAUSTING CAREER.

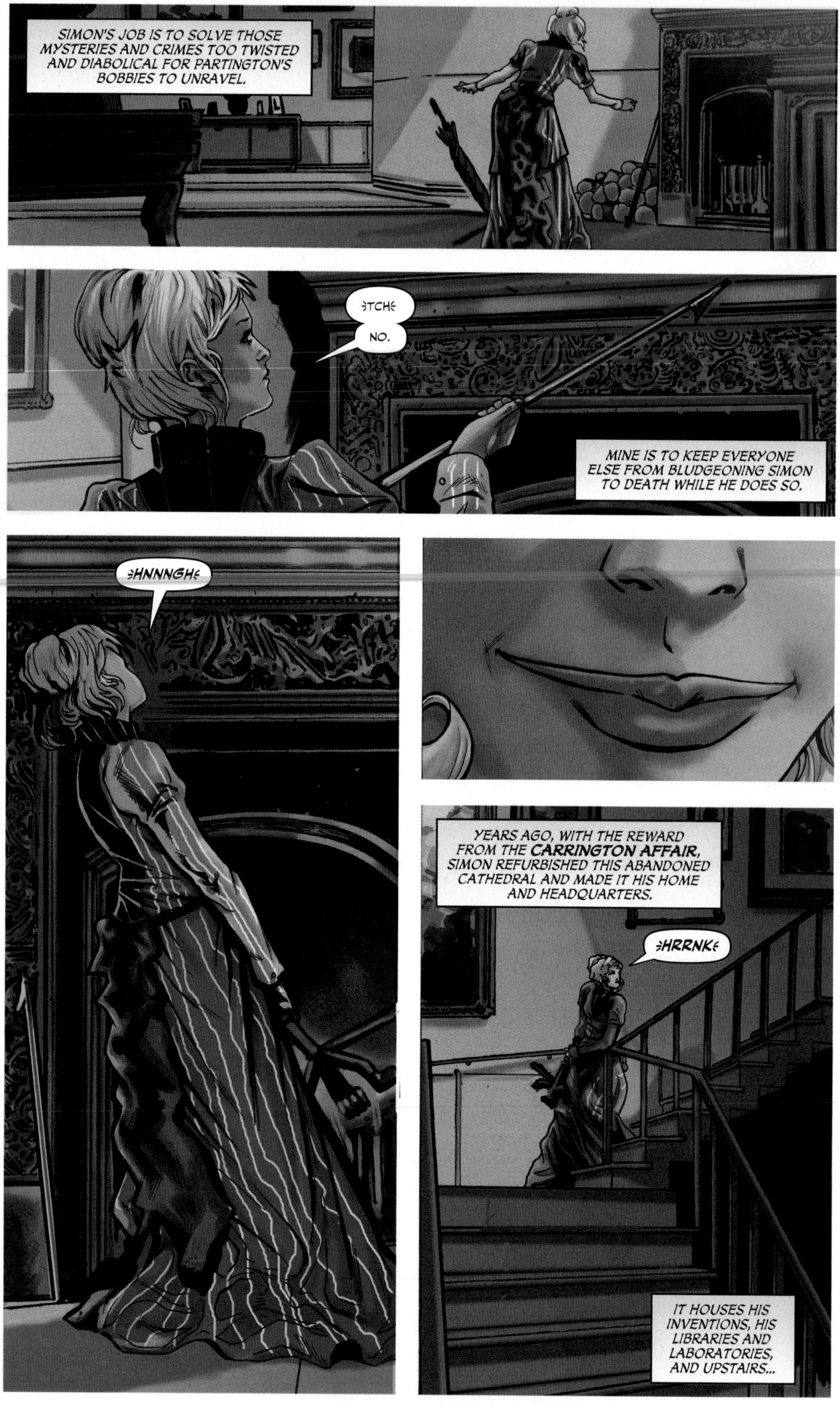
SIMON'S JOB IS TO SOLVE THOSE MYSTERIES AND CRIMES TOO TWISTED AND DIABOLICAL FOR PARTINGTON'S BOBBIES TO UNRAVEL.
TCH
NO.
MINE IS TO KEEP EVERYONE ELSE FROM BLUDGEONING SIMON TO DEATH WHILE HE DOES SO.
HNNNGH
YEARS AGO, WITH THE REWARD FROM THE CARRINGTON AFFAIR, SIMON REFURBISHED THIS ABANDONED CATHEDRAL AND MADE IT HIS HOME AND HEADQUARTERS.
HRRNK
IT HOUSES HIS INVENTIONS, HIS LIBRARIES AND LABORATORIES, AND UPSTAIRS...

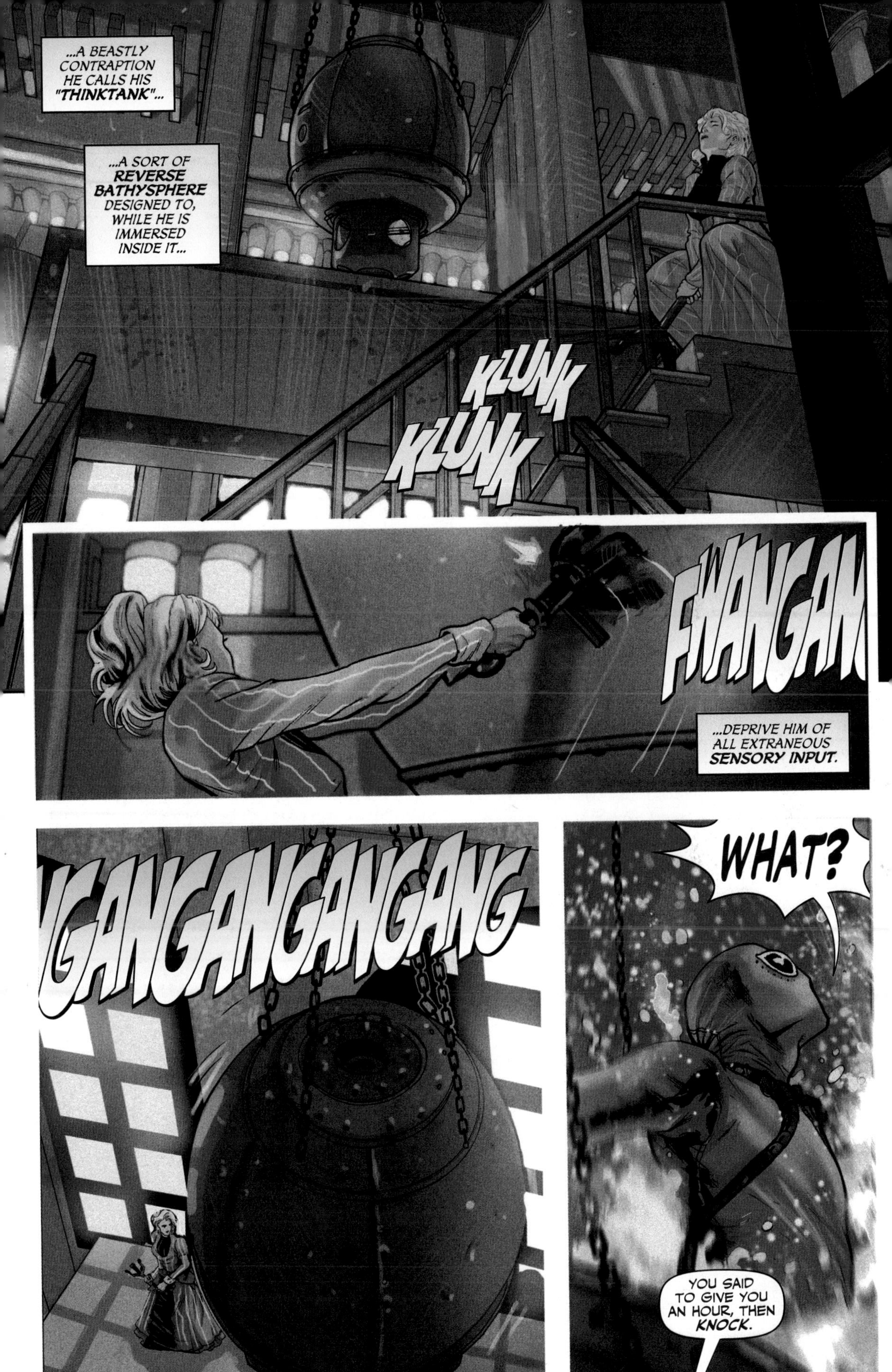
...A BEASTLY CONTRAPTION HE CALLS HIS "THINKTANK"...
...A SORT OF REVERSE BATHYSPHERE DESIGNED TO, WHILE HE IS IMMERSED INSIDE IT...
KLUNK
KLUNK
FWANGAM
...DEPRIVE HIM OF ALL EXTRANEOUS SENSORY INPUT.
GANGANGANGANGANG
WHAT?
YOU SAID TO GIVE YOU AN HOUR, THEN KNOCK.

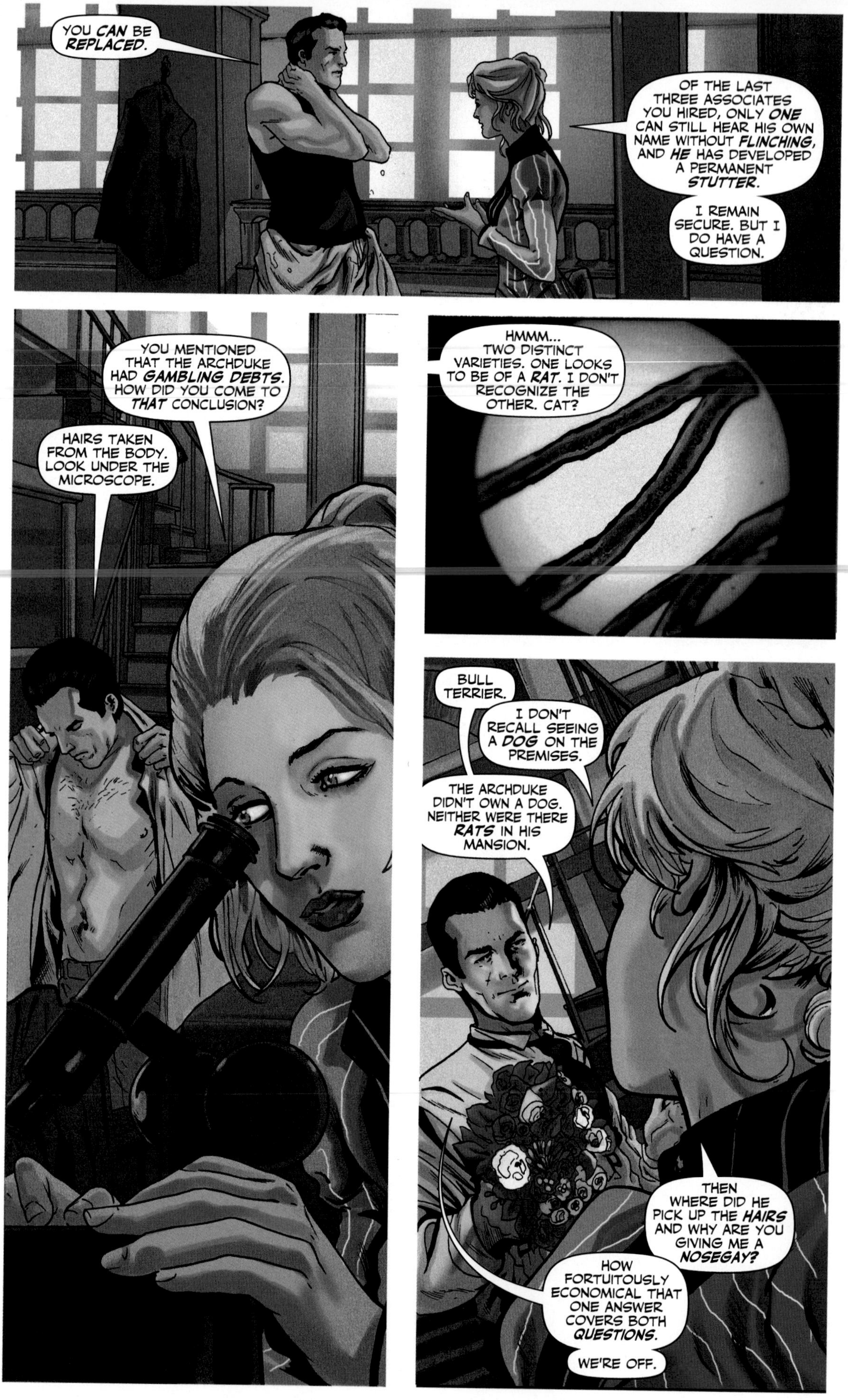
YOU CAN BE REPLACED.
OF THE LAST THREE ASSOCIATES YOU HIRED, ONLY ONE CAN STILL HEAR HIS OWN NAME WITHOUT FLINCHING, AND HE HAS DEVELOPED A PERMANENT STUTTER.
I REMAIN SECURE. BUT I DO HAVE A QUESTION.
YOU MENTIONED THAT THE ARCHDUKE HAD GAMBLING DEBTS. HOW DID YOU COME TO THAT CONCLUSION?
HAIRS TAKEN FROM THE BODY. LOOK UNDER THE MICROSCOPE.
HMMM... TWO DISTINCT VARIETIES. ONE LOOKS TO BE OF A RAT. I DON'T RECOGNIZE THE OTHER. CAT?
BULL TERRIER.
I DON'T RECALL SEEING A DOG ON THE PREMISES.
THE ARCHDUKE DIDN'T OWN A DOG. NEITHER WERE THERE RATS IN HIS MANSION.
THEN WHERE DID HE PICK UP THE HAIRS AND WHY ARE YOU GIVING ME A NOSEGAY?
HOW FORTUITOUSLY ECONOMICAL THAT ONE ANSWER COVERS BOTH QUESTIONS.
WE'RE OFF.

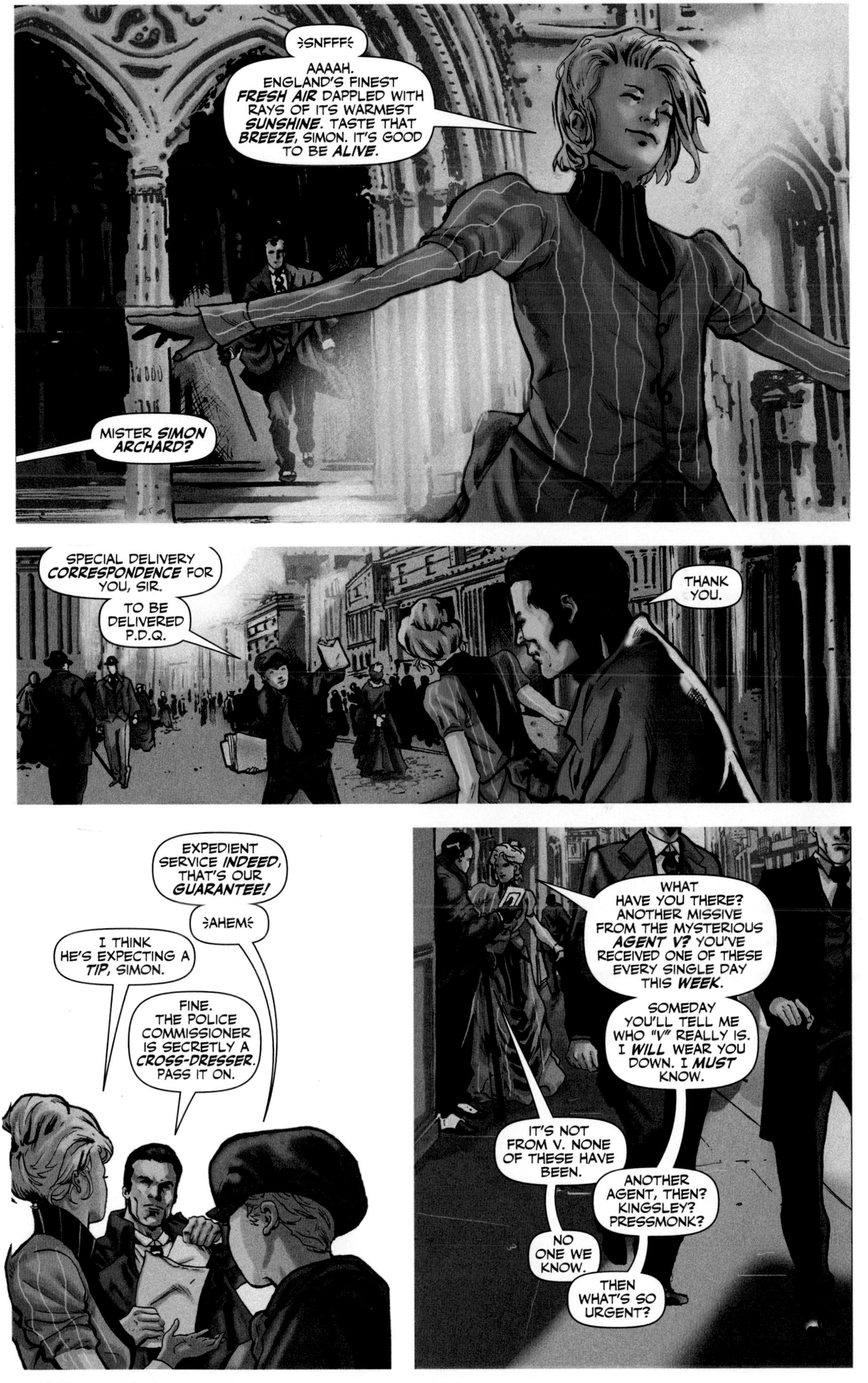

≶SNFFF≶
AAAAH. ENGLAND'S FINEST FRESH AIR DAPPLED WITH RAYS OF ITS WARMEST SUNSHINE. TASTE THAT BREEZE, SIMON. IT'S GOOD TO BE ALIVE.
MISTER SIMON ARCHARD?
SPECIAL DELIVERY CORRESPONDENCE FOR YOU, SIR.
TO BE DELIVERED P.D.Q.
THANK YOU.
EXPEDIENT SERVICE INDEED, THAT'S OUR GUARANTEE!
≶AHEM≶
I THINK HE'S EXPECTING A TIP, SIMON.
FINE. THE POLICE COMMISSIONER IS SECRETLY A CROSS-DRESSER. PASS IT ON.
WHAT HAVE YOU THERE? ANOTHER MISSIVE FROM THE MYSTERIOUS AGENT V? YOU'VE RECEIVED ONE OF THESE EVERY SINGLE DAY THIS WEEK.
SOMEDAY YOU'LL TELL ME WHO "V" REALLY IS. I WILL WEAR YOU DOWN. I MUST KNOW.
IT'S NOT FROM V. NONE OF THESE HAVE BEEN.
ANOTHER AGENT, THEN? KINGSLEY? PRESSMONK?
NO ONE WE KNOW.
THEN WHAT'S SO URGENT?

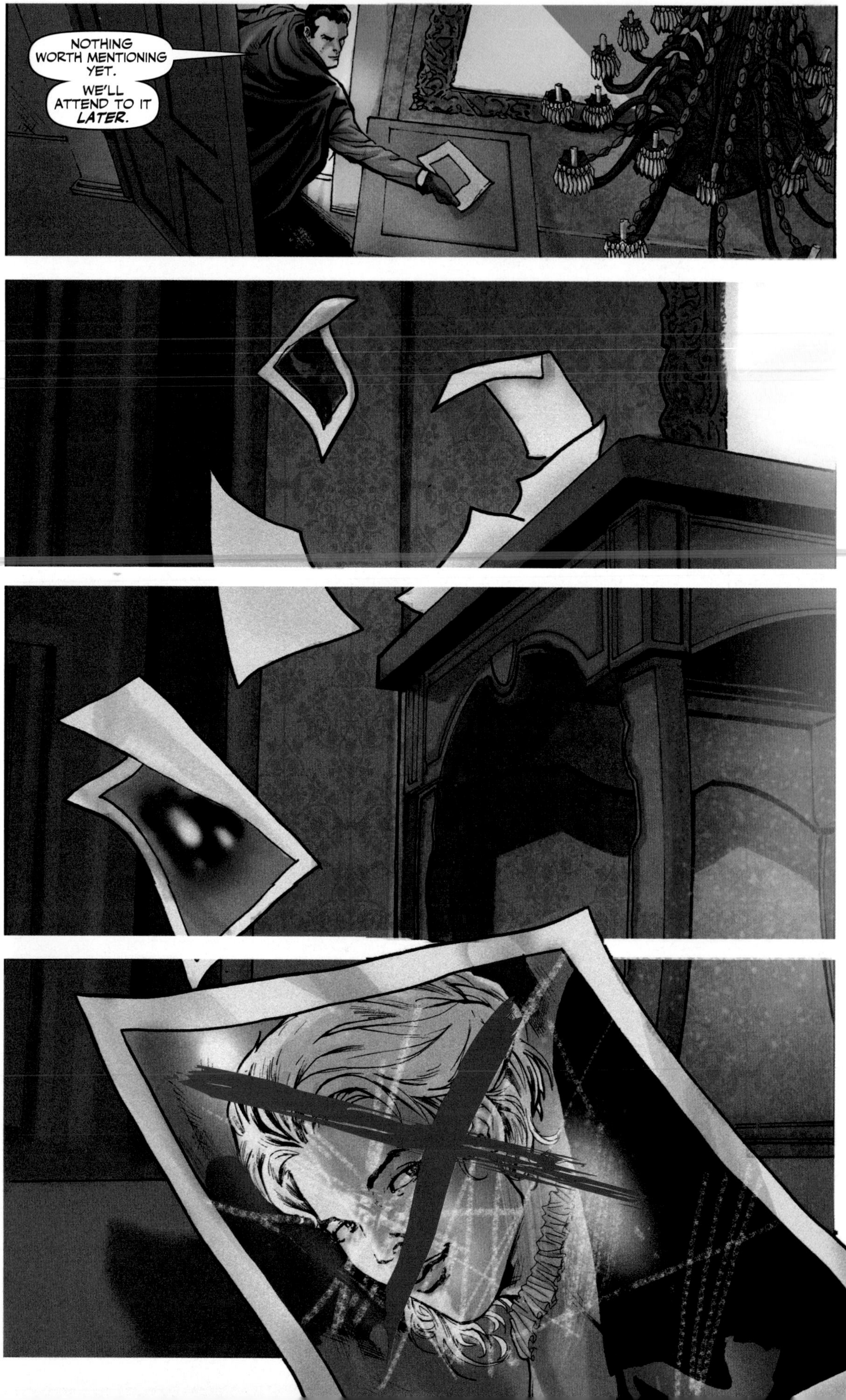
NOTHING WORTH MENTIONING YET.
WE'LL ATTEND TO IT ***LATER***.

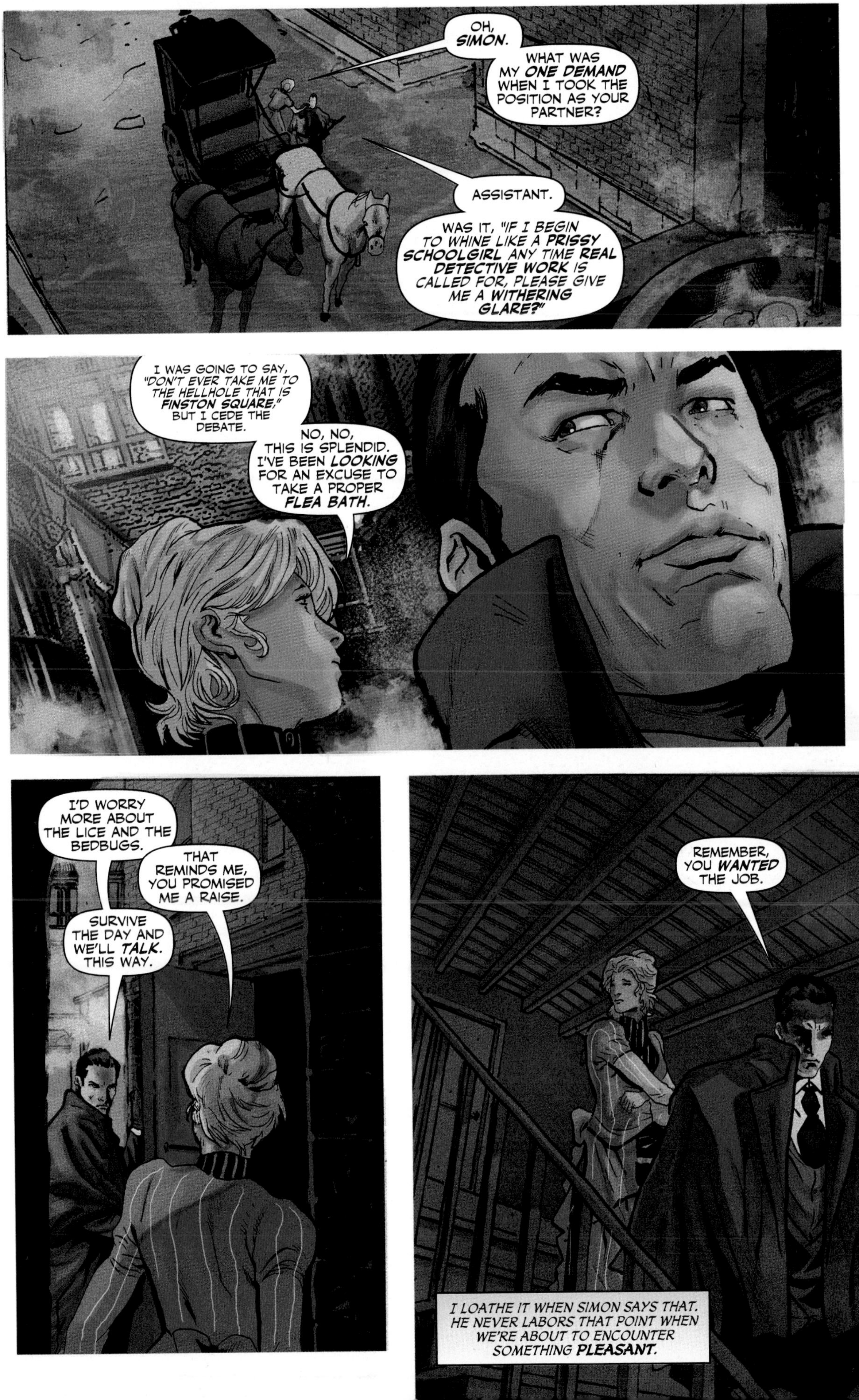

OH, SIMON.
WHAT WAS MY ONE DEMAND WHEN I TOOK THE POSITION AS YOUR PARTNER?
ASSISTANT.
WAS IT, "IF I BEGIN TO WHINE LIKE A PRISSY SCHOOLGIRL ANY TIME REAL DETECTIVE WORK IS CALLED FOR, PLEASE GIVE ME A WITHERING GLARE?"
I WAS GOING TO SAY, "DON'T EVER TAKE ME TO THE HELLHOLE THAT IS FINSTON SQUARE," BUT I CEDE THE DEBATE.
NO, NO, THIS IS SPLENDID. I'VE BEEN LOOKING FOR AN EXCUSE TO TAKE A PROPER FLEA BATH.
I'D WORRY MORE ABOUT THE LICE AND THE BEDBUGS.
THAT REMINDS ME, YOU PROMISED ME A RAISE.
SURVIVE THE DAY AND WE'LL TALK. THIS WAY.
REMEMBER, YOU WANTED THE JOB.
I LOATHE IT WHEN SIMON SAYS THAT. HE NEVER LABORS THAT POINT WHEN WE'RE ABOUT TO ENCOUNTER SOMETHING PLEASANT.

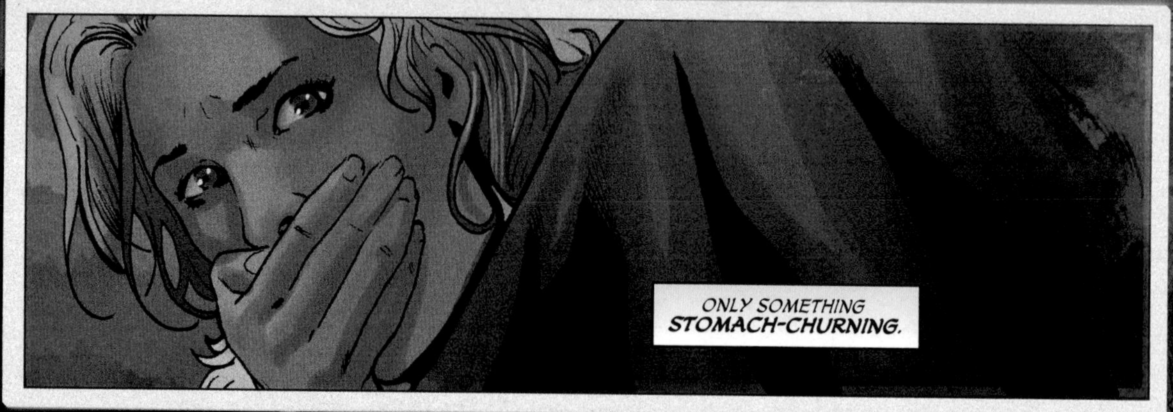
ONLY SOMETHING
STOMACH-CHURNING.

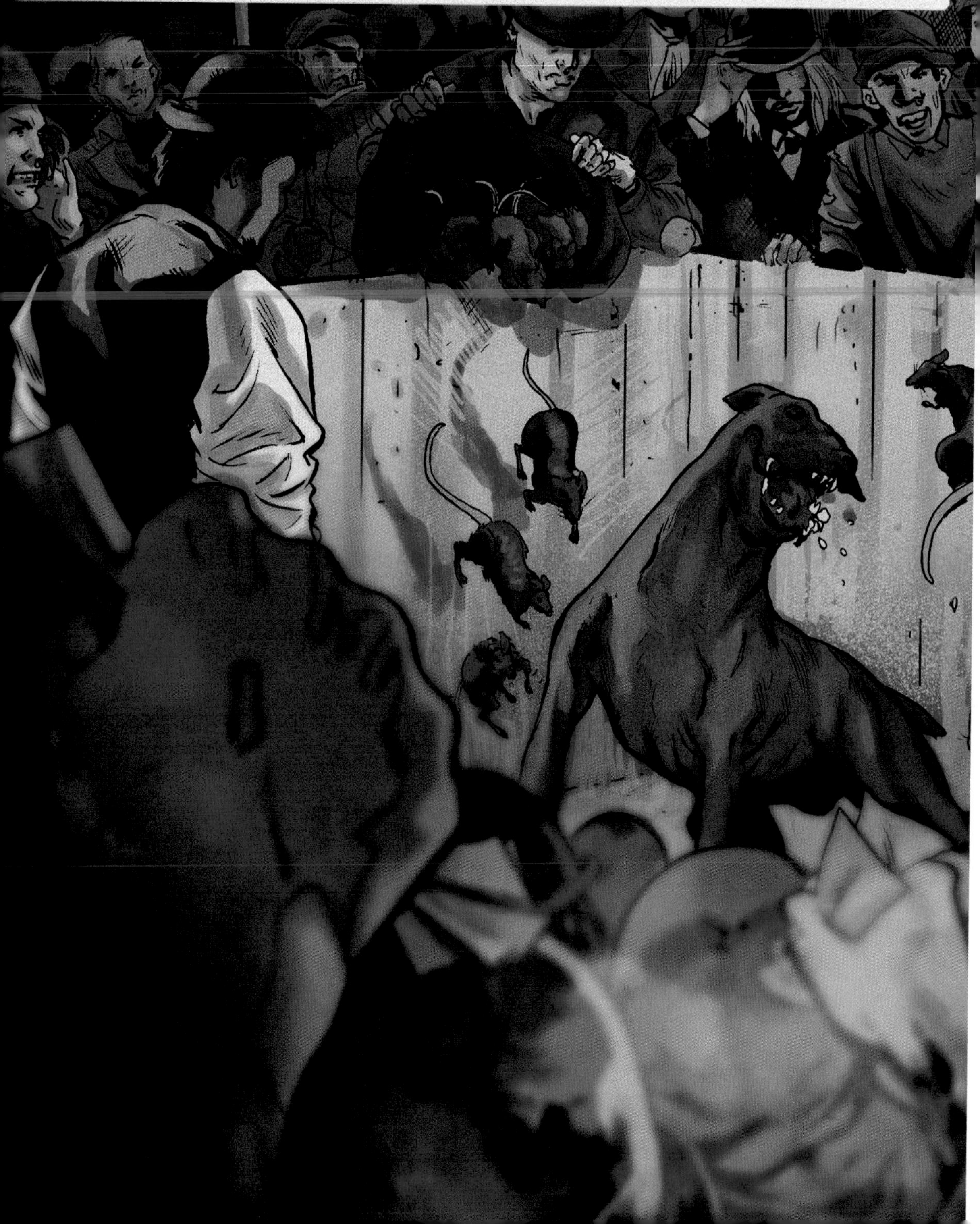

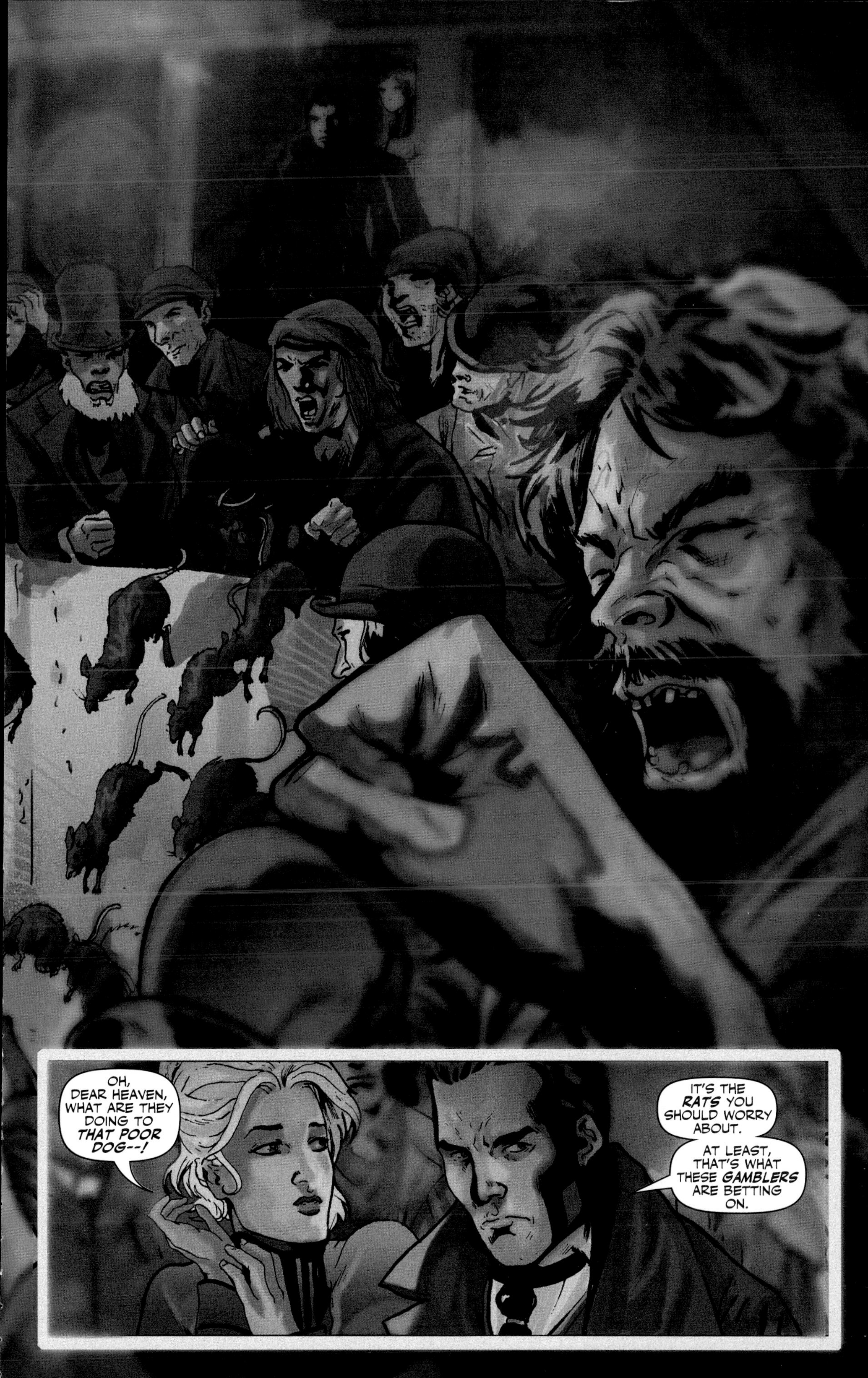

OH, DEAR HEAVEN, WHAT ARE THEY DOING TO THAT POOR DOG--!
IT'S THE RATS YOU SHOULD WORRY ABOUT.
AT LEAST, THAT'S WHAT THESE GAMBLERS ARE BETTING ON.

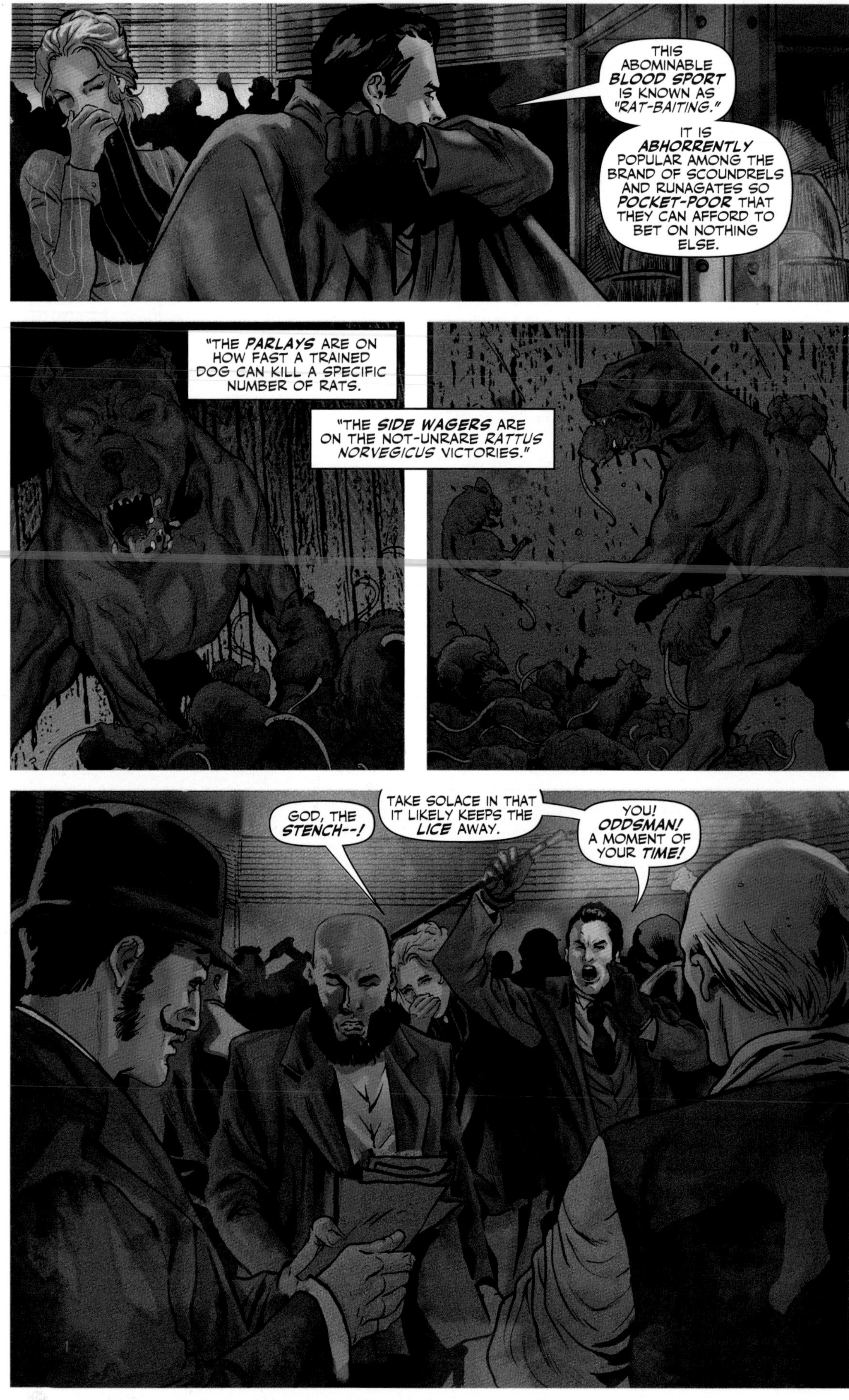
THIS ABOMINABLE BLOOD SPORT IS KNOWN AS "RAT-BAITING."
IT IS ABHORRENTLY POPULAR AMONG THE BRAND OF SCOUNDRELS AND RUNAGATES SO POCKET-POOR THAT THEY CAN AFFORD TO BET ON NOTHING ELSE.
"THE PARLAYS ARE ON HOW FAST A TRAINED DOG CAN KILL A SPECIFIC NUMBER OF RATS.
"THE SIDE WAGERS ARE ON THE NOT-UNRARE RATTUS NORVEGICUS VICTORIES."
GOD, THE STENCH--!
TAKE SOLACE IN THAT IT LIKELY KEEPS THE LICE AWAY.
YOU! ODDSMAN! A MOMENT OF YOUR TIME!

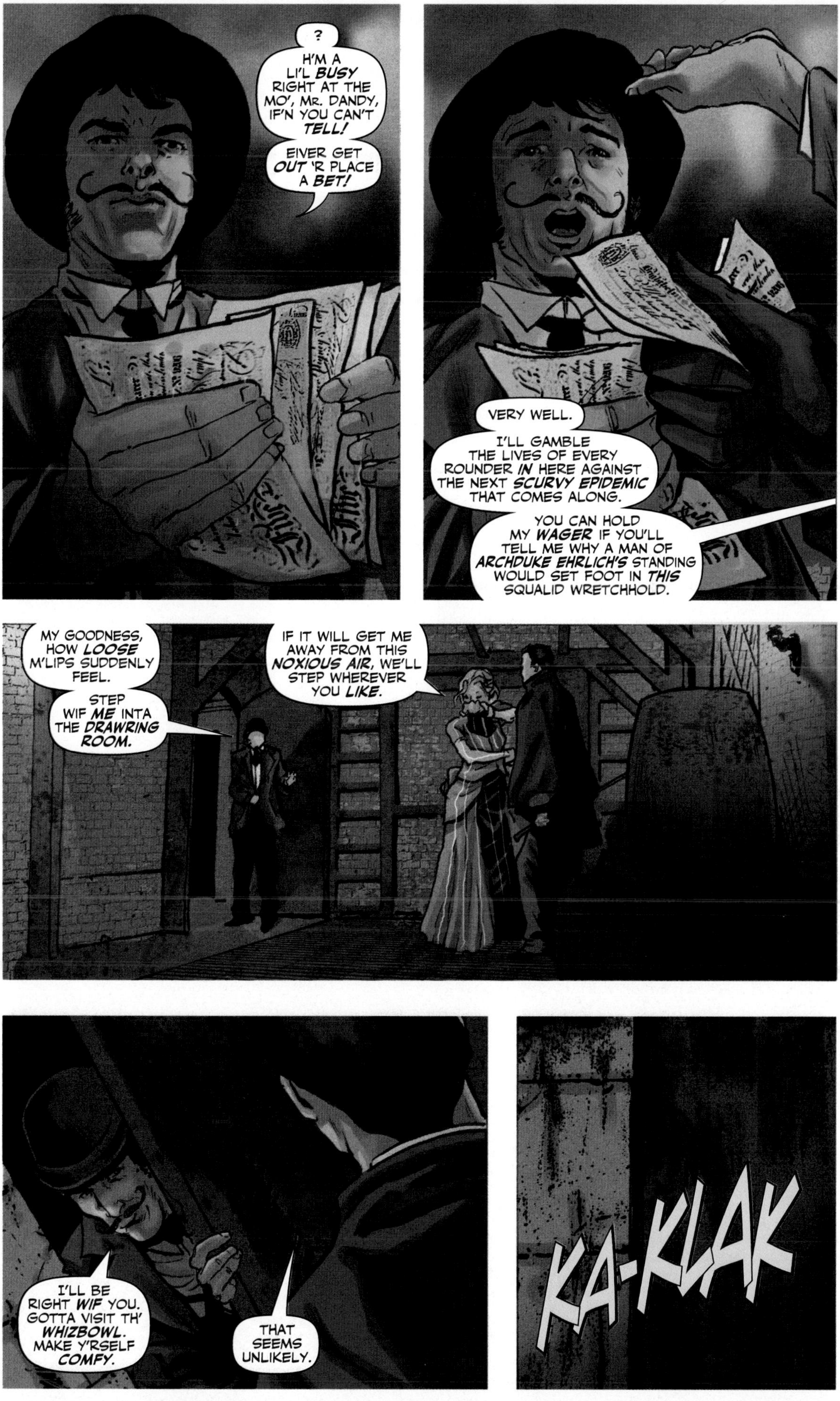
?
H'M A LI'L BUSY RIGHT AT THE MO', Mr. DANDY, IF'N YOU CAN'T TELL!
EIVER GET OUT 'R PLACE A BET!
VERY WELL.
I'LL GAMBLE THE LIVES OF EVERY ROUNDER IN HERE AGAINST THE NEXT SCURVY EPIDEMIC THAT COMES ALONG.
YOU CAN HOLD MY WAGER IF YOU'LL TELL ME WHY A MAN OF ARCHDUKE EHRLICH'S STANDING WOULD SET FOOT IN THIS SQUALID WRETCHHOLD.
MY GOODNESS, HOW LOOSE M'LIPS SUDDENLY FEEL.
STEP WIF ME INTA THE DRAWRING ROOM.
IF IT WILL GET ME AWAY FROM THIS NOXIOUS AIR, WE'LL STEP WHEREVER YOU LIKE.
I'LL BE RIGHT WIF YOU. GOTTA VISIT TH' WHIZBOWL. MAKE Y'RSELF COMFY.
THAT SEEMS UNLIKELY.
KA-KLAK

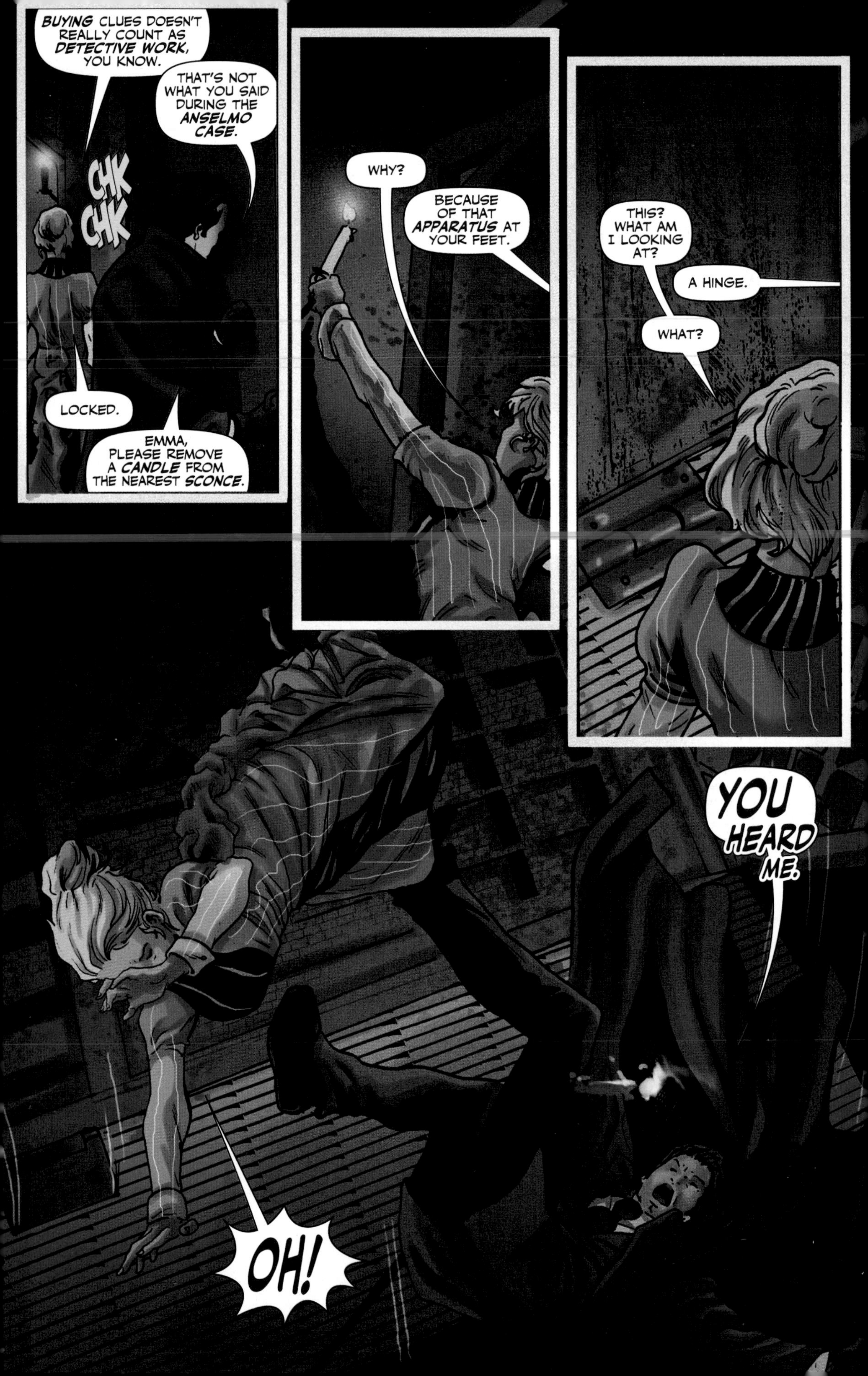
BUYING CLUES DOESN'T REALLY COUNT AS DETECTIVE WORK, YOU KNOW.
THAT'S NOT WHAT YOU SAID DURING THE ANSELMO CASE.
CHK CHK
LOCKED.
EMMA, PLEASE REMOVE A CANDLE FROM THE NEAREST SCONCE.
WHY?
BECAUSE OF THAT APPARATUS AT YOUR FEET.
THIS? WHAT AM I LOOKING AT?
A HINGE.
WHAT?
YOU HEARD ME.
OH!

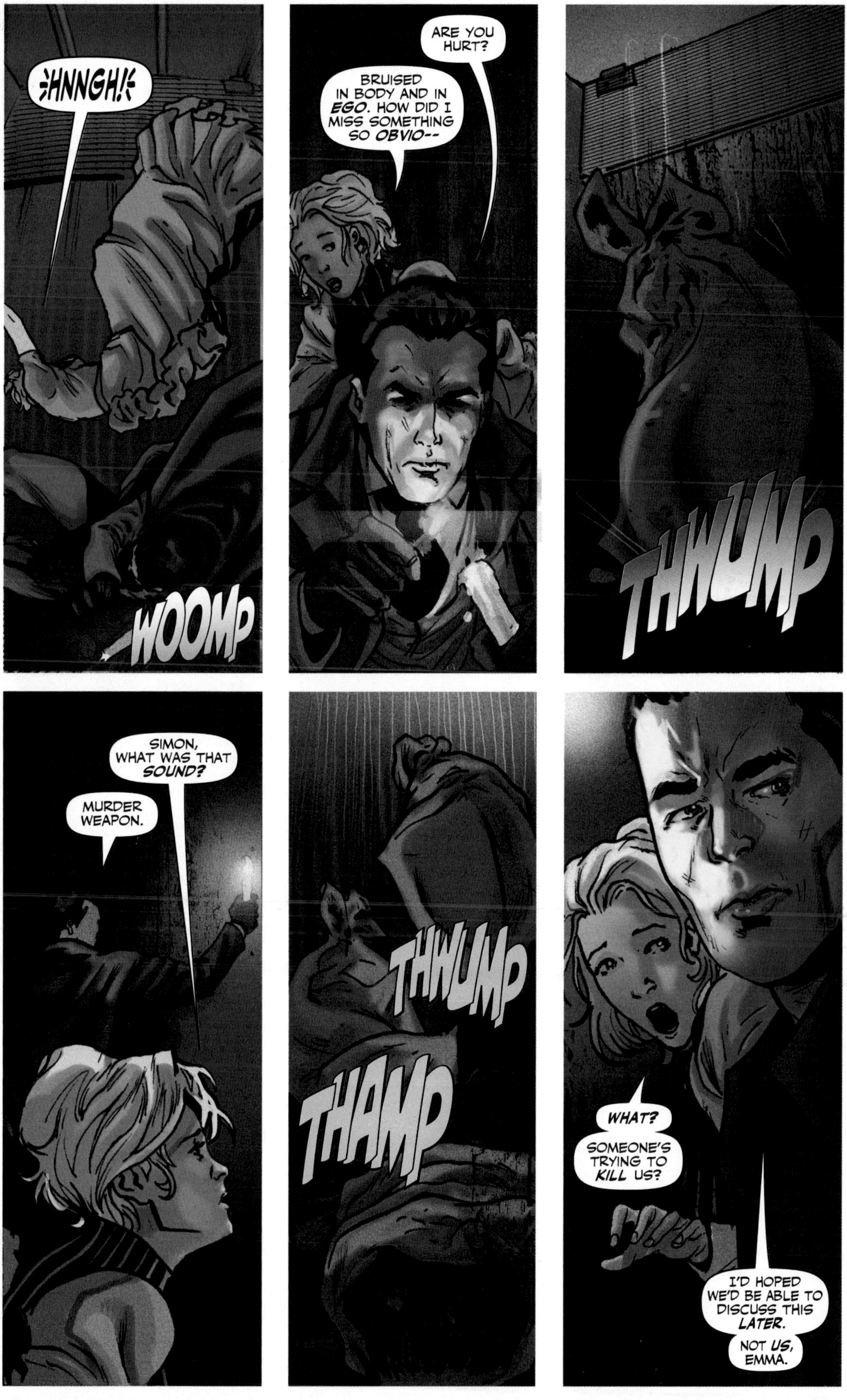
HNNGH!
WOOMP
ARE YOU HURT?
BRUISED IN BODY AND IN EGO. HOW DID I MISS SOMETHING SO OBVIO--
THWUMP
SIMON, WHAT WAS THAT SOUND?
MURDER WEAPON.
THWUMP
THAMP
WHAT?
SOMEONE'S TRYING TO KILL US?
I'D HOPED WE'D BE ABLE TO DISCUSS THIS LATER.
NOT US, EMMA.

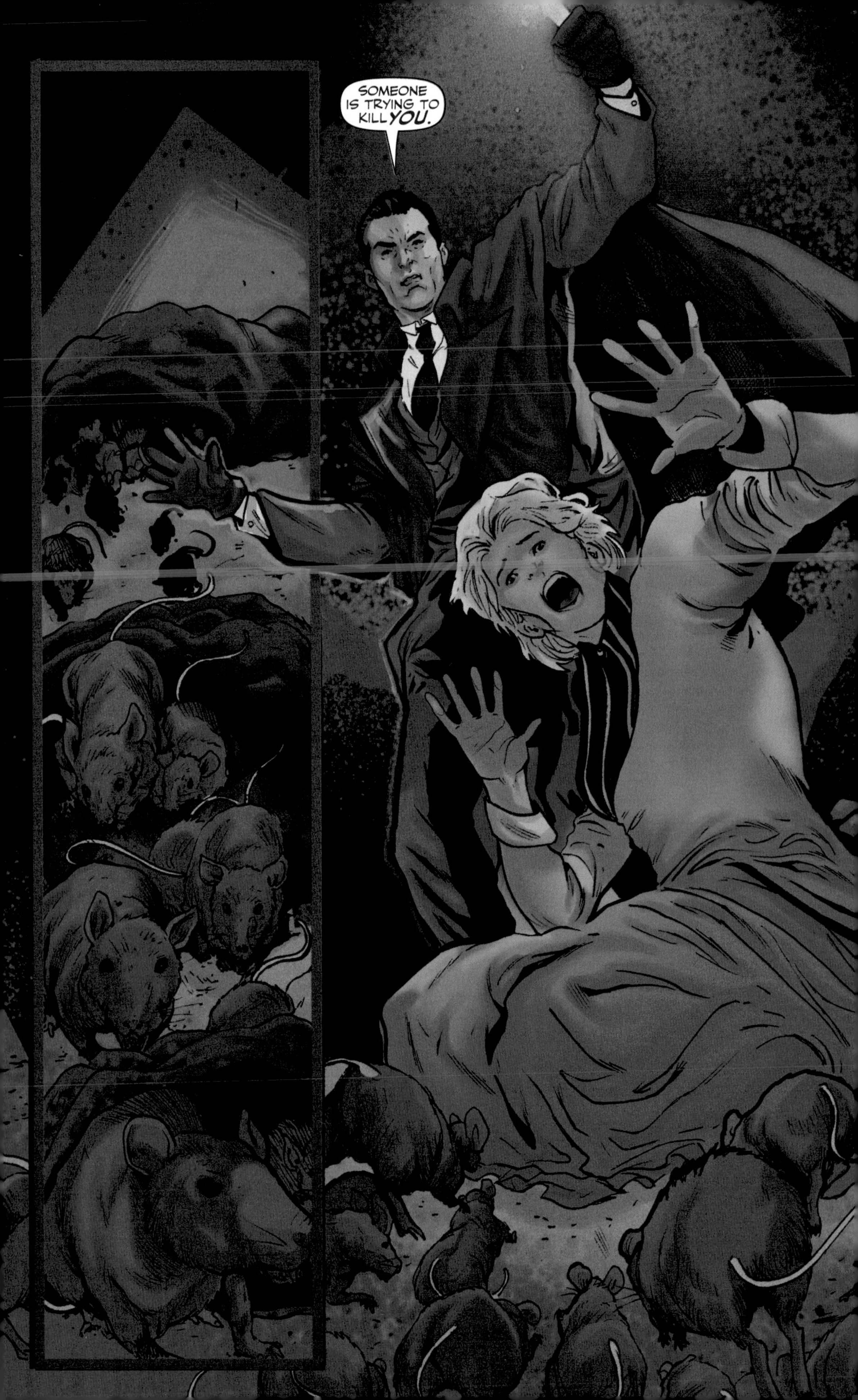
SOMEONE IS TRYING TO KILL YOU.

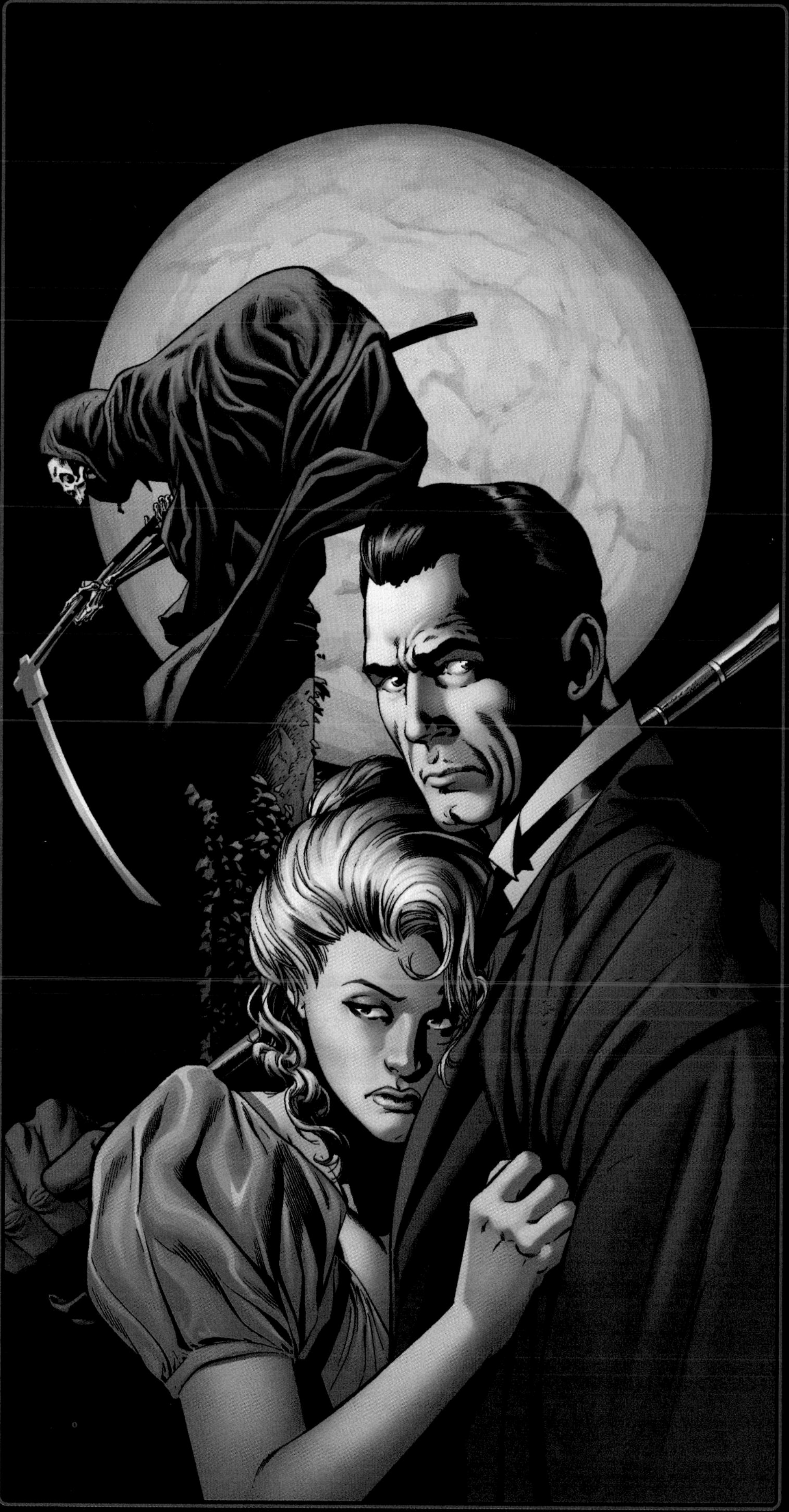

TWO

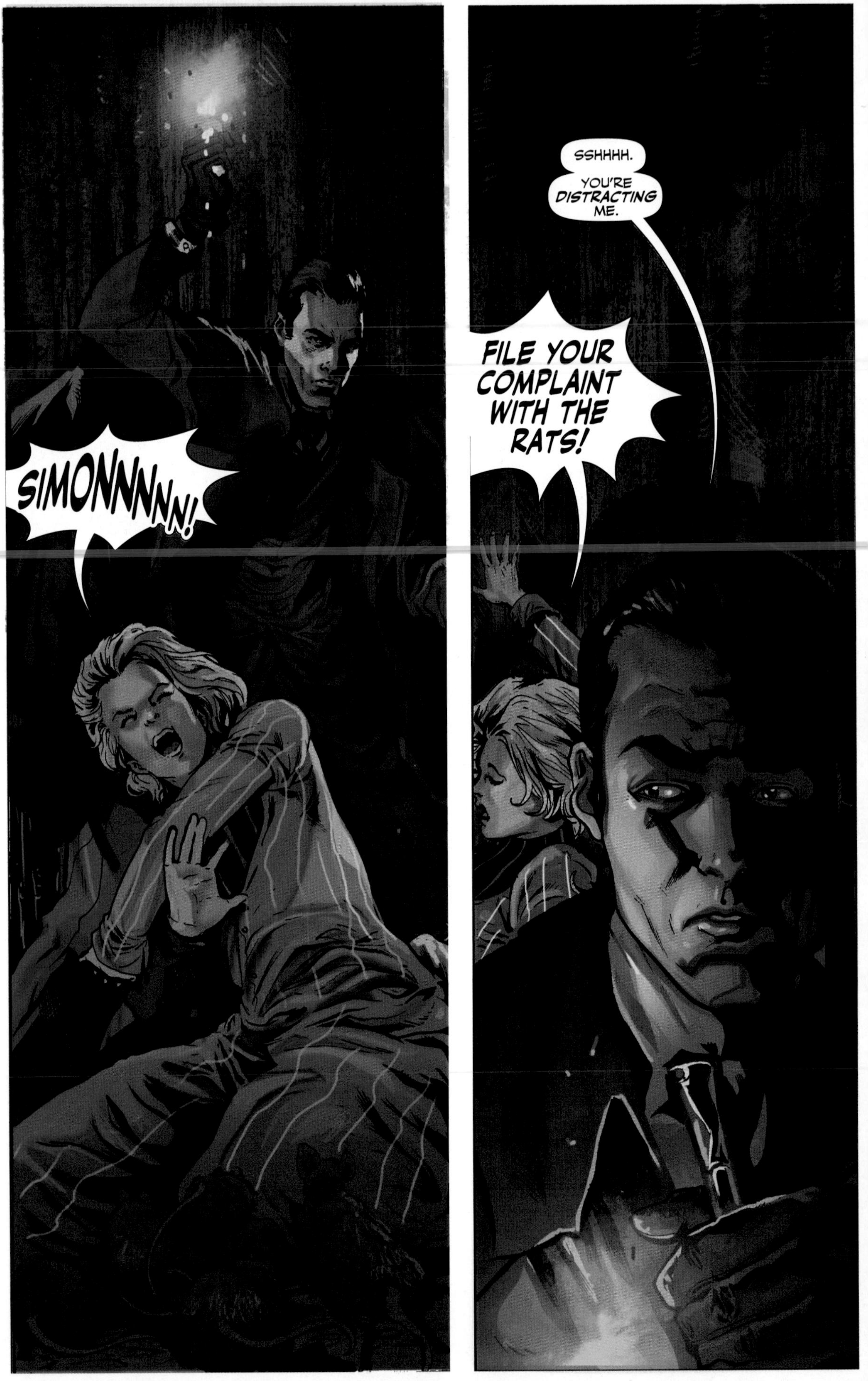
SIMONNNNNN!
SSHHHH.
YOU'RE DISTRACTING ME.
FILE YOUR COMPLAINT WITH THE RATS!

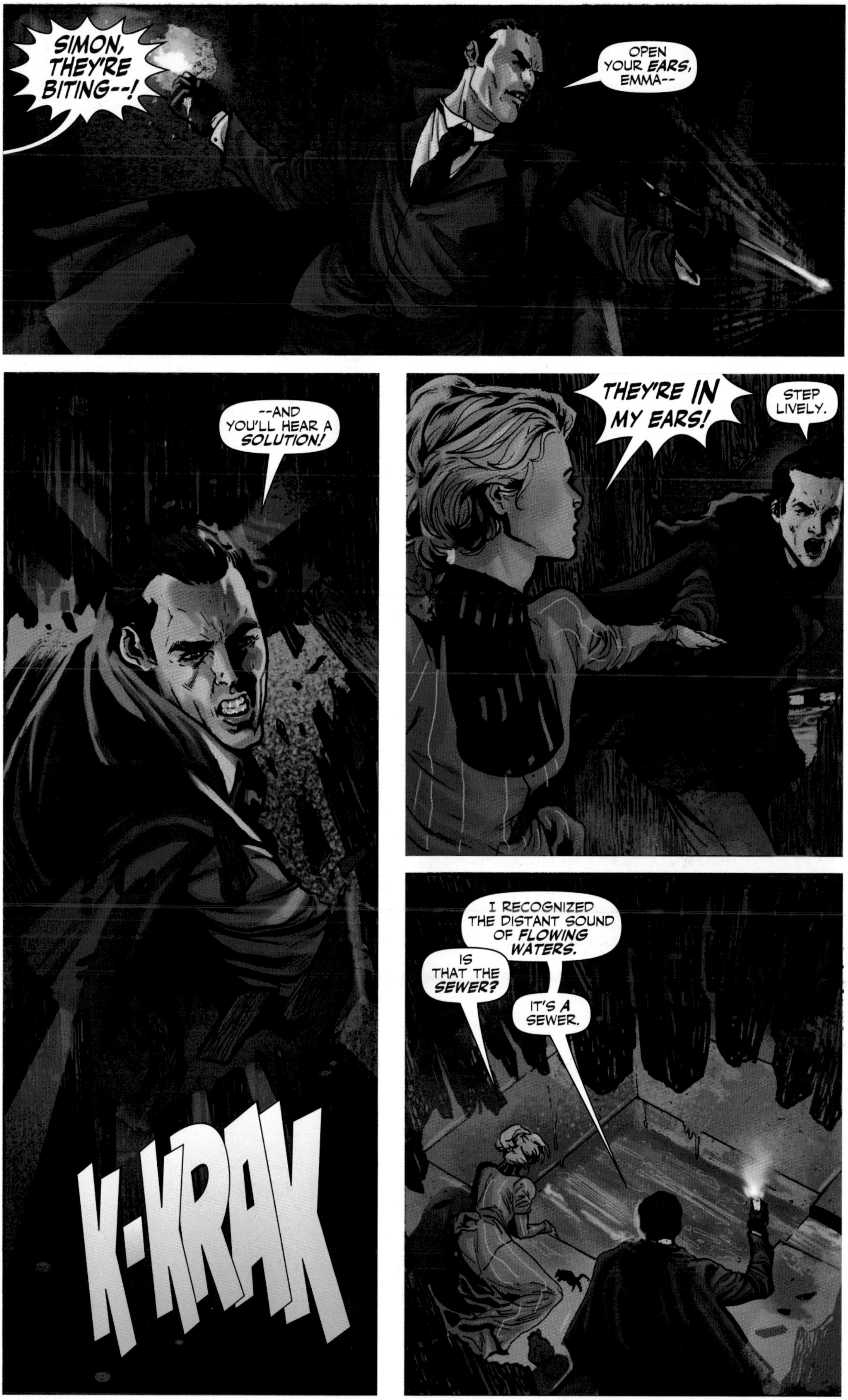

SIMON, THEY'RE BITING--!
OPEN YOUR EARS, EMMA--
--AND YOU'LL HEAR A SOLUTION!
K-KRAK
THEY'RE IN MY EARS!
STEP LIVELY.
I RECOGNIZED THE DISTANT SOUND OF FLOWING WATERS.
IS THAT THE SEWER?
IT'S A SEWER.

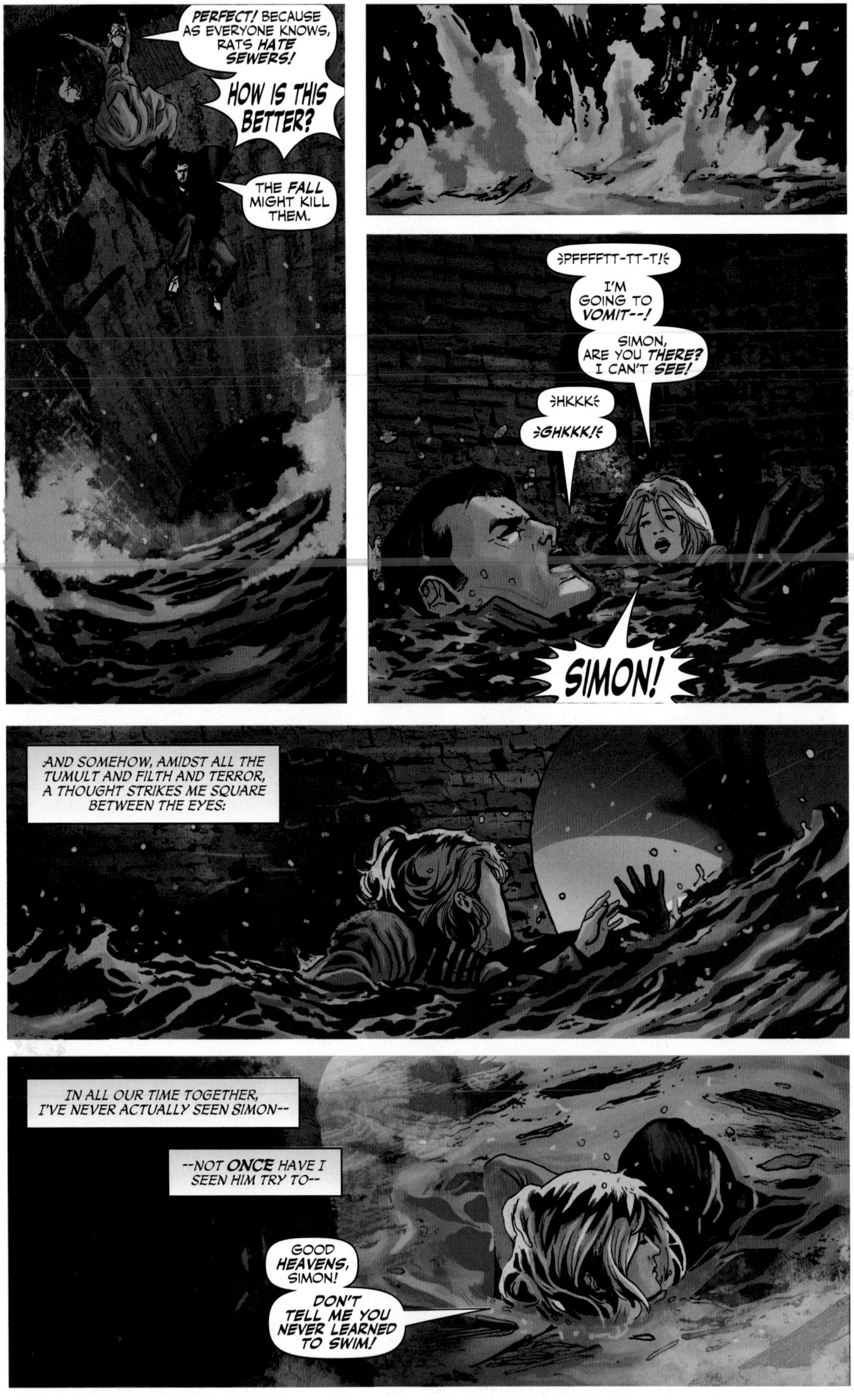
PERFECT! BECAUSE AS EVERYONE KNOWS, RATS HATE SEWERS!
HOW IS THIS BETTER?
THE FALL MIGHT KILL THEM.
PFFFFTT-TT-T!
I'M GOING TO VOMIT--!
SIMON, ARE YOU THERE? I CAN'T SEE!
HKKK
GHKKK!
SIMON!
AND SOMEHOW, AMIDST ALL THE TUMULT AND FILTH AND TERROR, A THOUGHT STRIKES ME SQUARE BETWEEN THE EYES:
IN ALL OUR TIME TOGETHER, I'VE NEVER ACTUALLY SEEN SIMON--
--NOT ONCE HAVE I SEEN HIM TRY TO--
GOOD HEAVENS, SIMON!
DON'T TELL ME YOU NEVER LEARNED TO SWIM!

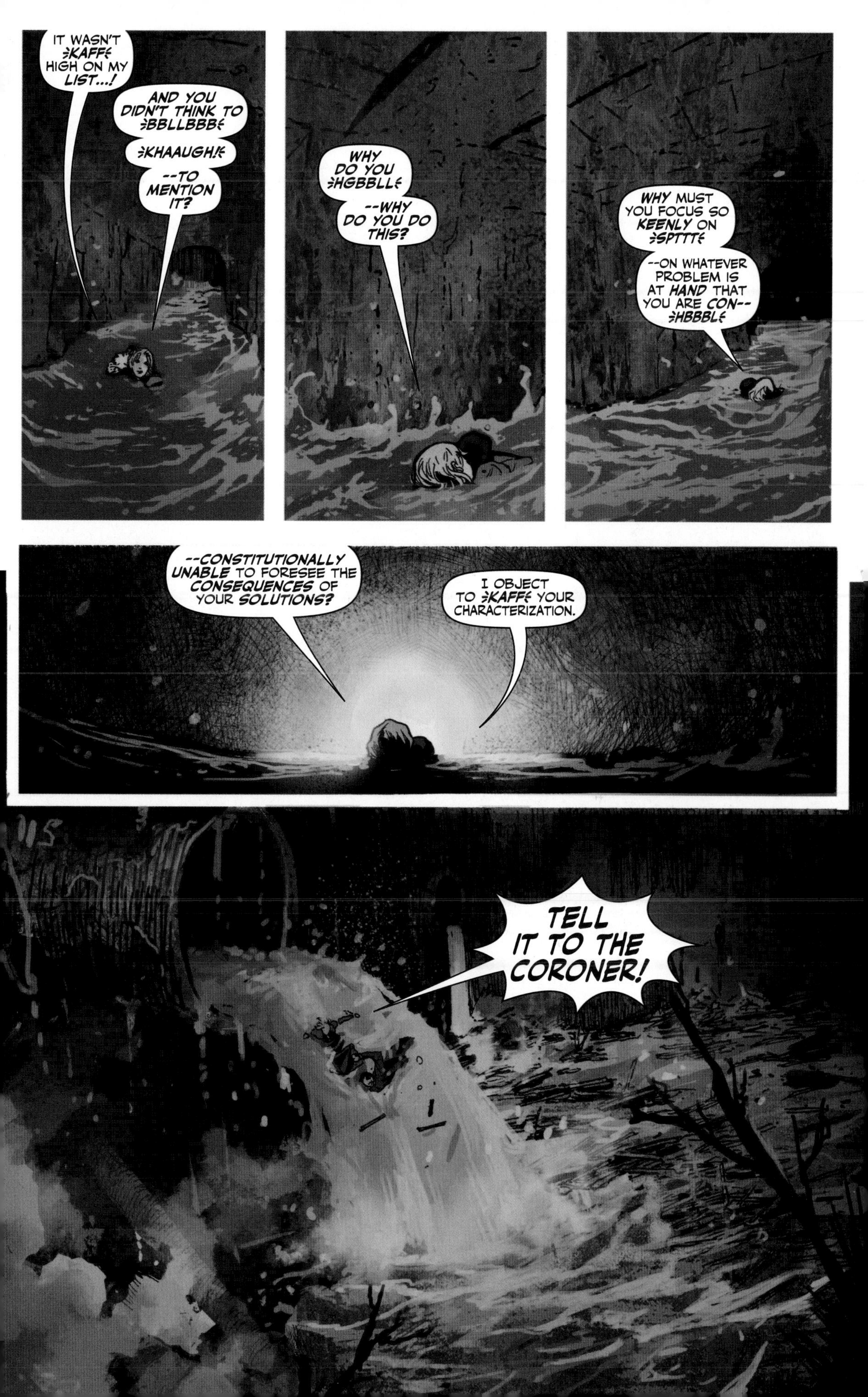
IT WASN'T ≽KAFF≼ HIGH ON MY LIST...!
AND YOU DIDN'T THINK TO ≽BBLLBBB≼
≽KHAAUGH!≼
--TO MENTION IT?
WHY DO YOU ≽HGBBLL≼
--WHY DO YOU DO THIS?
WHY MUST YOU FOCUS SO KEENLY ON ≽SPTTT≼
--ON WHATEVER PROBLEM IS AT HAND THAT YOU ARE CON-- ≽HBBBL≼
--CONSTITUTIONALLY UNABLE TO FORESEE THE CONSEQUENCES OF YOUR SOLUTIONS?
I OBJECT TO ≽KAFF≼ YOUR CHARACTERIZATION.
TELL IT TO THE CORONER!

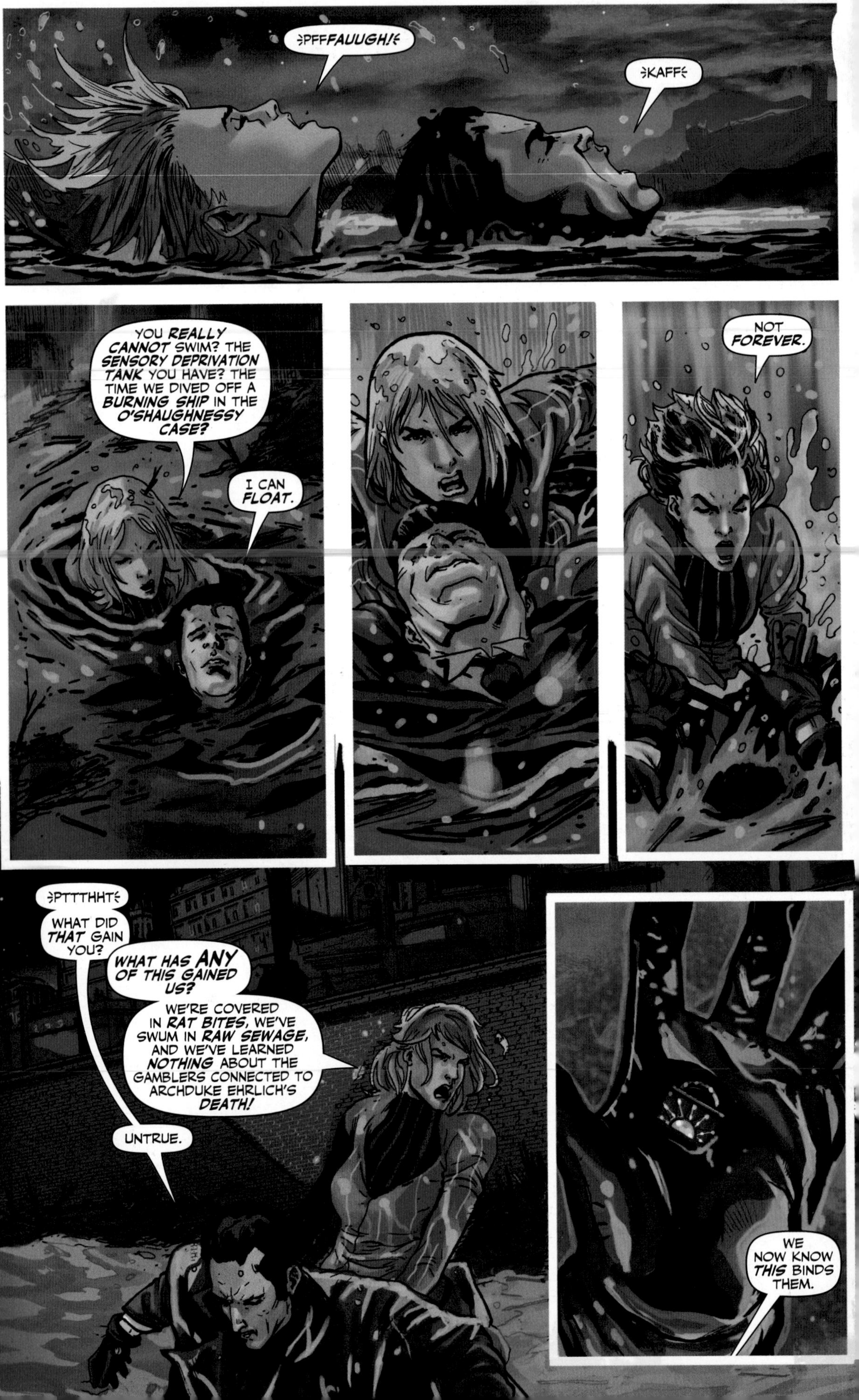
PFFFAUUGH!
KAFF
YOU REALLY CANNOT SWIM? THE SENSORY DEPRIVATION TANK YOU HAVE? THE TIME WE DIVED OFF A BURNING SHIP IN THE O'SHAUGHNESSY CASE?
I CAN FLOAT.
NOT FOREVER.
PTTTHHT
WHAT DID THAT GAIN YOU?
WHAT HAS ANY OF THIS GAINED US?
WE'RE COVERED IN RAT BITES, WE'VE SWUM IN RAW SEWAGE, AND WE'VE LEARNED NOTHING ABOUT THE GAMBLERS CONNECTED TO ARCHDUKE EHRLICH'S DEATH!
UNTRUE.
WE NOW KNOW THIS BINDS THEM.

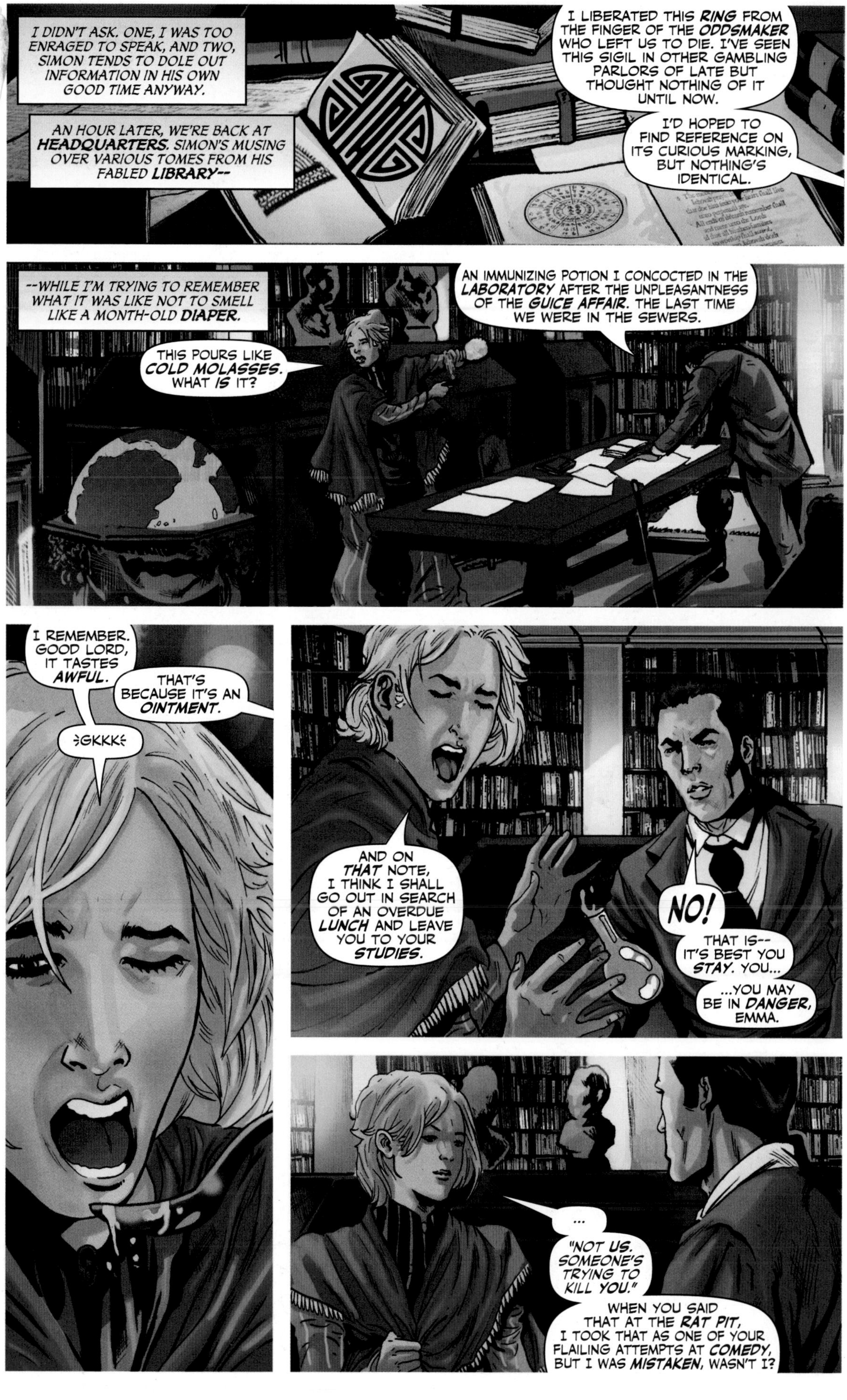

I DIDN'T ASK. ONE, I WAS TOO ENRAGED TO SPEAK, AND TWO, SIMON TENDS TO DOLE OUT INFORMATION IN HIS OWN GOOD TIME ANYWAY.
AN HOUR LATER, WE'RE BACK AT HEADQUARTERS. SIMON'S MUSING OVER VARIOUS TOMES FROM HIS FABLED LIBRARY--
I LIBERATED THIS RING FROM THE FINGER OF THE ODDSMAKER WHO LEFT US TO DIE. I'VE SEEN THIS SIGIL IN OTHER GAMBLING PARLORS OF LATE BUT THOUGHT NOTHING OF IT UNTIL NOW.
I'D HOPED TO FIND REFERENCE ON ITS CURIOUS MARKING, BUT NOTHING'S IDENTICAL.
--WHILE I'M TRYING TO REMEMBER WHAT IT WAS LIKE NOT TO SMELL LIKE A MONTH-OLD DIAPER.
THIS POURS LIKE COLD MOLASSES. WHAT IS IT?
AN IMMUNIZING POTION I CONCOCTED IN THE LABORATORY AFTER THE UNPLEASANTNESS OF THE GUICE AFFAIR. THE LAST TIME WE WERE IN THE SEWERS.
I REMEMBER. GOOD LORD, IT TASTES AWFUL.
THAT'S BECAUSE IT'S AN OINTMENT.
GKKK
AND ON THAT NOTE, I THINK I SHALL GO OUT IN SEARCH OF AN OVERDUE LUNCH AND LEAVE YOU TO YOUR STUDIES.
NO!
THAT IS-- IT'S BEST YOU STAY. YOU...
...YOU MAY BE IN DANGER, EMMA.
...
"NOT US. SOMEONE'S TRYING TO KILL YOU."
WHEN YOU SAID THAT AT THE RAT PIT, I TOOK THAT AS ONE OF YOUR FLAILING ATTEMPTS AT COMEDY, BUT I WAS MISTAKEN, WASN'T I?

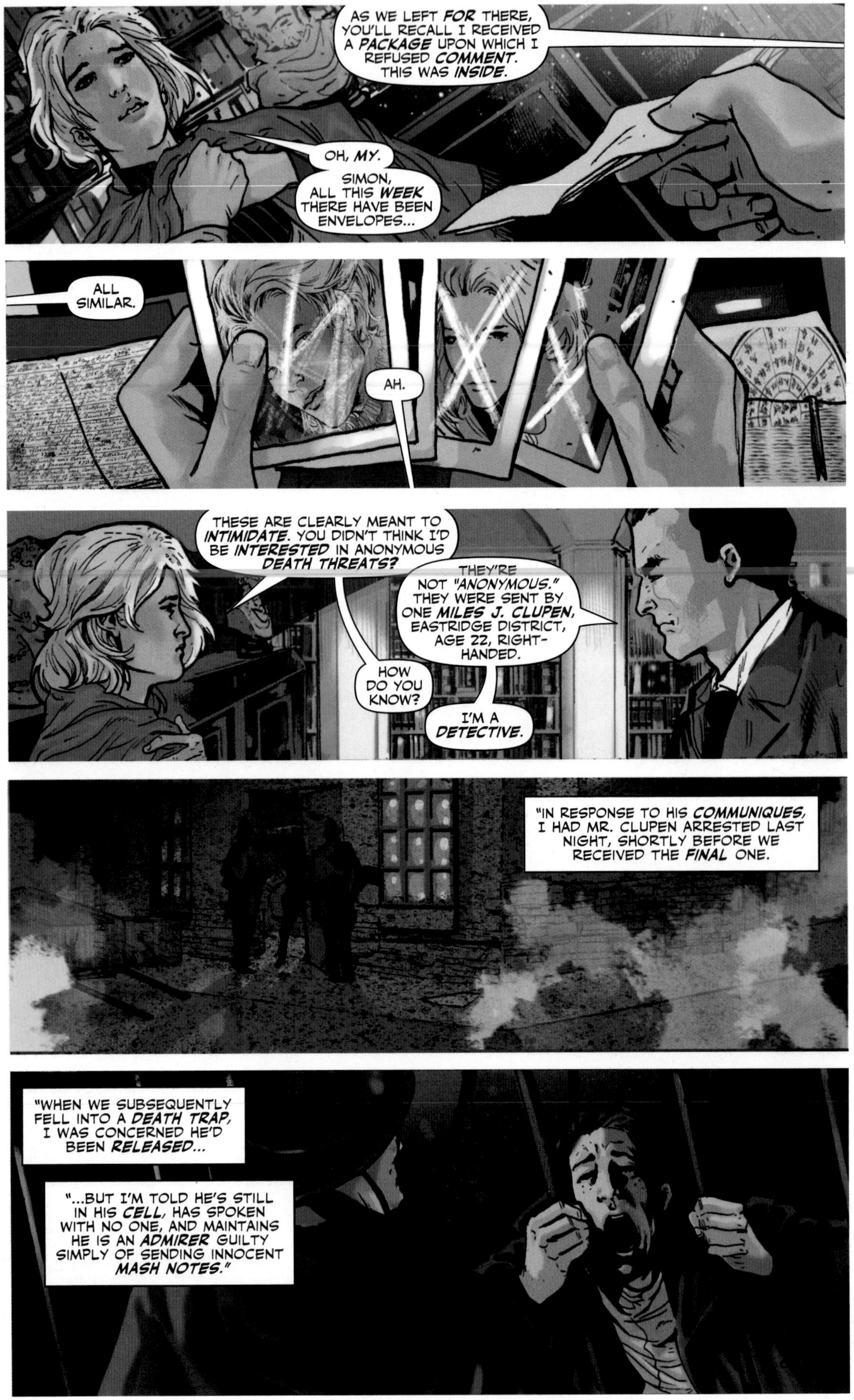
AS WE LEFT FOR THERE, YOU'LL RECALL I RECEIVED A PACKAGE UPON WHICH I REFUSED COMMENT. THIS WAS INSIDE.
OH, MY.
SIMON, ALL THIS WEEK THERE HAVE BEEN ENVELOPES...
ALL SIMILAR.
AH.
THESE ARE CLEARLY MEANT TO INTIMIDATE. YOU DIDN'T THINK I'D BE INTERESTED IN ANONYMOUS DEATH THREATS?
THEY'RE NOT "ANONYMOUS." THEY WERE SENT BY ONE MILES J. CLUPEN, EASTRIDGE DISTRICT, AGE 22, RIGHT-HANDED.
HOW DO YOU KNOW?
I'M A DETECTIVE.
"IN RESPONSE TO HIS COMMUNIQUES, I HAD MR. CLUPEN ARRESTED LAST NIGHT, SHORTLY BEFORE WE RECEIVED THE FINAL ONE.
"WHEN WE SUBSEQUENTLY FELL INTO A DEATH TRAP, I WAS CONCERNED HE'D BEEN RELEASED...
"...BUT I'M TOLD HE'S STILL IN HIS CELL, HAS SPOKEN WITH NO ONE, AND MAINTAINS HE IS AN ADMIRER GUILTY SIMPLY OF SENDING INNOCENT MASH NOTES."

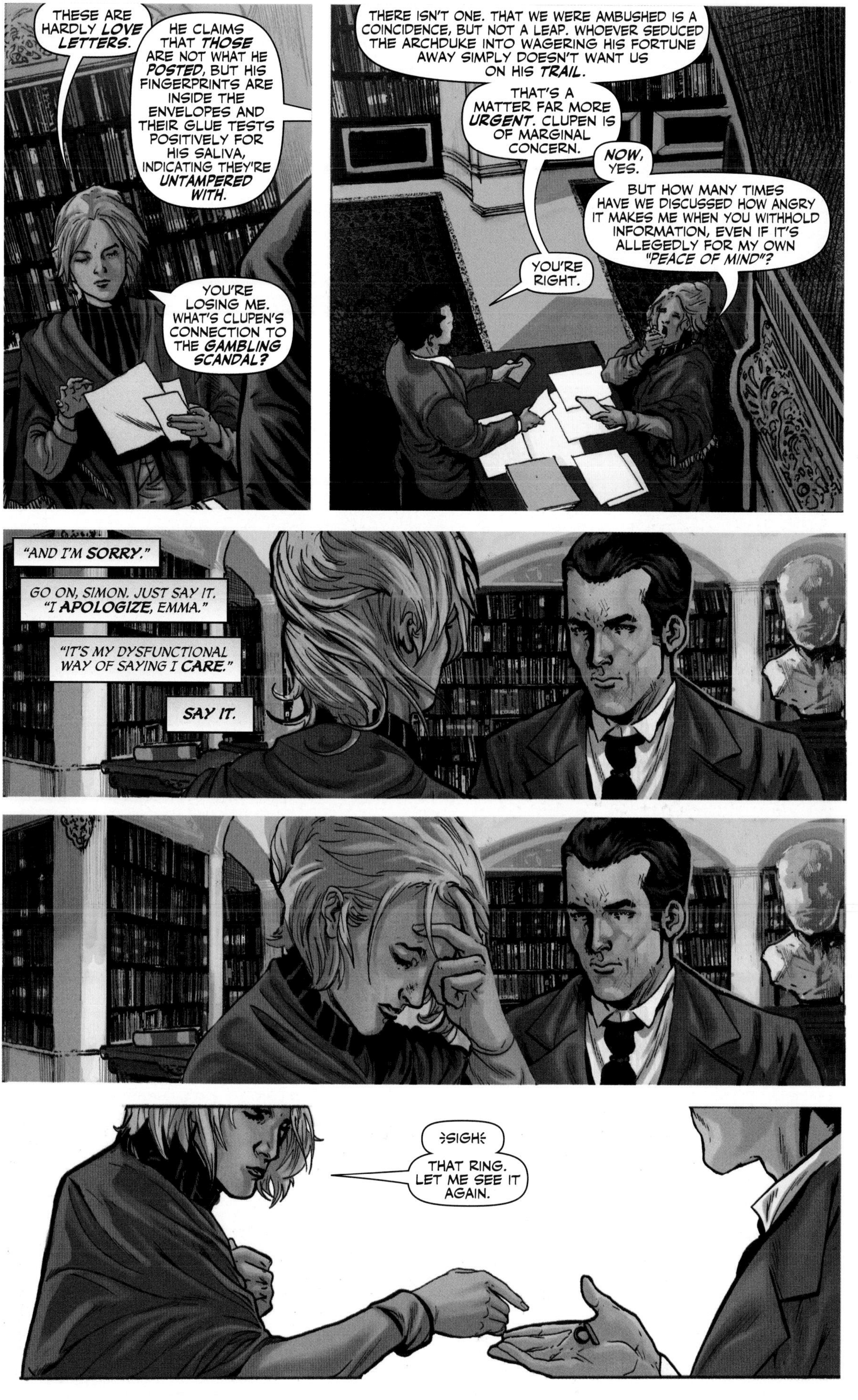
THESE ARE HARDLY LOVE LETTERS.
HE CLAIMS THAT THOSE ARE NOT WHAT HE POSTED, BUT HIS FINGERPRINTS ARE INSIDE THE ENVELOPES AND THEIR GLUE TESTS POSITIVELY FOR HIS SALIVA, INDICATING THEY'RE UNTAMPERED WITH.
YOU'RE LOSING ME. WHAT'S CLUPEN'S CONNECTION TO THE GAMBLING SCANDAL?
THERE ISN'T ONE. THAT WE WERE AMBUSHED IS A COINCIDENCE, BUT NOT A LEAP. WHOEVER SEDUCED THE ARCHDUKE INTO WAGERING HIS FORTUNE AWAY SIMPLY DOESN'T WANT US ON HIS TRAIL.
THAT'S A MATTER FAR MORE URGENT. CLUPEN IS OF MARGINAL CONCERN.
NOW, YES.
BUT HOW MANY TIMES HAVE WE DISCUSSED HOW ANGRY IT MAKES ME WHEN YOU WITHHOLD INFORMATION, EVEN IF IT'S ALLEGEDLY FOR MY OWN "PEACE OF MIND"?
YOU'RE RIGHT.
"AND I'M SORRY."
GO ON, SIMON. JUST SAY IT. "I APOLOGIZE, EMMA."
"IT'S MY DYSFUNCTIONAL WAY OF SAYING I CARE."
SAY IT.
SIGH
THAT RING. LET ME SEE IT AGAIN.

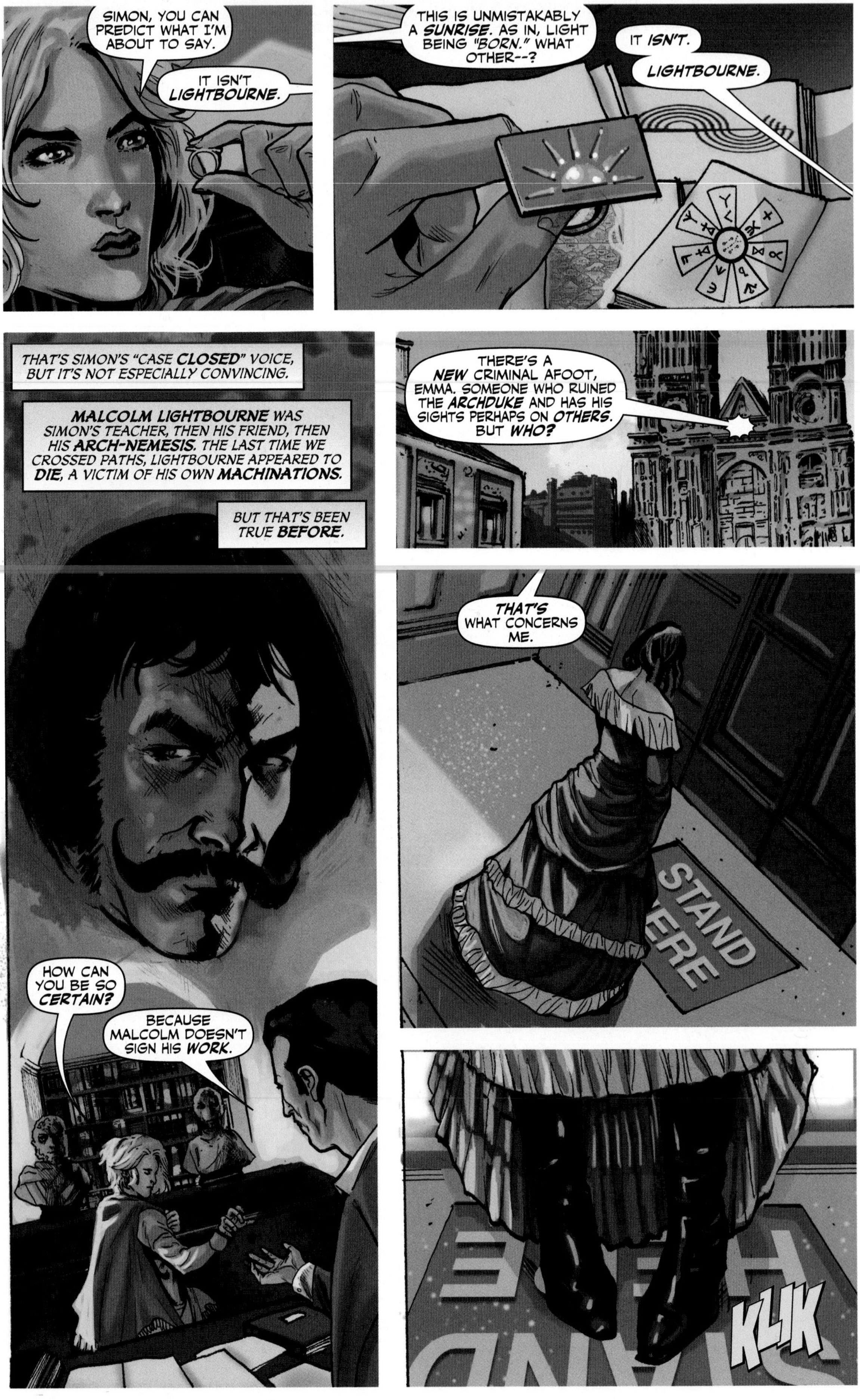
SIMON, YOU CAN PREDICT WHAT I'M ABOUT TO SAY.
IT ISN'T LIGHTBOURNE.
THIS IS UNMISTAKABLY A SUNRISE. AS IN, LIGHT BEING "BORN." WHAT OTHER--?
IT ISN'T.
LIGHTBOURNE.
THAT'S SIMON'S "CASE CLOSED" VOICE, BUT IT'S NOT ESPECIALLY CONVINCING.
MALCOLM LIGHTBOURNE WAS SIMON'S TEACHER, THEN HIS FRIEND, THEN HIS ARCH-NEMESIS. THE LAST TIME WE CROSSED PATHS, LIGHTBOURNE APPEARED TO DIE, A VICTIM OF HIS OWN MACHINATIONS.
BUT THAT'S BEEN TRUE BEFORE.
HOW CAN YOU BE SO CERTAIN?
BECAUSE MALCOLM DOESN'T SIGN HIS WORK.
THERE'S A NEW CRIMINAL AFOOT, EMMA. SOMEONE WHO RUINED THE ARCHDUKE AND HAS HIS SIGHTS PERHAPS ON OTHERS. BUT WHO?
THAT'S WHAT CONCERNS ME.
STAND HERE
KLIK

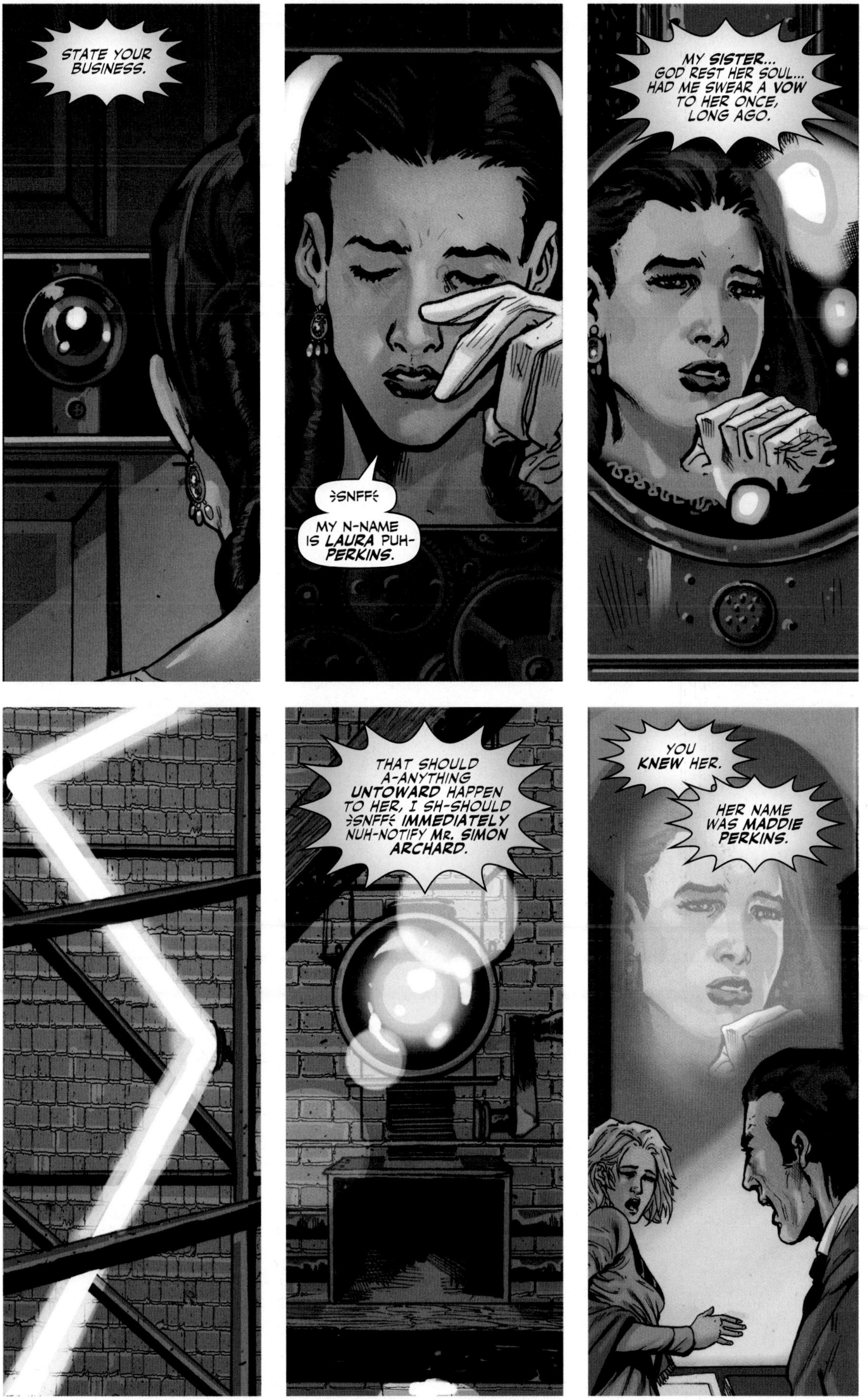
STATE YOUR BUSINESS.
SNFF
MY N-NAME IS LAURA PUH-PERKINS.
MY SISTER... GOD REST HER SOUL... HAD ME SWEAR A VOW TO HER ONCE, LONG AGO.
THAT SHOULD A-ANYTHING UNTOWARD HAPPEN TO HER, I SH-SHOULD *SNFF* IMMEDIATELY NUH-NOTIFY MR. SIMON ARCHARD.
YOU KNEW HER.
HER NAME WAS MADDIE PERKINS.

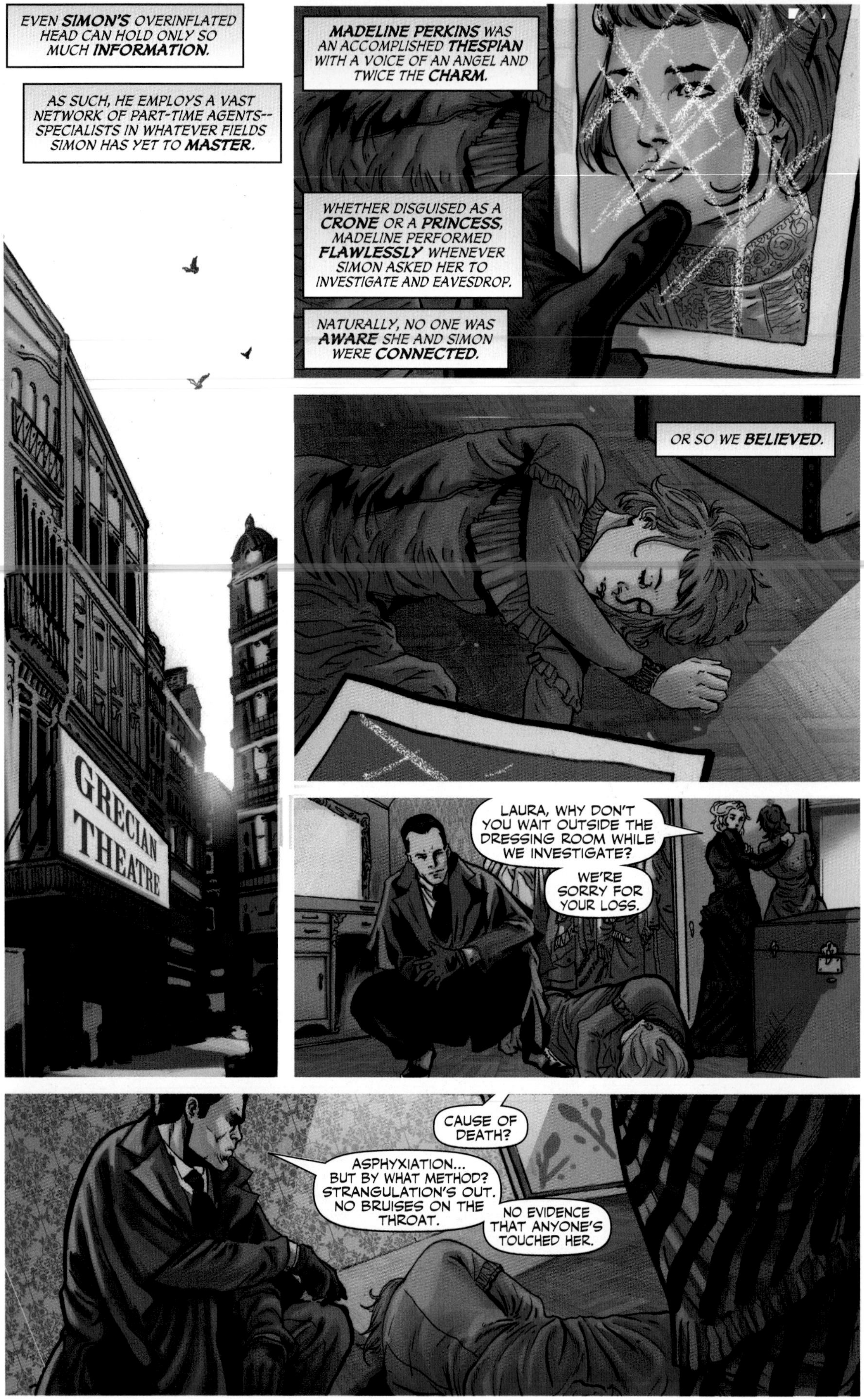
EVEN SIMON'S OVERINFLATED HEAD CAN HOLD ONLY SO MUCH INFORMATION.
AS SUCH, HE EMPLOYS A VAST NETWORK OF PART-TIME AGENTS-- SPECIALISTS IN WHATEVER FIELDS SIMON HAS YET TO MASTER.
GRECIAN THEATRE
MADELINE PERKINS WAS AN ACCOMPLISHED THESPIAN WITH A VOICE OF AN ANGEL AND TWICE THE CHARM.
WHETHER DISGUISED AS A CRONE OR A PRINCESS, MADELINE PERFORMED FLAWLESSLY WHENEVER SIMON ASKED HER TO INVESTIGATE AND EAVESDROP.
NATURALLY, NO ONE WAS AWARE SHE AND SIMON WERE CONNECTED.
OR SO WE BELIEVED.
LAURA, WHY DON'T YOU WAIT OUTSIDE THE DRESSING ROOM WHILE WE INVESTIGATE?
WE'RE SORRY FOR YOUR LOSS.
CAUSE OF DEATH?
ASPHYXIATION... BUT BY WHAT METHOD? STRANGULATION'S OUT. NO BRUISES ON THE THROAT.
NO EVIDENCE THAT ANYONE'S TOUCHED HER.

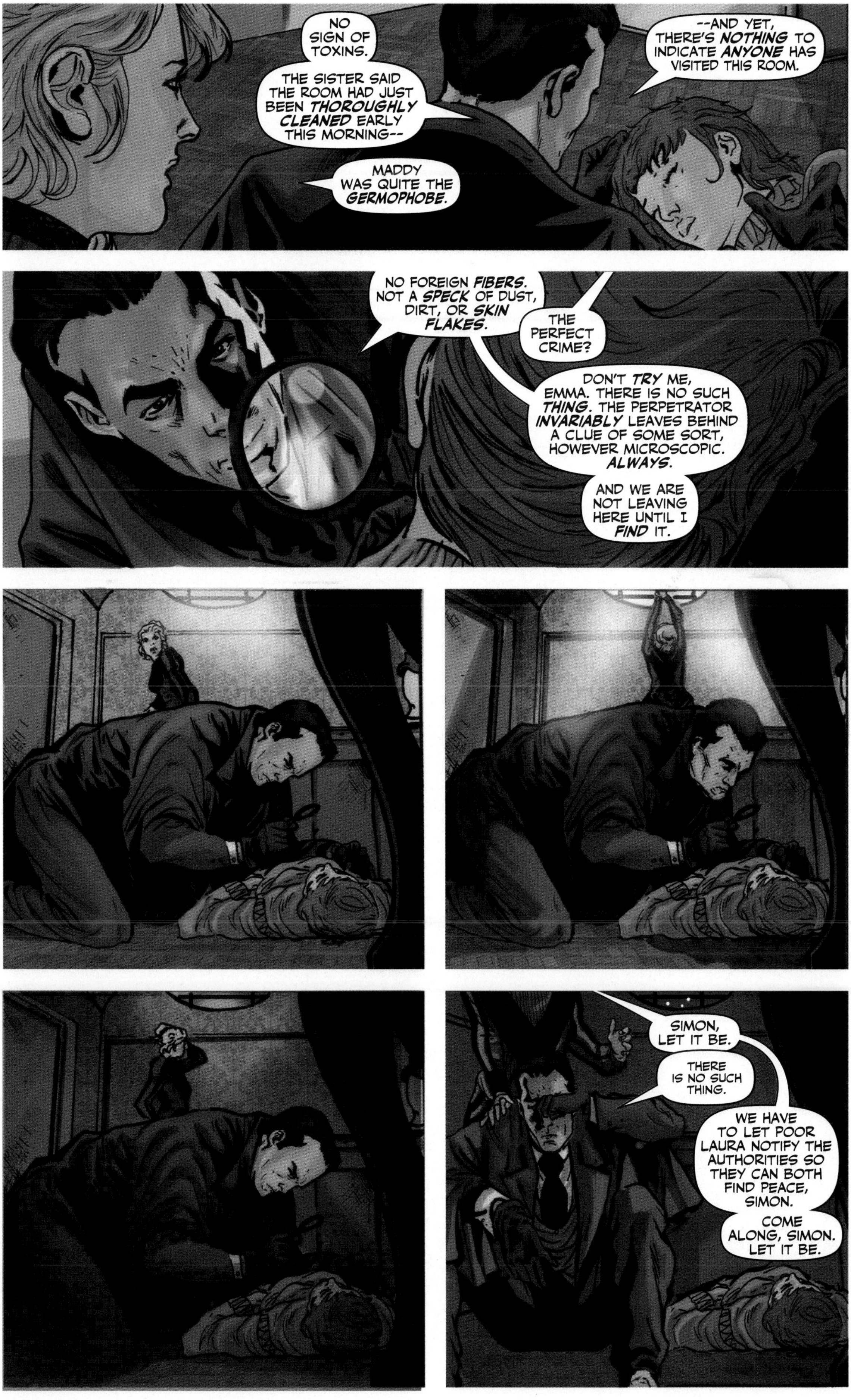
NO SIGN OF TOXINS.
THE SISTER SAID THE ROOM HAD JUST BEEN THOROUGHLY CLEANED EARLY THIS MORNING--
MADDY WAS QUITE THE GERMOPHOBE.
--AND YET, THERE'S NOTHING TO INDICATE ANYONE HAS VISITED THIS ROOM.
NO FOREIGN FIBERS. NOT A SPECK OF DUST, DIRT, OR SKIN FLAKES.
THE PERFECT CRIME?
DON'T TRY ME, EMMA. THERE IS NO SUCH THING. THE PERPETRATOR INVARIABLY LEAVES BEHIND A CLUE OF SOME SORT, HOWEVER MICROSCOPIC. ALWAYS.
AND WE ARE NOT LEAVING HERE UNTIL I FIND IT.
SIMON, LET IT BE.
THERE IS NO SUCH THING.
WE HAVE TO LET POOR LAURA NOTIFY THE AUTHORITIES SO THEY CAN BOTH FIND PEACE, SIMON.
COME ALONG, SIMON. LET IT BE.

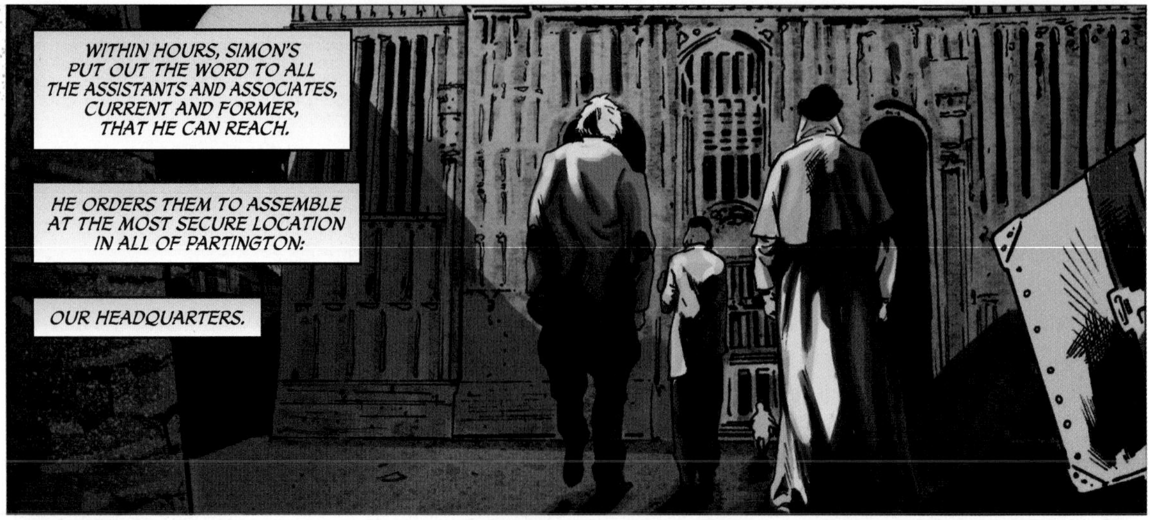
WITHIN HOURS, SIMON'S PUT OUT THE WORD TO ALL THE ASSISTANTS AND ASSOCIATES, CURRENT AND FORMER, THAT HE CAN REACH.
HE ORDERS THEM TO ASSEMBLE AT THE MOST SECURE LOCATION IN ALL OF PARTINGTON:
OUR HEADQUARTERS.

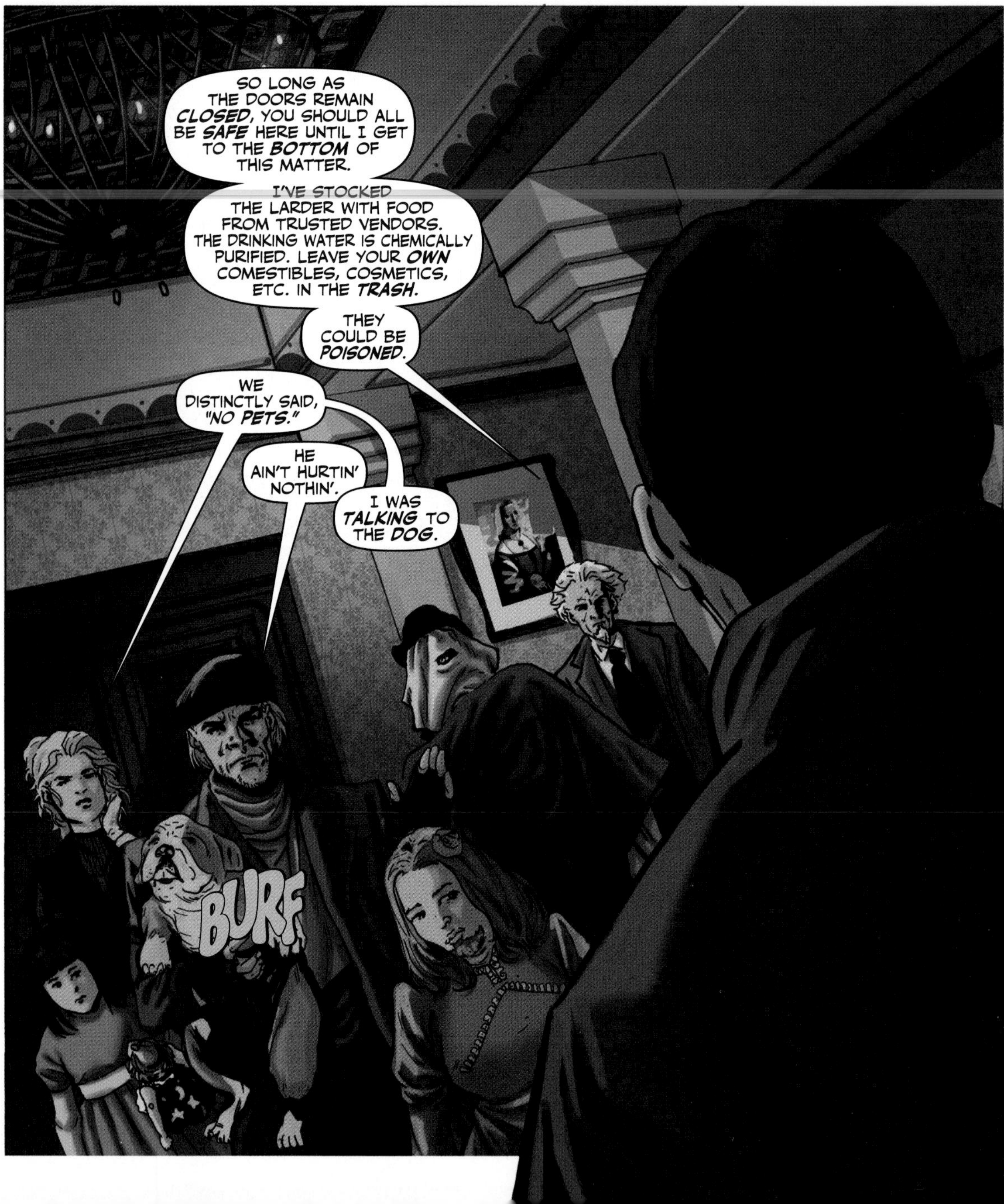
SO LONG AS THE DOORS REMAIN *CLOSED*, YOU SHOULD ALL BE *SAFE* HERE UNTIL I GET TO THE *BOTTOM* OF THIS MATTER.
I'VE STOCKED THE LARDER WITH FOOD FROM TRUSTED VENDORS. THE DRINKING WATER IS CHEMICALLY PURIFIED. LEAVE YOUR *OWN* COMESTIBLES, COSMETICS, ETC. IN THE *TRASH*.
THEY COULD BE *POISONED*.
WE DISTINCTLY SAID, *"NO PETS."*
HE AIN'T HURTIN' NOTHIN'.
I WAS *TALKING* TO THE *DOG*.
BURF

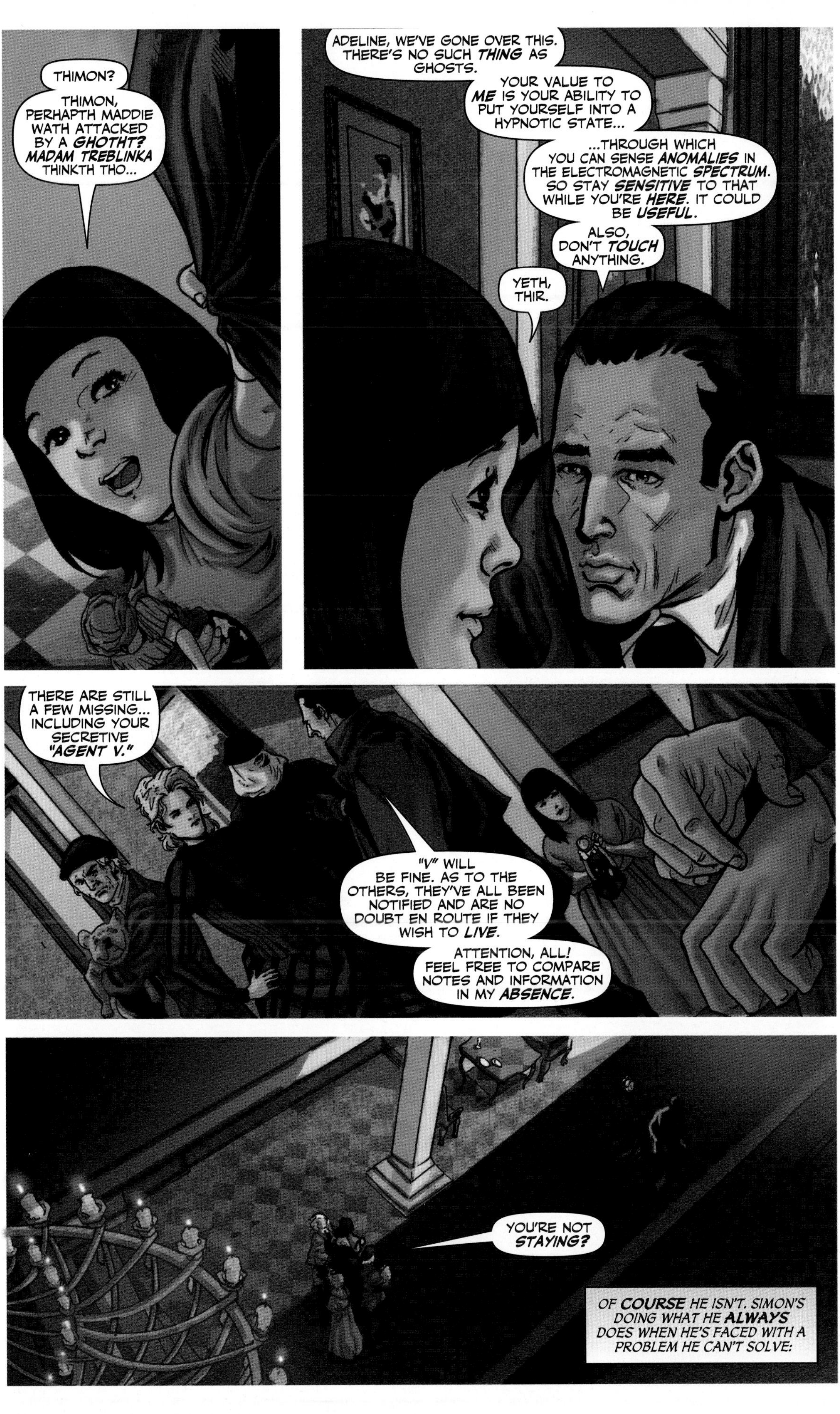
THIMON?
THIMON, PERHAPTH MADDIE WATH ATTACKED BY A GHOTHT? MADAM TREBLINKA THINKTH THO...
ADELINE, WE'VE GONE OVER THIS. THERE'S NO SUCH THING AS GHOSTS.
YOUR VALUE TO ME IS YOUR ABILITY TO PUT YOURSELF INTO A HYPNOTIC STATE...
...THROUGH WHICH YOU CAN SENSE ANOMALIES IN THE ELECTROMAGNETIC SPECTRUM. SO STAY SENSITIVE TO THAT WHILE YOU'RE HERE. IT COULD BE USEFUL.
ALSO, DON'T TOUCH ANYTHING.
YETH, THIR.
THERE ARE STILL A FEW MISSING... INCLUDING YOUR SECRETIVE "AGENT V."
"V" WILL BE FINE. AS TO THE OTHERS, THEY'VE ALL BEEN NOTIFIED AND ARE NO DOUBT EN ROUTE IF THEY WISH TO LIVE.
ATTENTION, ALL! FEEL FREE TO COMPARE NOTES AND INFORMATION IN MY ABSENCE.
YOU'RE NOT STAYING?
OF COURSE HE ISN'T. SIMON'S DOING WHAT HE ALWAYS DOES WHEN HE'S FACED WITH A PROBLEM HE CAN'T SOLVE:

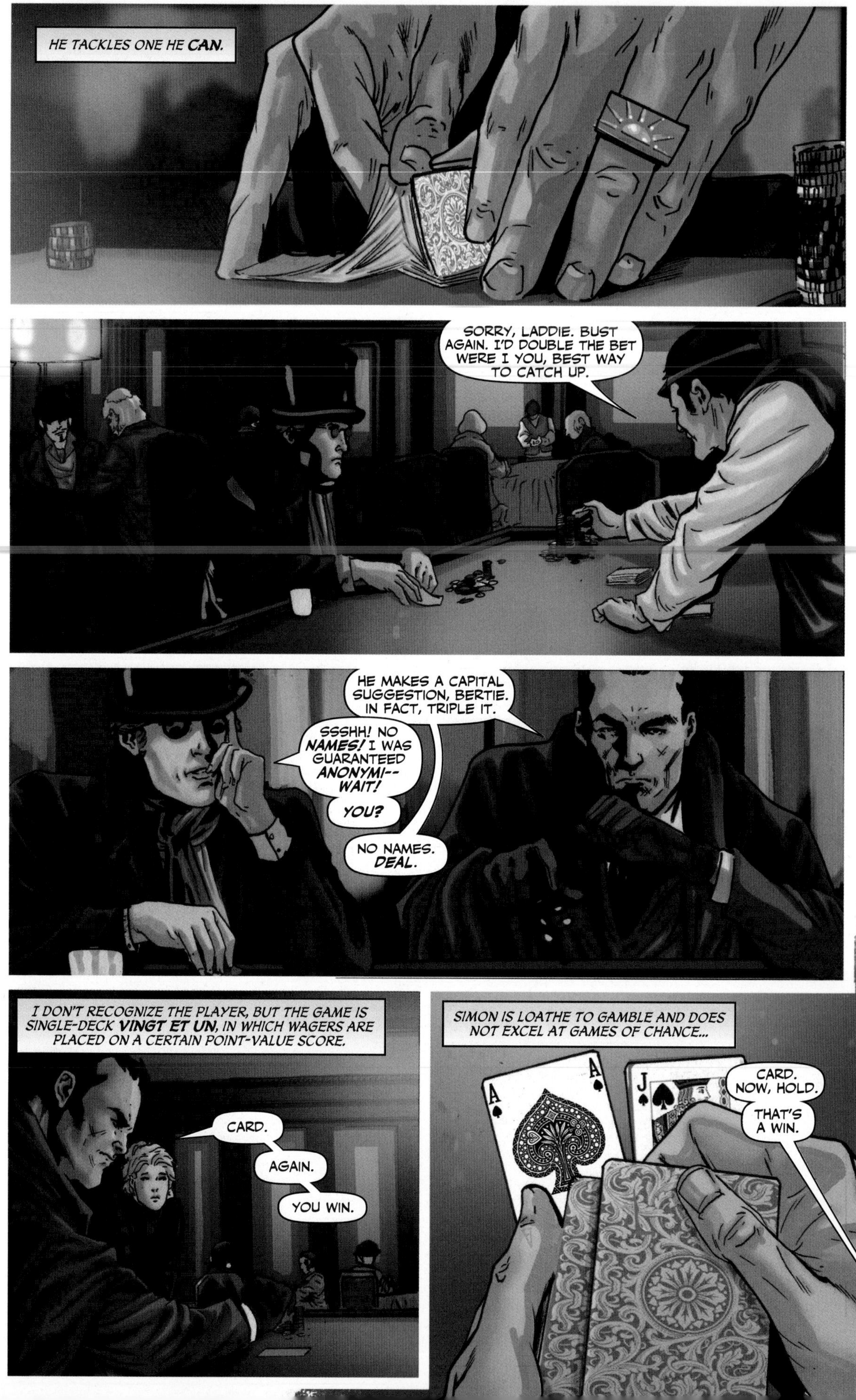
HE TACKLES ONE HE CAN.
SORRY, LADDIE. BUST AGAIN. I'D DOUBLE THE BET WERE I YOU, BEST WAY TO CATCH UP.
HE MAKES A CAPITAL SUGGESTION, BERTIE. IN FACT, TRIPLE IT.
SSSHH! NO NAMES! I WAS GUARANTEED ANONYMI-- WAIT!
YOU?
NO NAMES. DEAL.
I DON'T RECOGNIZE THE PLAYER, BUT THE GAME IS SINGLE-DECK VINGT ET UN, IN WHICH WAGERS ARE PLACED ON A CERTAIN POINT-VALUE SCORE.
CARD.
AGAIN.
YOU WIN.
SIMON IS LOATHE TO GAMBLE AND DOES NOT EXCEL AT GAMES OF CHANCE...
CARD. NOW, HOLD.
THAT'S A WIN.

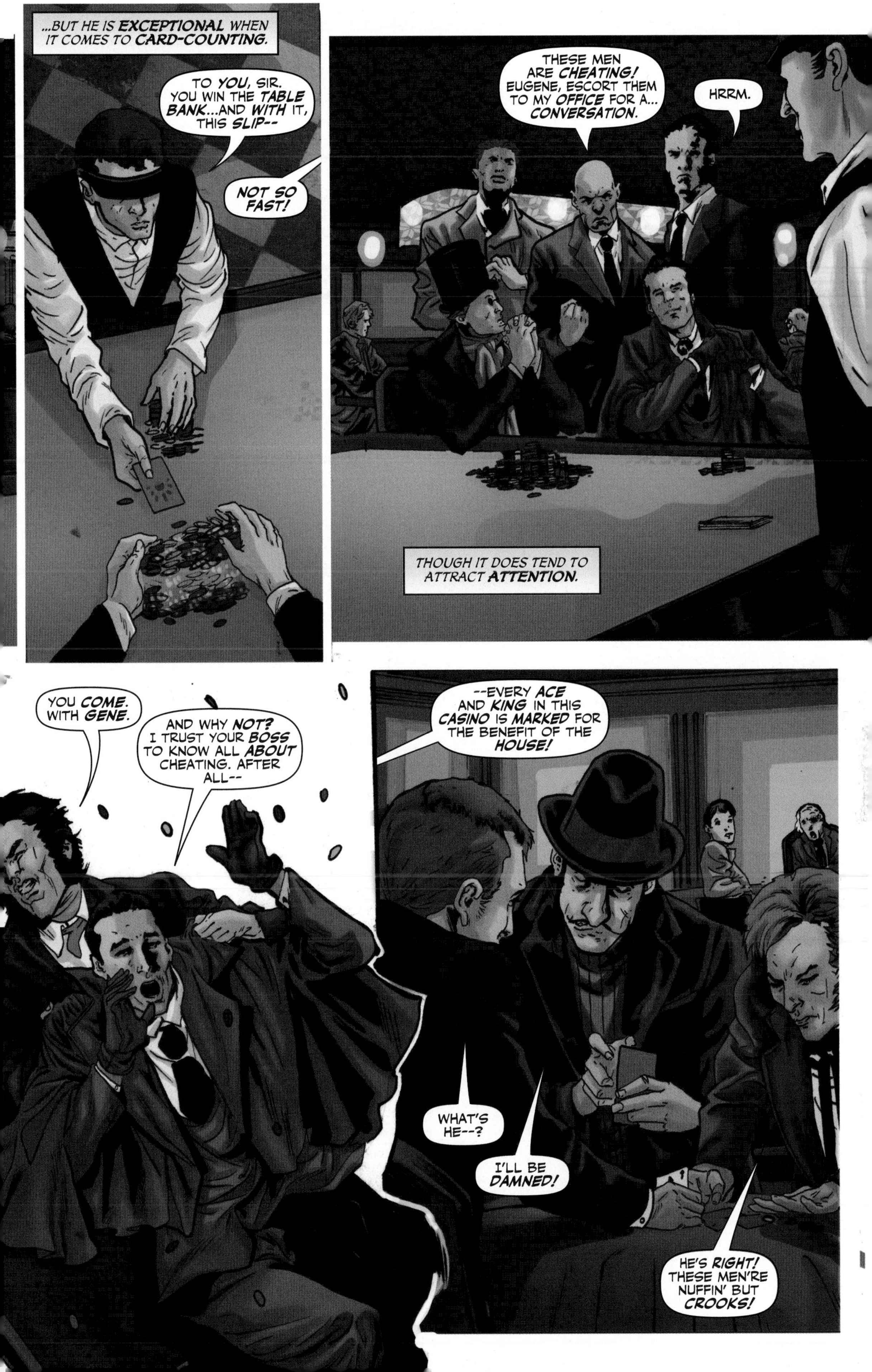
...BUT HE IS EXCEPTIONAL WHEN IT COMES TO CARD-COUNTING.
TO YOU, SIR. YOU WIN THE TABLE BANK...AND WITH IT, THIS SLIP--
NOT SO FAST!
THESE MEN ARE CHEATING! EUGENE, ESCORT THEM TO MY OFFICE FOR A... CONVERSATION.
HRRM.
THOUGH IT DOES TEND TO ATTRACT ATTENTION.
YOU COME. WITH GENE.
AND WHY NOT? I TRUST YOUR BOSS TO KNOW ALL ABOUT CHEATING. AFTER ALL--
--EVERY ACE AND KING IN THIS CASINO IS MARKED FOR THE BENEFIT OF THE HOUSE!
WHAT'S HE--?
I'LL BE DAMNED!
HE'S RIGHT! THESE MEN'RE NUFFIN' BUT CROOKS!

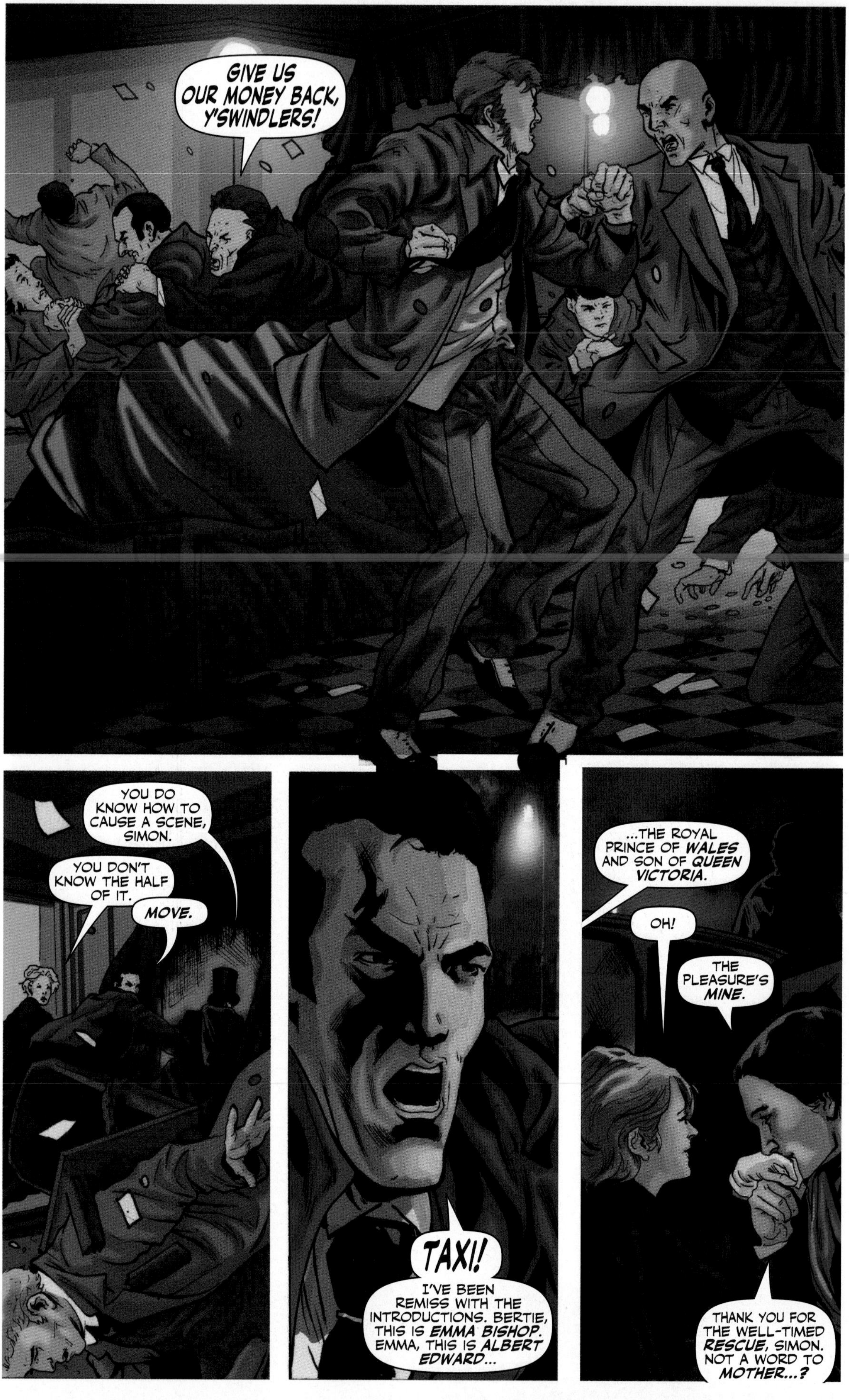

GIVE US OUR MONEY BACK, Y'SWINDLERS!
YOU DO KNOW HOW TO CAUSE A SCENE, SIMON.
YOU DON'T KNOW THE HALF OF IT.
MOVE.
TAXI!
I'VE BEEN REMISS WITH THE INTRODUCTIONS. BERTIE, THIS IS EMMA BISHOP. EMMA, THIS IS ALBERT EDWARD...
...THE ROYAL PRINCE OF WALES AND SON OF QUEEN VICTORIA.
OH!
THE PLEASURE'S MINE.
THANK YOU FOR THE WELL-TIMED RESCUE, SIMON. NOT A WORD TO MOTHER...?

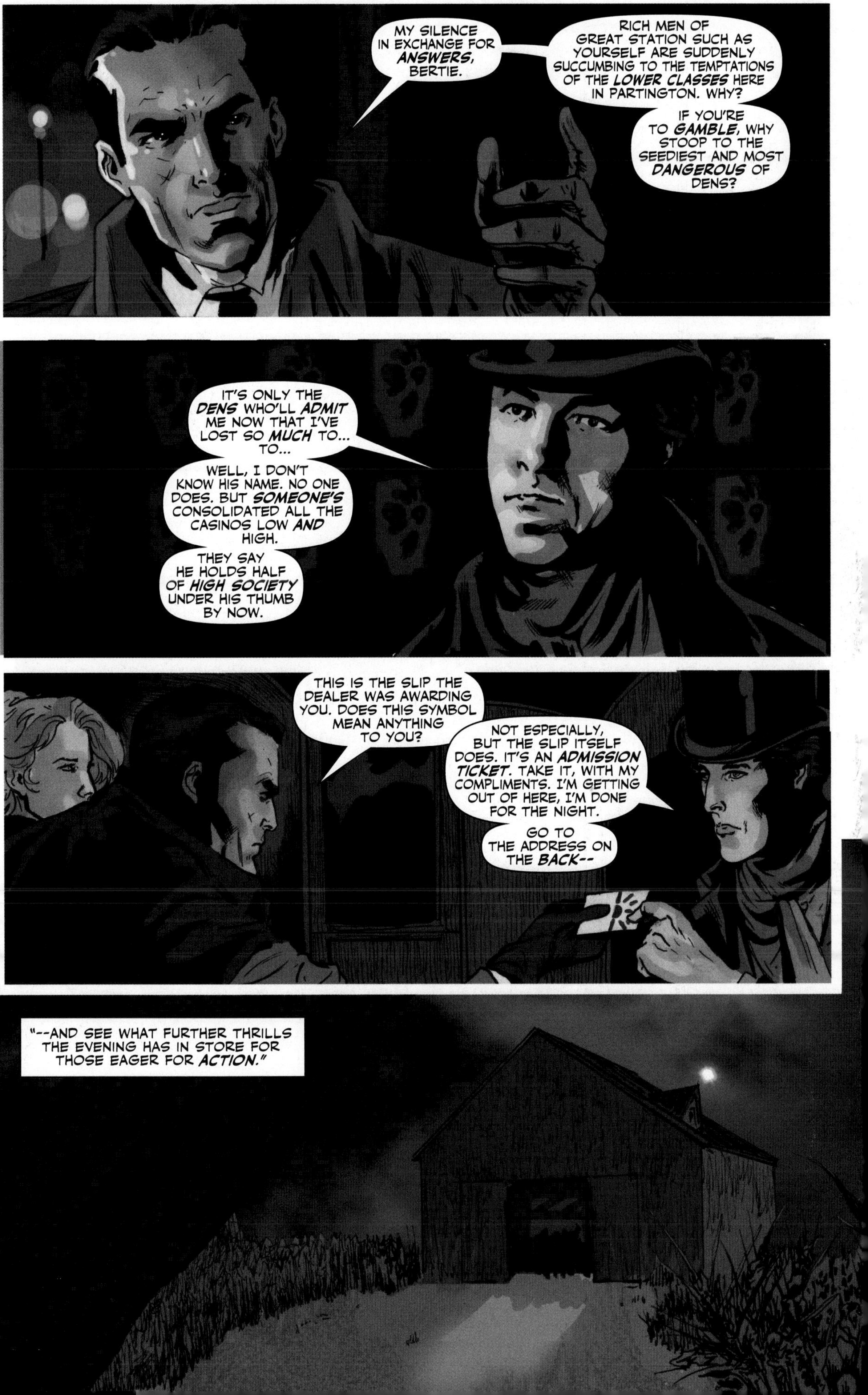
MY SILENCE IN EXCHANGE FOR ANSWERS, BERTIE.
RICH MEN OF GREAT STATION SUCH AS YOURSELF ARE SUDDENLY SUCCUMBING TO THE TEMPTATIONS OF THE LOWER CLASSES HERE IN PARTINGTON. WHY?
IF YOU'RE TO GAMBLE, WHY STOOP TO THE SEEDIEST AND MOST DANGEROUS OF DENS?
IT'S ONLY THE DENS WHO'LL ADMIT ME NOW THAT I'VE LOST SO MUCH TO... TO...
WELL, I DON'T KNOW HIS NAME. NO ONE DOES. BUT SOMEONE'S CONSOLIDATED ALL THE CASINOS LOW AND HIGH.
THEY SAY HE HOLDS HALF OF HIGH SOCIETY UNDER HIS THUMB BY NOW.
THIS IS THE SLIP THE DEALER WAS AWARDING YOU. DOES THIS SYMBOL MEAN ANYTHING TO YOU?
NOT ESPECIALLY, BUT THE SLIP ITSELF DOES. IT'S AN ADMISSION TICKET. TAKE IT, WITH MY COMPLIMENTS. I'M GETTING OUT OF HERE, I'M DONE FOR THE NIGHT.
GO TO THE ADDRESS ON THE BACK--
"--AND SEE WHAT FURTHER THRILLS THE EVENING HAS IN STORE FOR THOSE EAGER FOR ACTION."

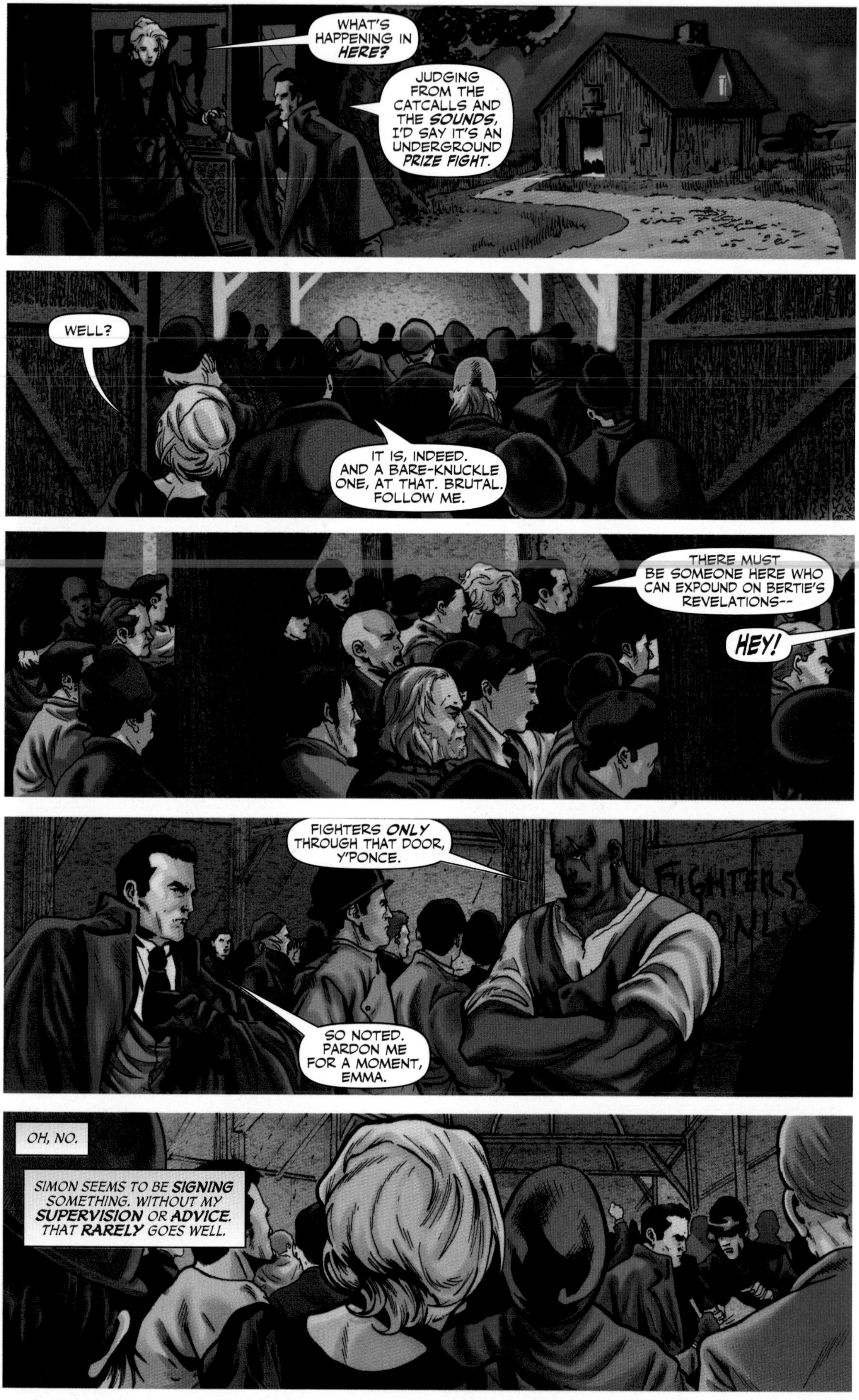
WHAT'S HAPPENING IN HERE?
JUDGING FROM THE CATCALLS AND THE SOUNDS, I'D SAY IT'S AN UNDERGROUND PRIZE FIGHT.
WELL?
IT IS, INDEED. AND A BARE-KNUCKLE ONE, AT THAT. BRUTAL. FOLLOW ME.
THERE MUST BE SOMEONE HERE WHO CAN EXPOUND ON BERTIE'S REVELATIONS--
HEY!
FIGHTERS ONLY THROUGH THAT DOOR, Y'PONCE.
FIGHTERS ONLY
SO NOTED. PARDON ME FOR A MOMENT, EMMA.
OH, NO.
SIMON SEEMS TO BE SIGNING SOMETHING. WITHOUT MY SUPERVISION OR ADVICE. THAT RARELY GOES WELL.

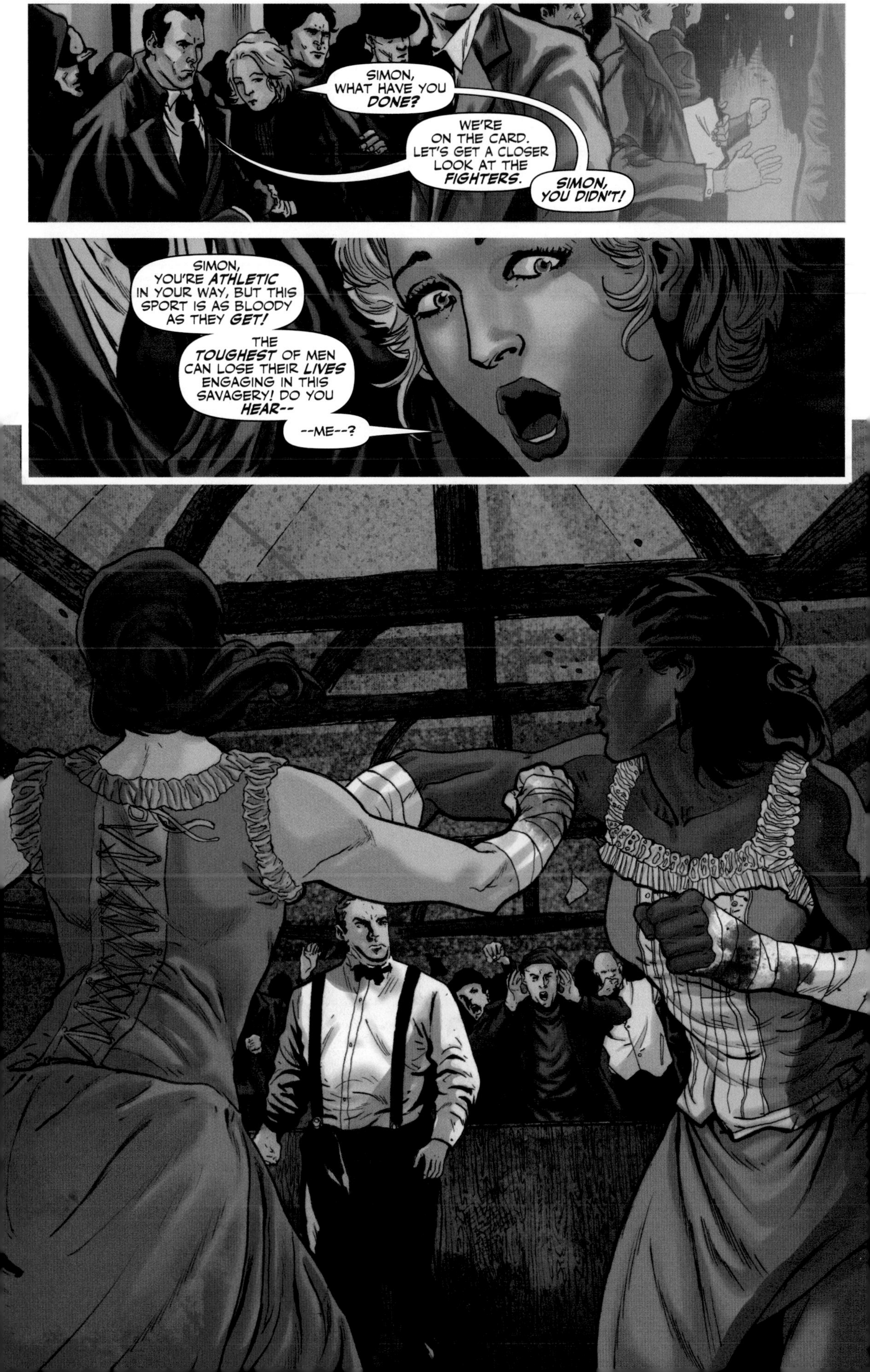
SIMON, WHAT HAVE YOU DONE?
WE'RE ON THE CARD. LET'S GET A CLOSER LOOK AT THE FIGHTERS.
SIMON, YOU DIDN'T!
SIMON, YOU'RE ATHLETIC IN YOUR WAY, BUT THIS SPORT IS AS BLOODY AS THEY GET!
THE TOUGHEST OF MEN CAN LOSE THEIR LIVES ENGAGING IN THIS SAVAGERY! DO YOU HEAR--
--ME--?

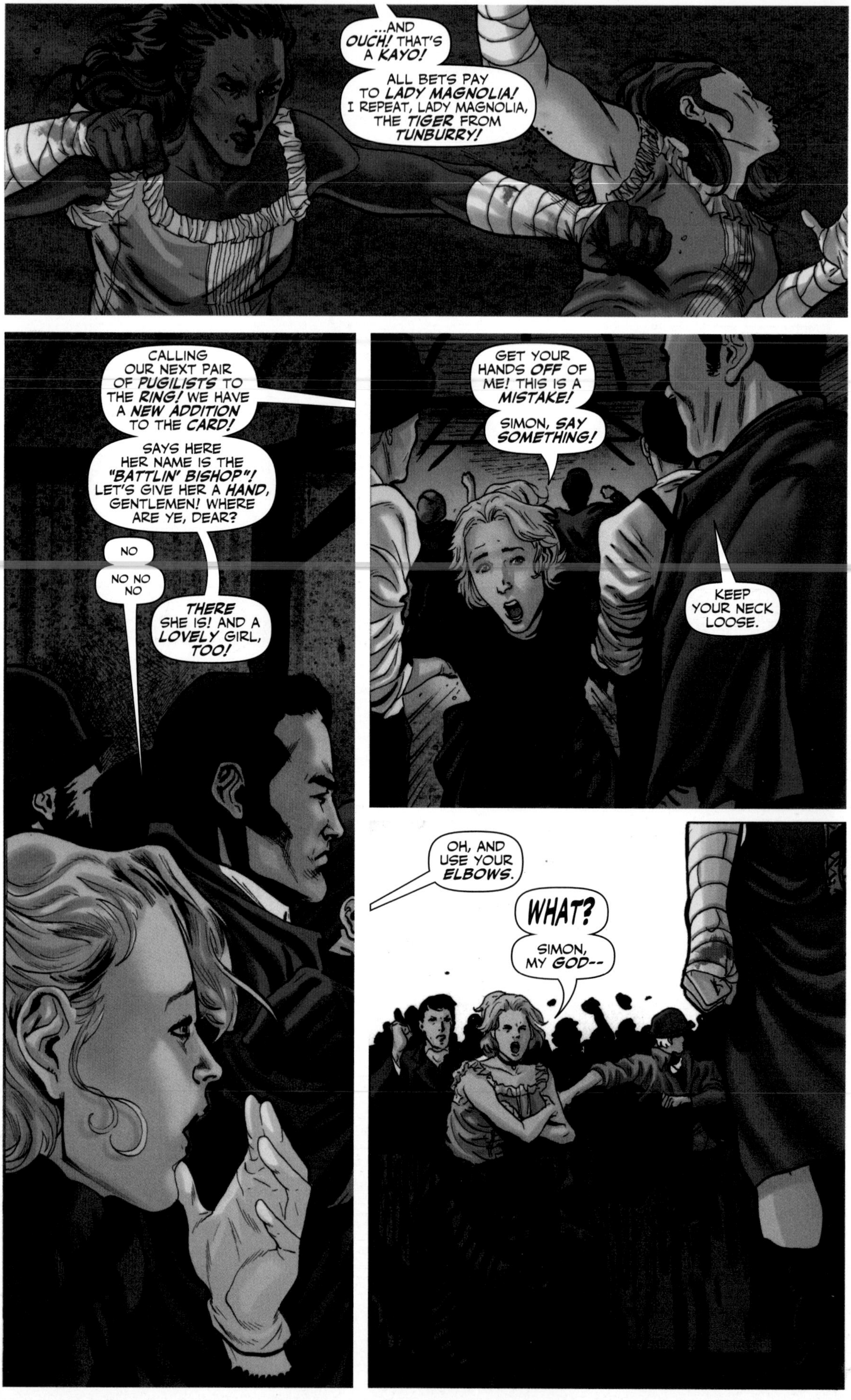
...AND OUCH! THAT'S A KAYO!
ALL BETS PAY TO LADY MAGNOLIA! I REPEAT, LADY MAGNOLIA, THE TIGER FROM TUNBURRY!
CALLING OUR NEXT PAIR OF PUGILISTS TO THE RING! WE HAVE A NEW ADDITION TO THE CARD!
SAYS HERE HER NAME IS THE "BATTLIN' BISHOP"! LET'S GIVE HER A HAND, GENTLEMEN! WHERE ARE YE, DEAR?
NO
NO NO NO
THERE SHE IS! AND A LOVELY GIRL, TOO!
GET YOUR HANDS OFF OF ME! THIS IS A MISTAKE!
SIMON, SAY SOMETHING!
KEEP YOUR NECK LOOSE.
OH, AND USE YOUR ELBOWS.
WHAT?
SIMON, MY GOD--

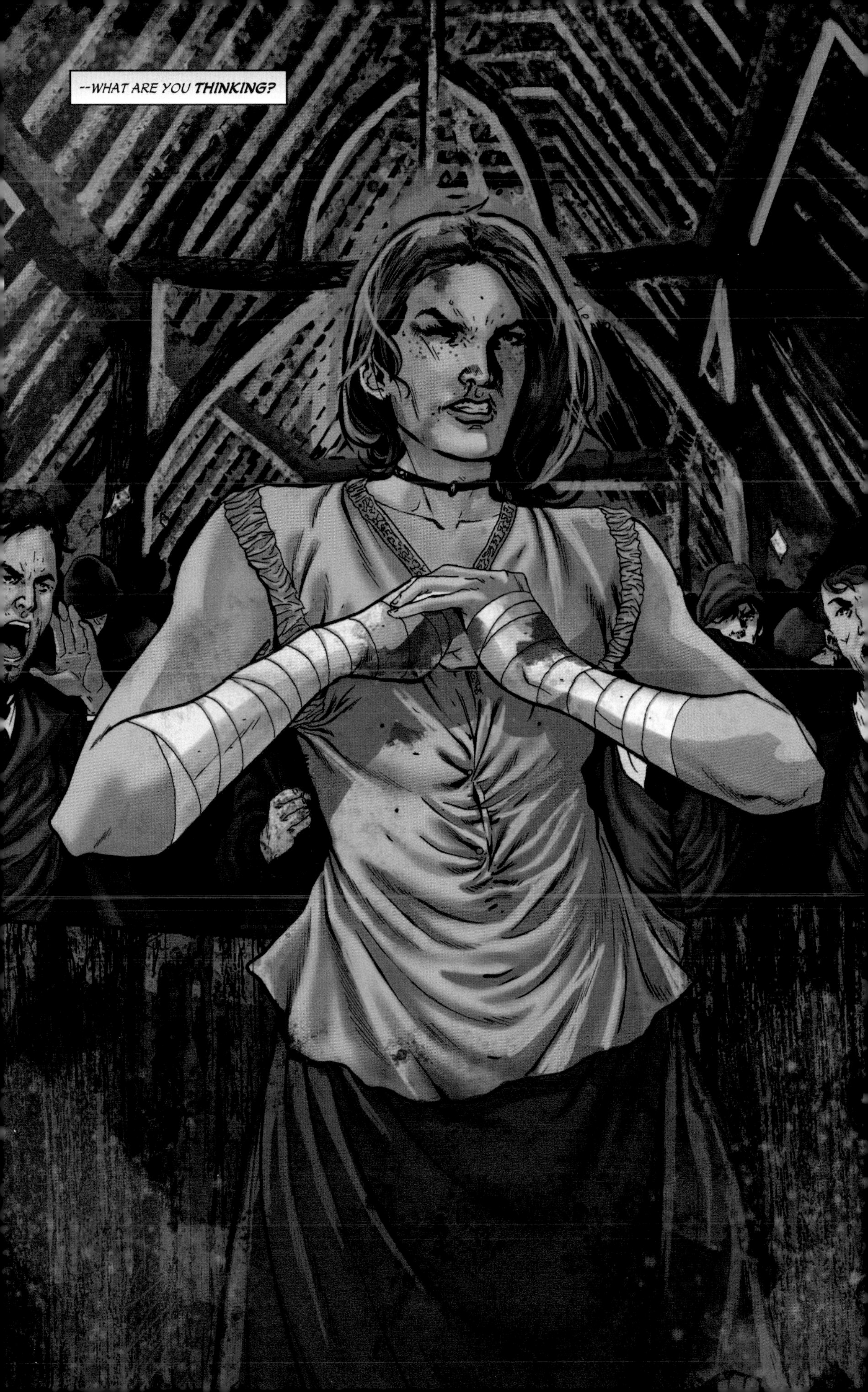
--WHAT ARE YOU THINKING?

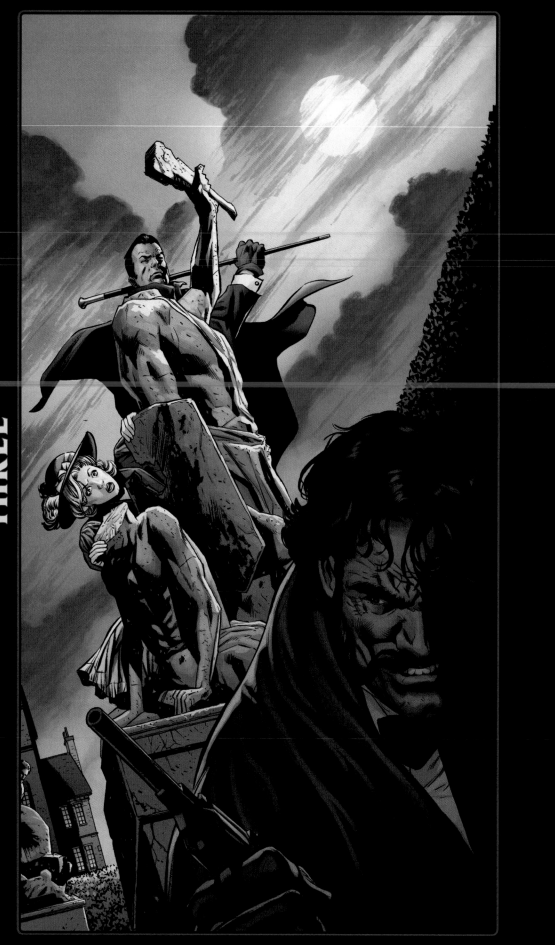

THREE

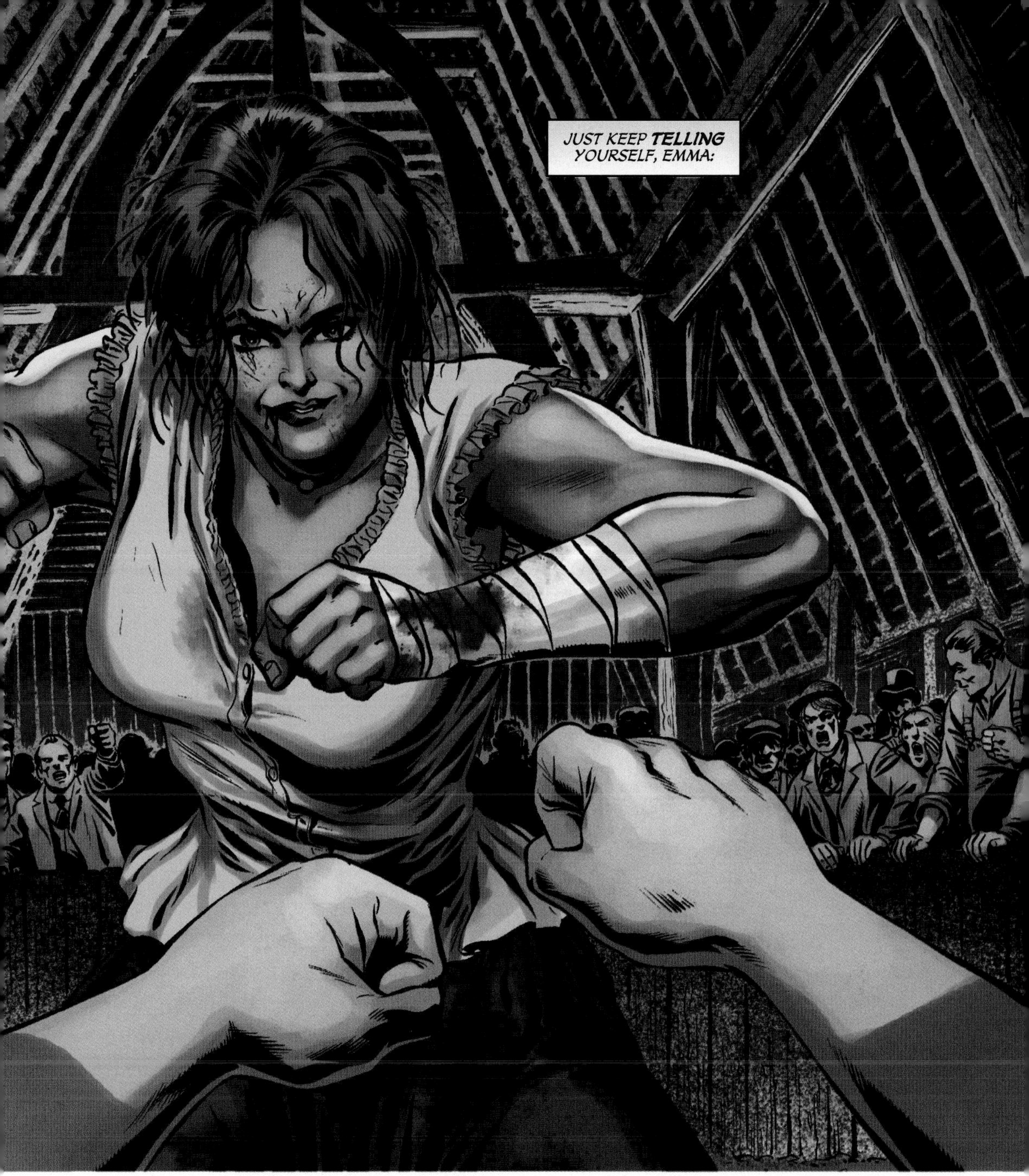
JUST KEEP **TELLING** YOURSELF, EMMA:

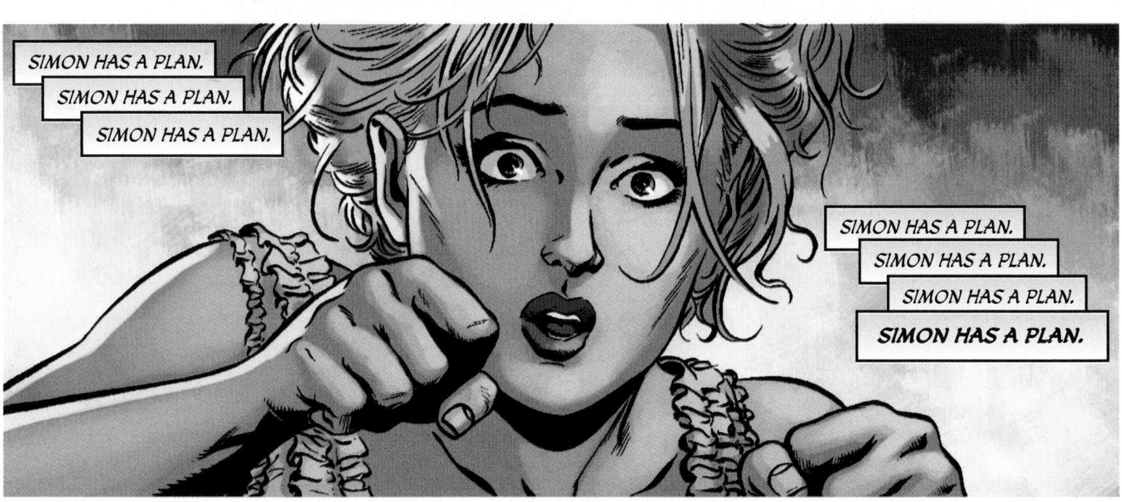
SIMON HAS A PLAN.
SIMON HAS A PLAN.
SIMON HAS A PLAN.
SIMON HAS A PLAN.
SIMON HAS A PLAN.
SIMON HAS A PLAN.
SIMON HAS A PLAN.

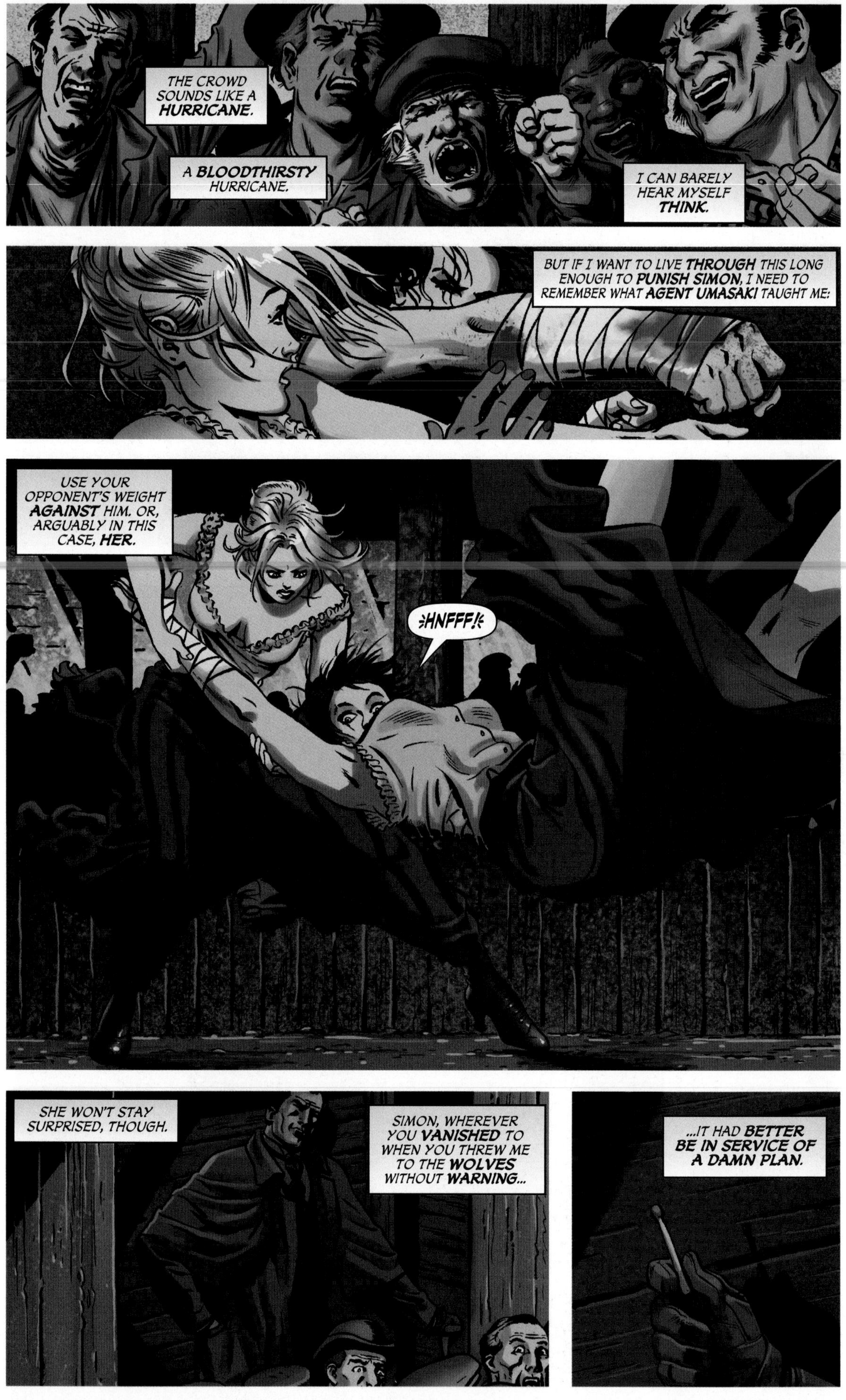
THE CROWD SOUNDS LIKE A HURRICANE.
A BLOODTHIRSTY HURRICANE.
I CAN BARELY HEAR MYSELF THINK.
BUT IF I WANT TO LIVE THROUGH THIS LONG ENOUGH TO PUNISH SIMON, I NEED TO REMEMBER WHAT AGENT UMASAKI TAUGHT ME:
USE YOUR OPPONENT'S WEIGHT AGAINST HIM. OR, ARGUABLY IN THIS CASE, HER.
HNFFF!
SHE WON'T STAY SURPRISED, THOUGH.
SIMON, WHEREVER YOU VANISHED TO WHEN YOU THREW ME TO THE WOLVES WITHOUT WARNING...
...IT HAD BETTER BE IN SERVICE OF A DAMN PLAN.

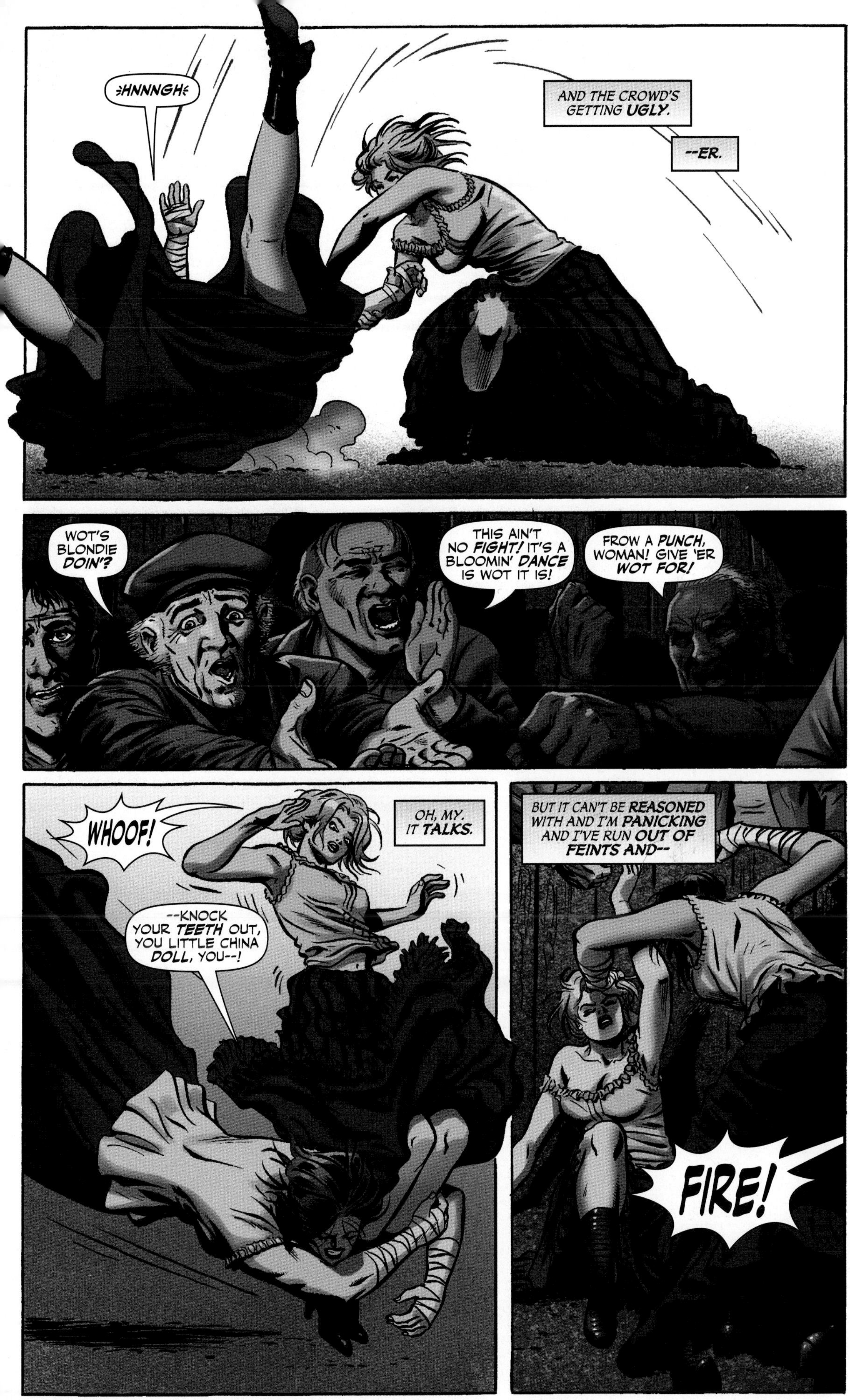
HNNNGH
AND THE CROWD'S GETTING UGLY.
--ER.
WOT'S BLONDIE DOIN'?
THIS AIN'T NO FIGHT! IT'S A BLOOMIN' DANCE IS WOT IT IS!
FROW A PUNCH, WOMAN! GIVE 'ER WOT FOR!
WHOOF!
OH, MY. IT TALKS.
--KNOCK YOUR TEETH OUT, YOU LITTLE CHINA DOLL, YOU--!
BUT IT CAN'T BE REASONED WITH AND I'M PANICKING AND I'VE RUN OUT OF FEINTS AND--
FIRE!

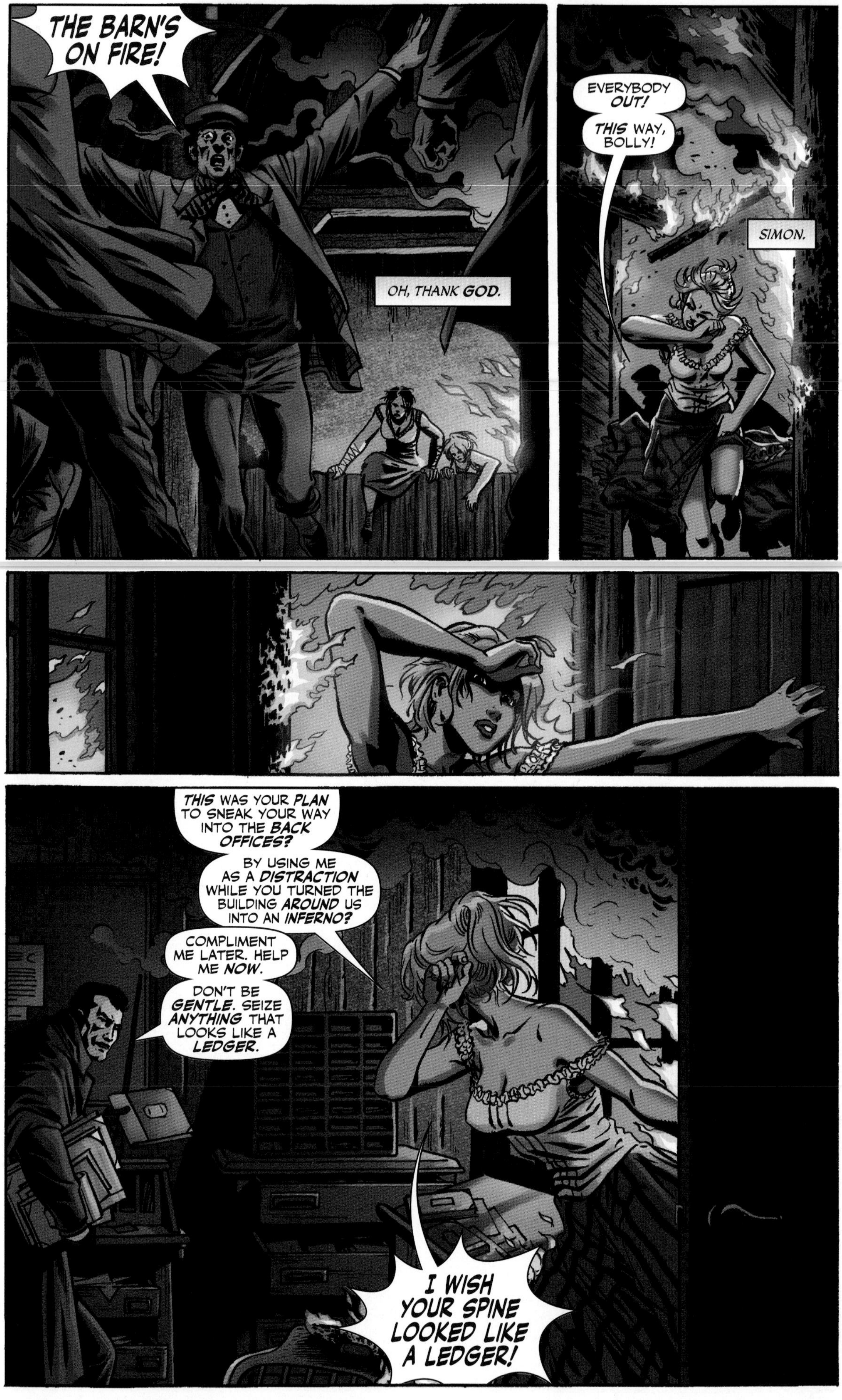
THE BARN'S ON FIRE!
OH, THANK GOD.
EVERYBODY OUT!
THIS WAY, BOLLY!
SIMON.
THIS WAS YOUR PLAN TO SNEAK YOUR WAY INTO THE BACK OFFICES?
BY USING ME AS A DISTRACTION WHILE YOU TURNED THE BUILDING AROUND US INTO AN INFERNO?
COMPLIMENT ME LATER. HELP ME NOW.
DON'T BE GENTLE. SEIZE ANYTHING THAT LOOKS LIKE A LEDGER.
I WISH YOUR SPINE LOOKED LIKE A LEDGER!

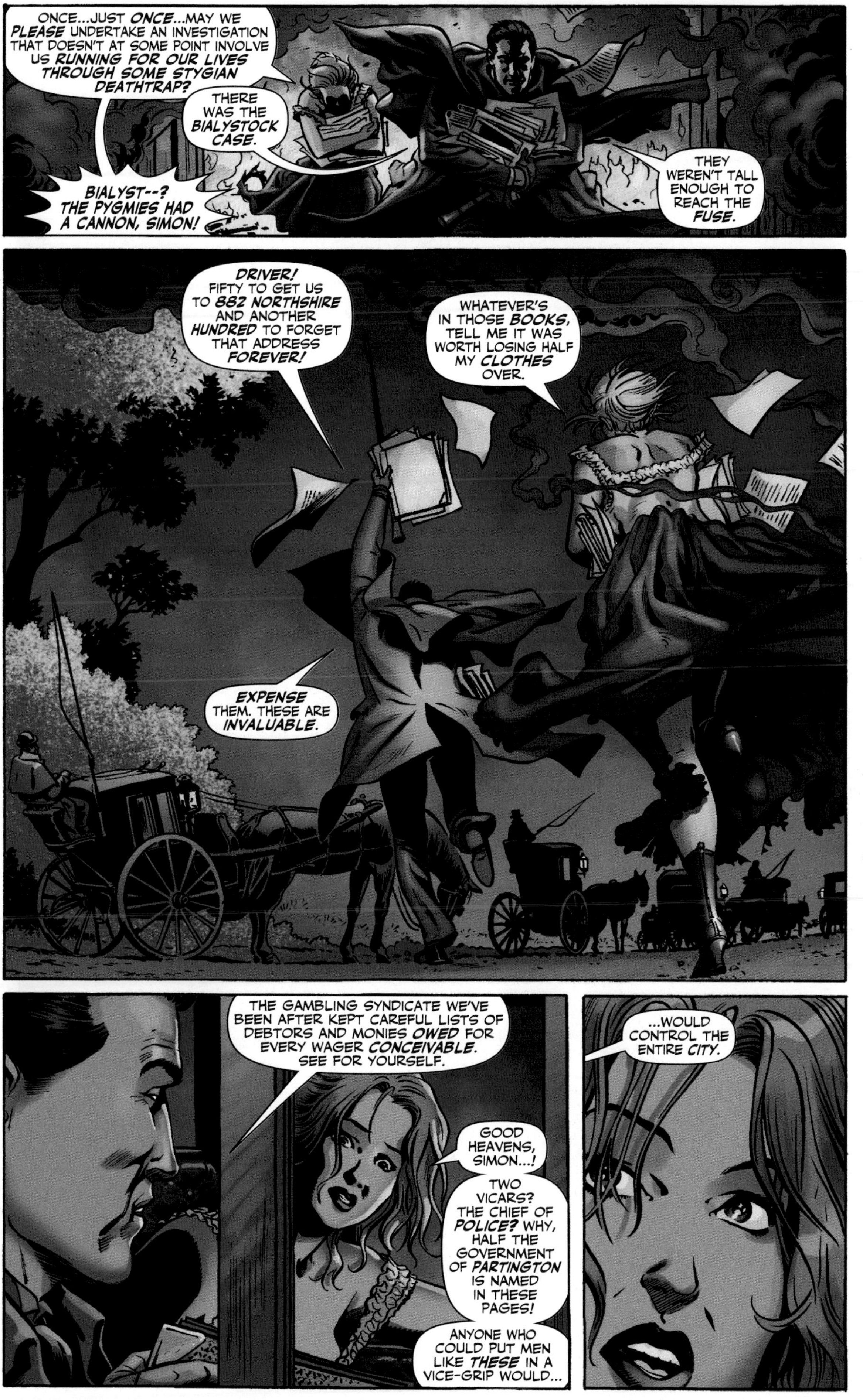
ONCE...JUST ONCE...MAY WE PLEASE UNDERTAKE AN INVESTIGATION THAT DOESN'T AT SOME POINT INVOLVE US RUNNING FOR OUR LIVES THROUGH SOME STYGIAN DEATHTRAP?
THERE WAS THE BIALYSTOCK CASE.
BIALYST--? THE PYGMIES HAD A CANNON, SIMON!
THEY WEREN'T TALL ENOUGH TO REACH THE FUSE.
DRIVER! FIFTY TO GET US TO 882 NORTHSHIRE AND ANOTHER HUNDRED TO FORGET THAT ADDRESS FOREVER!
WHATEVER'S IN THOSE BOOKS, TELL ME IT WAS WORTH LOSING HALF MY CLOTHES OVER.
EXPENSE THEM. THESE ARE INVALUABLE.
THE GAMBLING SYNDICATE WE'VE BEEN AFTER KEPT CAREFUL LISTS OF DEBTORS AND MONIES OWED FOR EVERY WAGER CONCEIVABLE. SEE FOR YOURSELF.
GOOD HEAVENS, SIMON...!
TWO VICARS? THE CHIEF OF POLICE? WHY, HALF THE GOVERNMENT OF PARTINGTON IS NAMED IN THESE PAGES!
ANYONE WHO COULD PUT MEN LIKE THESE IN A VICE-GRIP WOULD...
...WOULD CONTROL THE ENTIRE CITY.

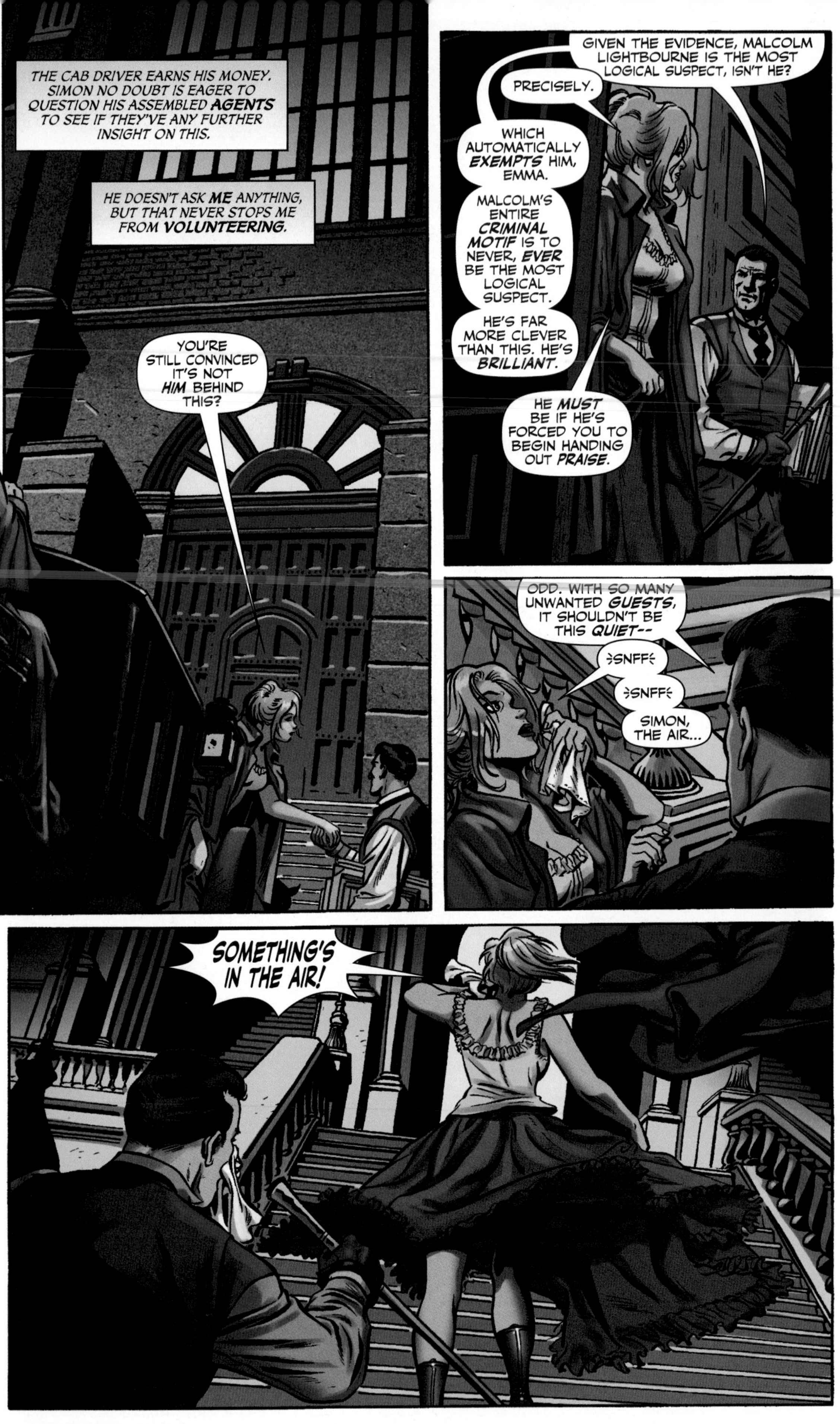
THE CAB DRIVER EARNS HIS MONEY. SIMON NO DOUBT IS EAGER TO QUESTION HIS ASSEMBLED AGENTS TO SEE IF THEY'VE ANY FURTHER INSIGHT ON THIS.
HE DOESN'T ASK ME ANYTHING, BUT THAT NEVER STOPS ME FROM VOLUNTEERING.
YOU'RE STILL CONVINCED IT'S NOT HIM BEHIND THIS?
GIVEN THE EVIDENCE, MALCOLM LIGHTBOURNE IS THE MOST LOGICAL SUSPECT, ISN'T HE?
PRECISELY.
WHICH AUTOMATICALLY EXEMPTS HIM, EMMA.
MALCOLM'S ENTIRE CRIMINAL MOTIF IS TO NEVER, EVER BE THE MOST LOGICAL SUSPECT.
HE'S FAR MORE CLEVER THAN THIS. HE'S BRILLIANT.
HE MUST BE IF HE'S FORCED YOU TO BEGIN HANDING OUT PRAISE.
ODD. WITH SO MANY UNWANTED GUESTS, IT SHOULDN'T BE THIS QUIET--
SNFF
SNFF
SIMON, THE AIR...
SOMETHING'S IN THE AIR!

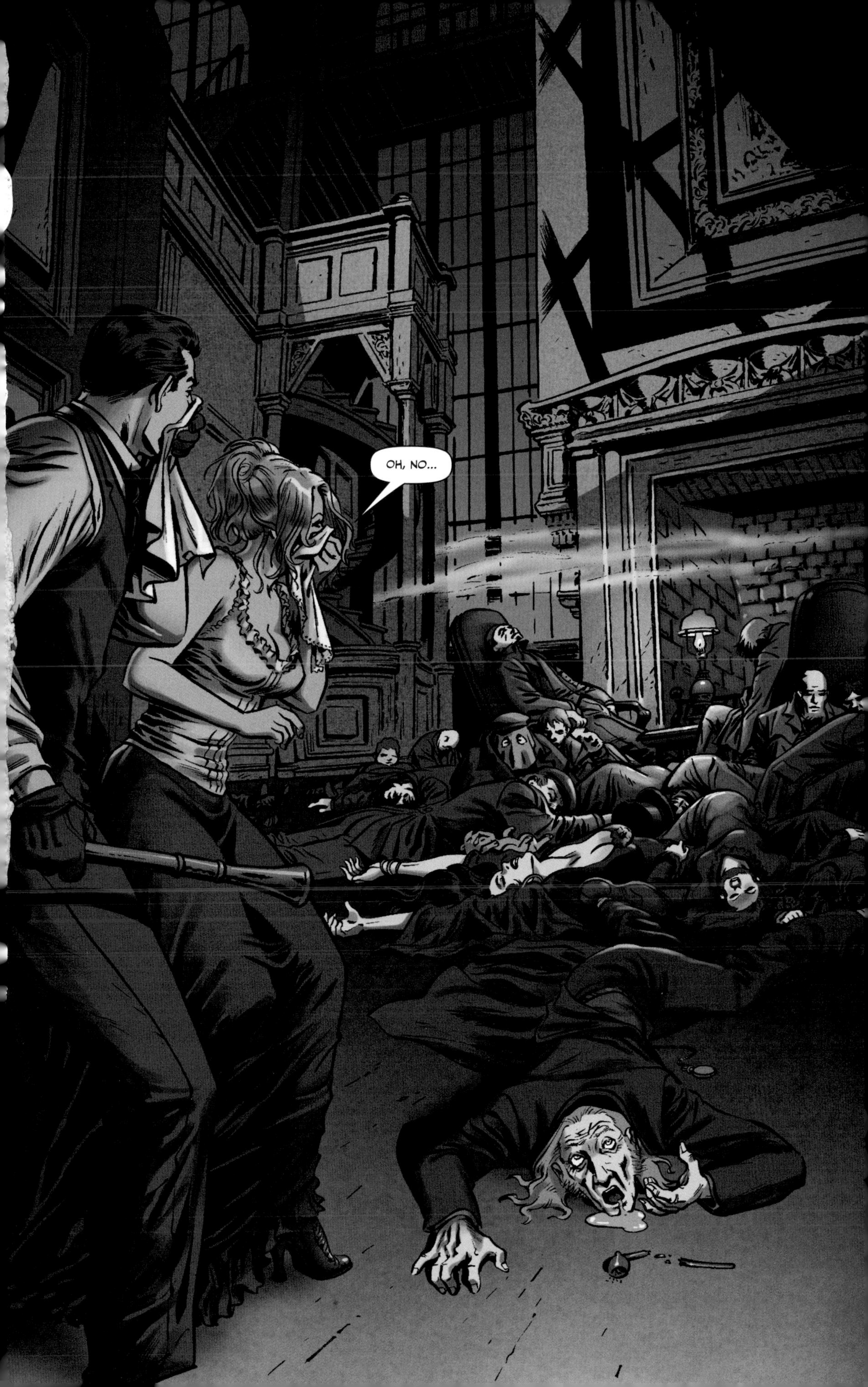
OH, NO...

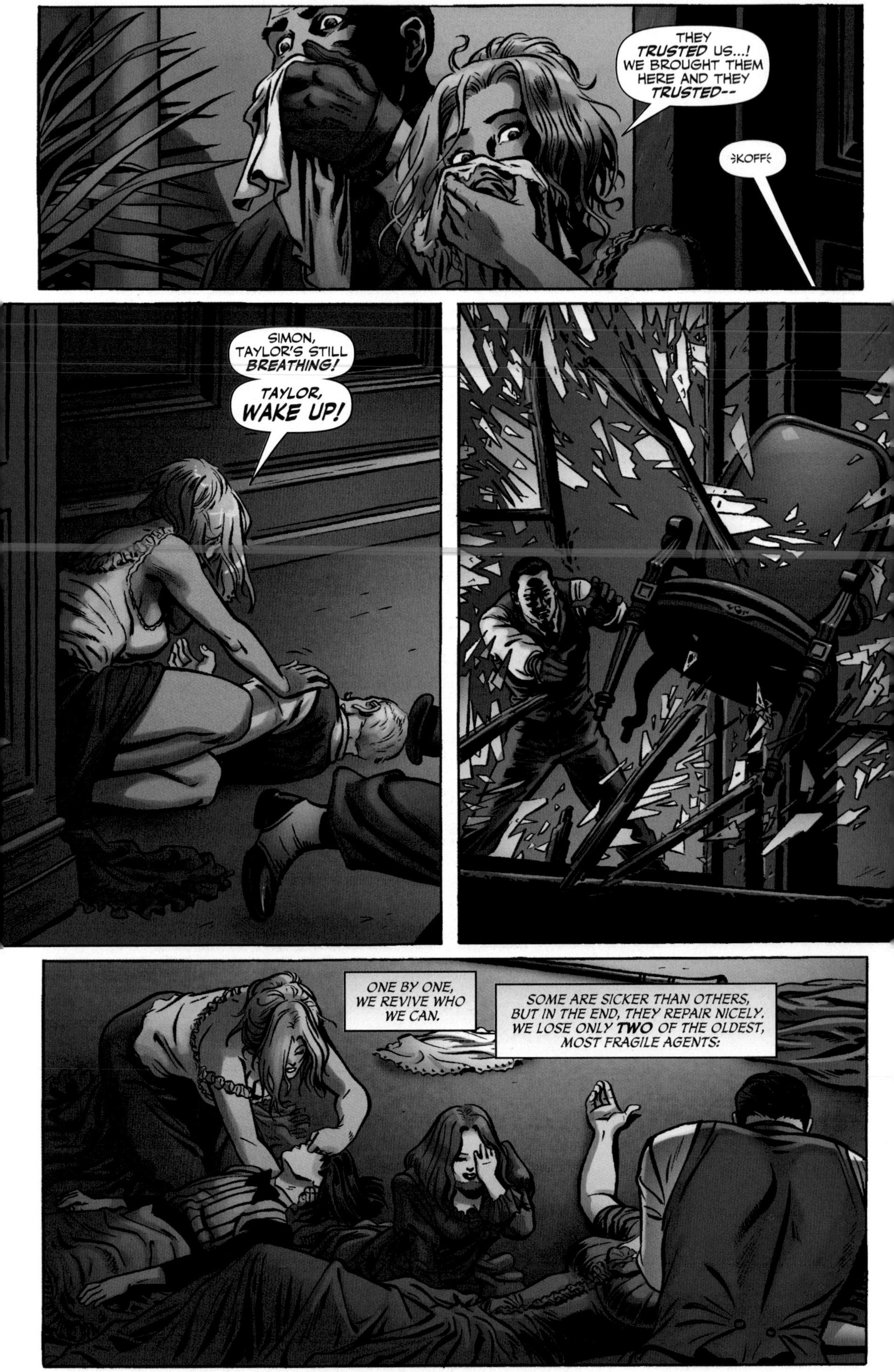
THEY TRUSTED US...! WE BROUGHT THEM HERE AND THEY TRUSTED--
KOFF
SIMON, TAYLOR'S STILL BREATHING!
TAYLOR, WAKE UP!
ONE BY ONE, WE REVIVE WHO WE CAN.
SOME ARE SICKER THAN OTHERS, BUT IN THE END, THEY REPAIR NICELY. WE LOSE ONLY TWO OF THE OLDEST, MOST FRAGILE AGENTS:

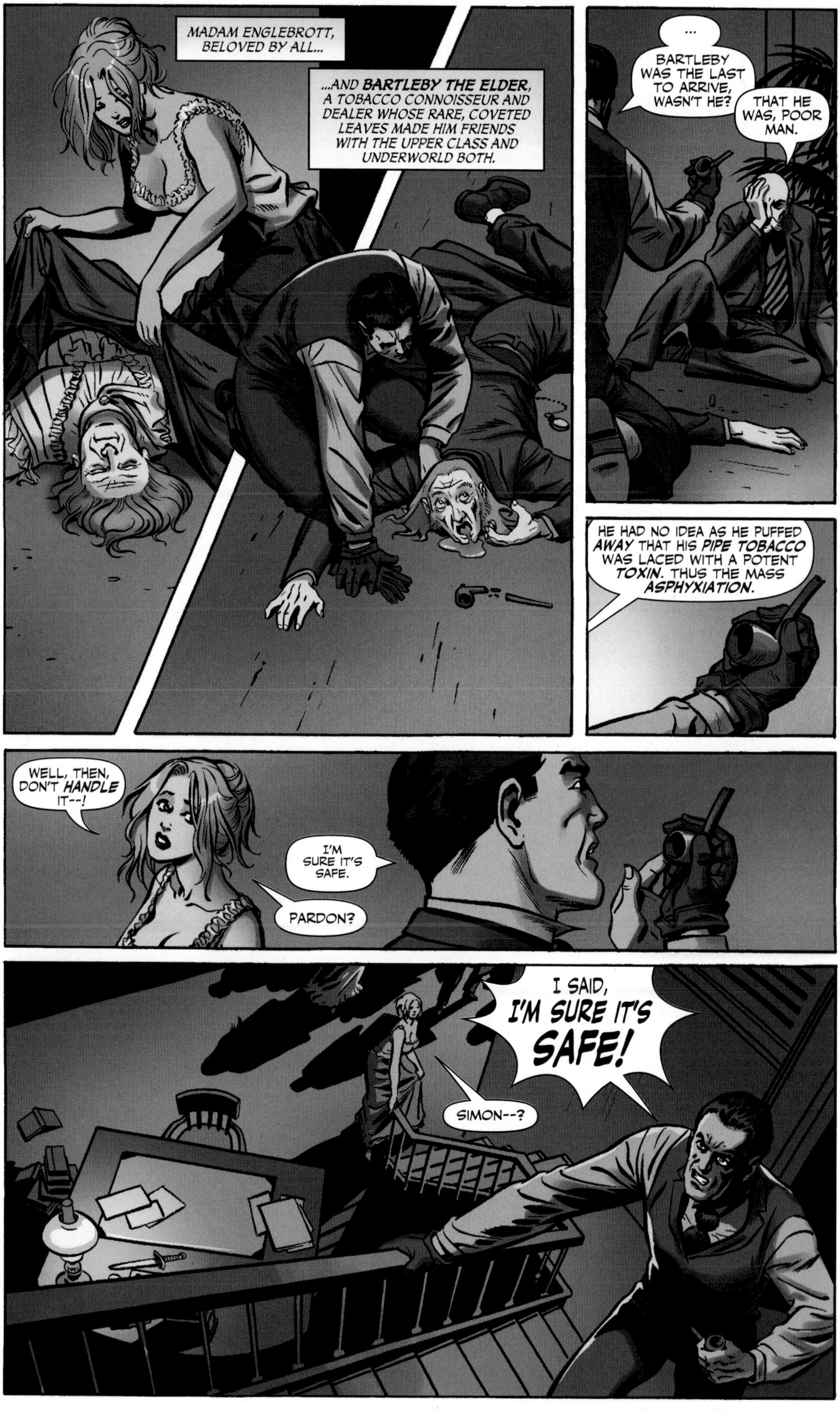
MADAM ENGLEBROTT, BELOVED BY ALL...
...AND BARTLEBY THE ELDER, A TOBACCO CONNOISSEUR AND DEALER WHOSE RARE, COVETED LEAVES MADE HIM FRIENDS WITH THE UPPER CLASS AND UNDERWORLD BOTH.
...
BARTLEBY WAS THE LAST TO ARRIVE, WASN'T HE?
THAT HE WAS, POOR MAN.
HE HAD NO IDEA AS HE PUFFED AWAY THAT HIS PIPE TOBACCO WAS LACED WITH A POTENT TOXIN. THUS THE MASS ASPHYXIATION.
WELL, THEN, DON'T HANDLE IT--!
I'M SURE IT'S SAFE.
PARDON?
I SAID, I'M SURE IT'S SAFE!
SIMON--?

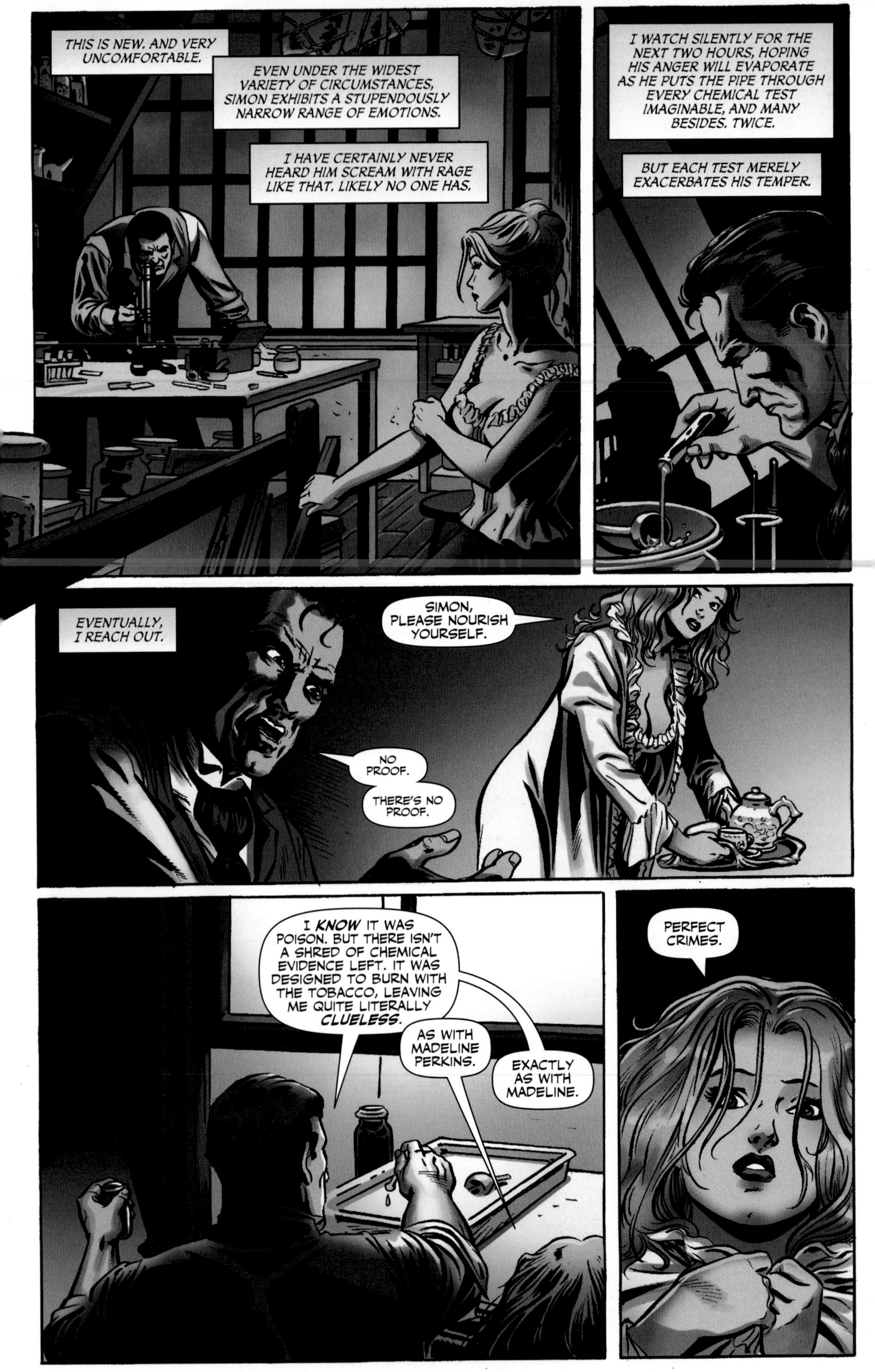
THIS IS NEW. AND VERY UNCOMFORTABLE.
EVEN UNDER THE WIDEST VARIETY OF CIRCUMSTANCES, SIMON EXHIBITS A STUPENDOUSLY NARROW RANGE OF EMOTIONS.
I HAVE CERTAINLY NEVER HEARD HIM SCREAM WITH RAGE LIKE THAT. LIKELY NO ONE HAS.
I WATCH SILENTLY FOR THE NEXT TWO HOURS, HOPING HIS ANGER WILL EVAPORATE AS HE PUTS THE PIPE THROUGH EVERY CHEMICAL TEST IMAGINABLE, AND MANY BESIDES. TWICE.
BUT EACH TEST MERELY EXACERBATES HIS TEMPER.
EVENTUALLY, I REACH OUT.
SIMON, PLEASE NOURISH YOURSELF.
NO PROOF.
THERE'S NO PROOF.
I KNOW IT WAS POISON. BUT THERE ISN'T A SHRED OF CHEMICAL EVIDENCE LEFT. IT WAS DESIGNED TO BURN WITH THE TOBACCO, LEAVING ME QUITE LITERALLY CLUELESS.
AS WITH MADELINE PERKINS.
EXACTLY AS WITH MADELINE.
PERFECT CRIMES.

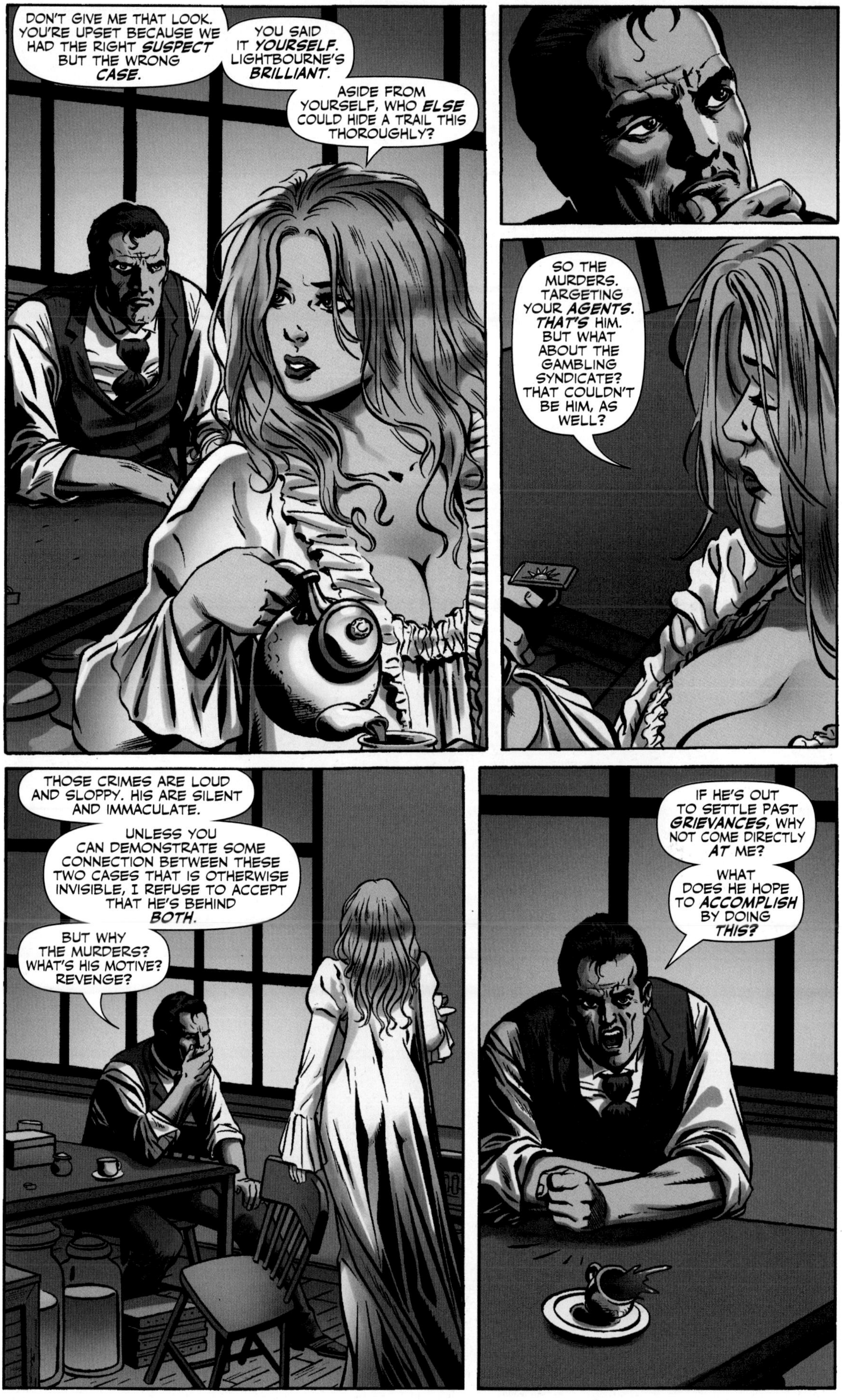
DON'T GIVE ME THAT LOOK. YOU'RE UPSET BECAUSE WE HAD THE RIGHT *SUSPECT* BUT THE WRONG *CASE*.
YOU SAID IT *YOURSELF*. LIGHTBOURNE'S *BRILLIANT*.
ASIDE FROM YOURSELF, WHO *ELSE* COULD HIDE A TRAIL THIS THOROUGHLY?
SO THE MURDERS. TARGETING YOUR *AGENTS*. *THAT'S* HIM. BUT WHAT ABOUT THE GAMBLING SYNDICATE? THAT COULDN'T BE HIM, AS WELL?
THOSE CRIMES ARE LOUD AND SLOPPY. HIS ARE SILENT AND IMMACULATE.
UNLESS YOU CAN DEMONSTRATE SOME CONNECTION BETWEEN THESE TWO CASES THAT IS OTHERWISE INVISIBLE, I REFUSE TO ACCEPT THAT HE'S BEHIND *BOTH*.
BUT WHY THE MURDERS? WHAT'S HIS MOTIVE? REVENGE?
IF HE'S OUT TO SETTLE PAST *GRIEVANCES*, WHY NOT COME DIRECTLY *AT* ME?
WHAT DOES HE HOPE TO *ACCOMPLISH* BY DOING *THIS?*

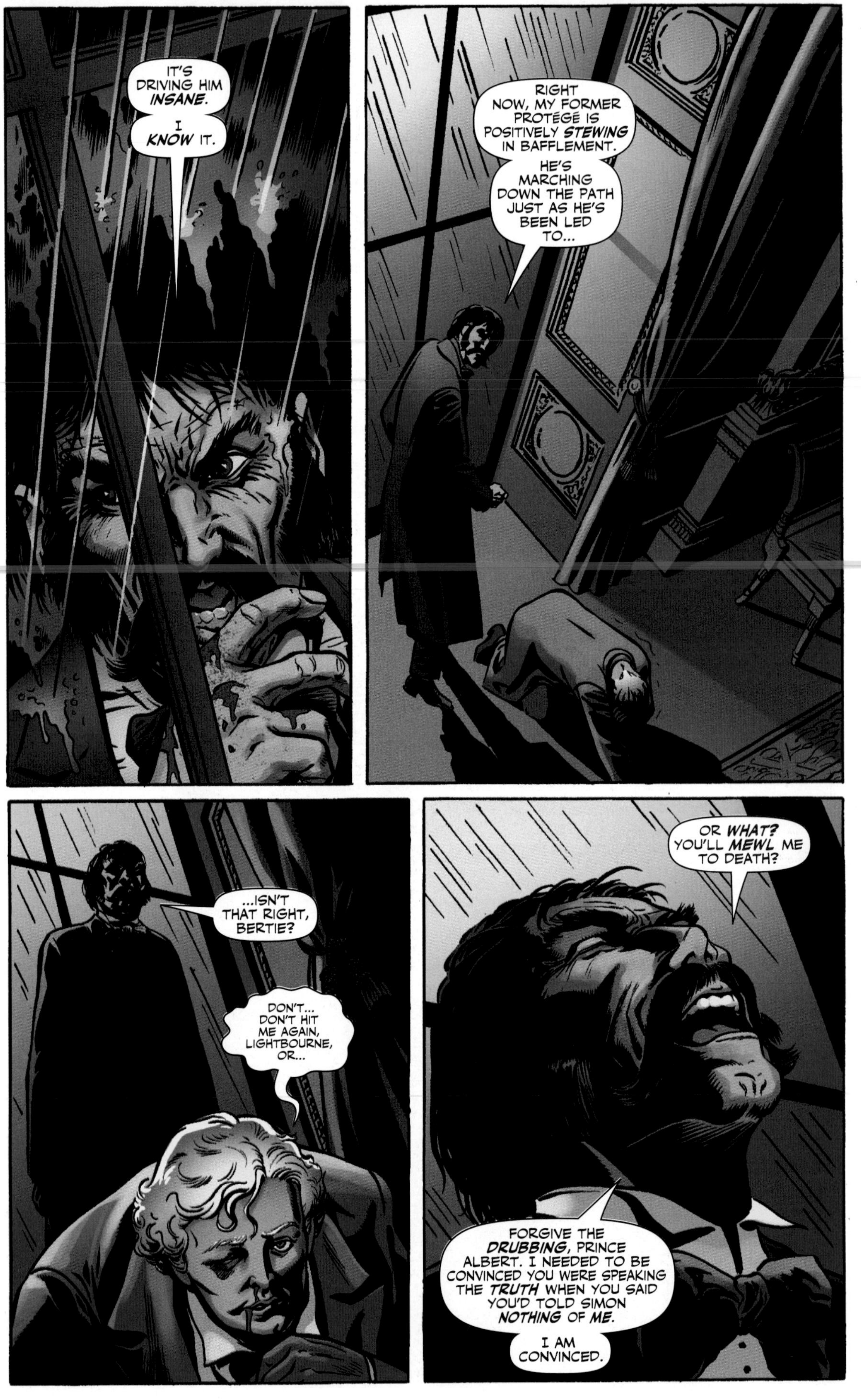
IT'S DRIVING HIM INSANE.
I KNOW IT.
RIGHT NOW, MY FORMER PROTÉGÉ IS POSITIVELY STEWING IN BAFFLEMENT.
HE'S MARCHING DOWN THE PATH JUST AS HE'S BEEN LED TO...
...ISN'T THAT RIGHT, BERTIE?
DON'T... DON'T HIT ME AGAIN, LIGHTBOURNE, OR...
OR WHAT? YOU'LL MEWL ME TO DEATH?
FORGIVE THE DRUBBING, PRINCE ALBERT. I NEEDED TO BE CONVINCED YOU WERE SPEAKING THE TRUTH WHEN YOU SAID YOU'D TOLD SIMON NOTHING OF ME.
I AM CONVINCED.

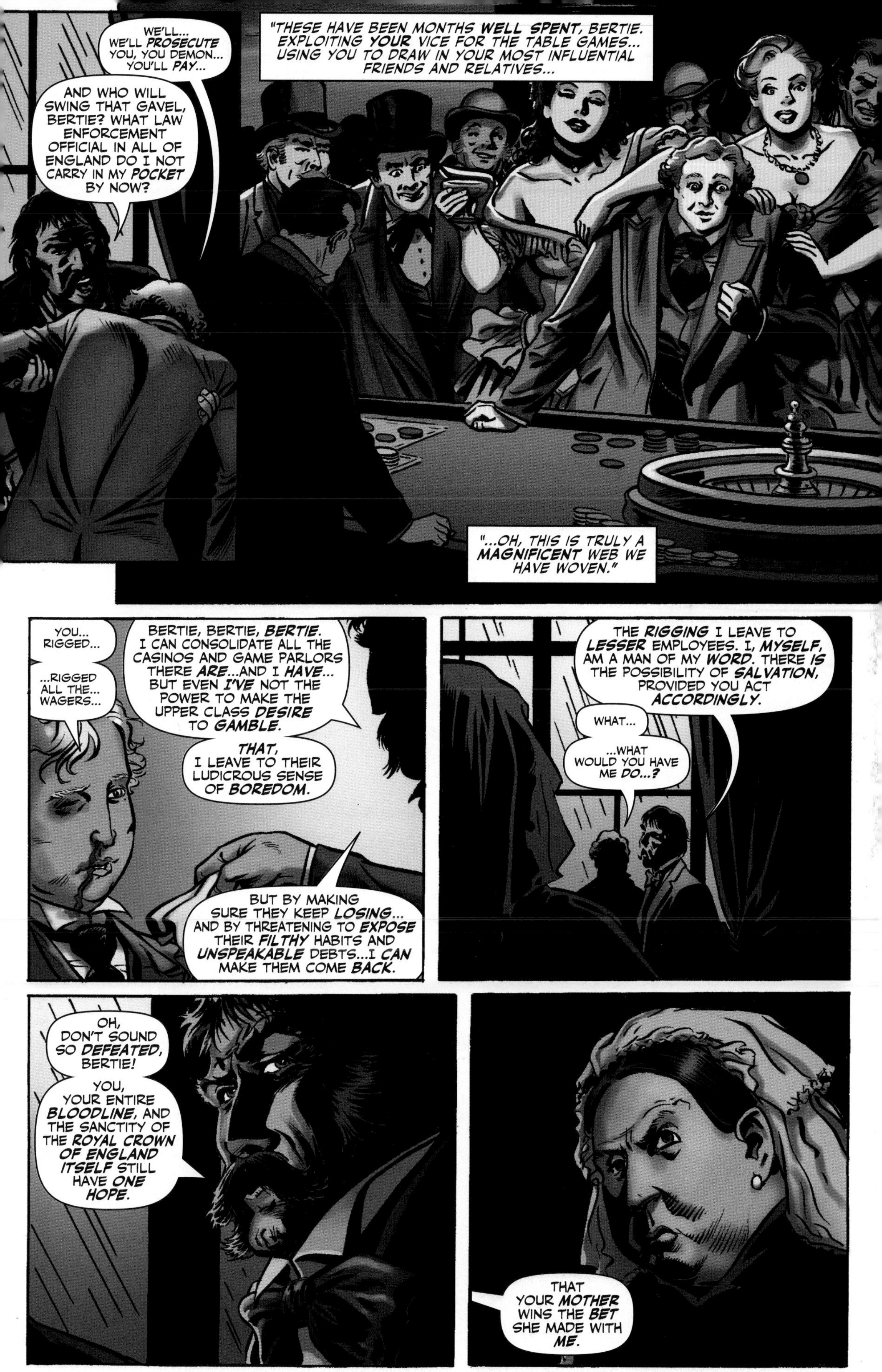
WE'LL... WE'LL PROSECUTE YOU, YOU DEMON... YOU'LL PAY...
AND WHO WILL SWING THAT GAVEL, BERTIE? WHAT LAW ENFORCEMENT OFFICIAL IN ALL OF ENGLAND DO I NOT CARRY IN MY POCKET BY NOW?
"THESE HAVE BEEN MONTHS WELL SPENT, BERTIE. EXPLOITING YOUR VICE FOR THE TABLE GAMES... USING YOU TO DRAW IN YOUR MOST INFLUENTIAL FRIENDS AND RELATIVES...
"...OH, THIS IS TRULY A MAGNIFICENT WEB WE HAVE WOVEN."
YOU... RIGGED...
...RIGGED ALL THE... WAGERS...
BERTIE, BERTIE, BERTIE. I CAN CONSOLIDATE ALL THE CASINOS AND GAME PARLORS THERE ARE...AND I HAVE... BUT EVEN I'VE NOT THE POWER TO MAKE THE UPPER CLASS DESIRE TO GAMBLE.
THAT, I LEAVE TO THEIR LUDICROUS SENSE OF BOREDOM.
BUT BY MAKING SURE THEY KEEP LOSING... AND BY THREATENING TO EXPOSE THEIR FILTHY HABITS AND UNSPEAKABLE DEBTS...I CAN MAKE THEM COME BACK.
THE RIGGING I LEAVE TO LESSER EMPLOYEES. I, MYSELF, AM A MAN OF MY WORD. THERE IS THE POSSIBILITY OF SALVATION, PROVIDED YOU ACT ACCORDINGLY.
WHAT...
...WHAT WOULD YOU HAVE ME DO...?
OH, DON'T SOUND SO DEFEATED, BERTIE!
YOU, YOUR ENTIRE BLOODLINE, AND THE SANCTITY OF THE ROYAL CROWN OF ENGLAND ITSELF STILL HAVE ONE HOPE.
THAT YOUR MOTHER WINS THE BET SHE MADE WITH ME.

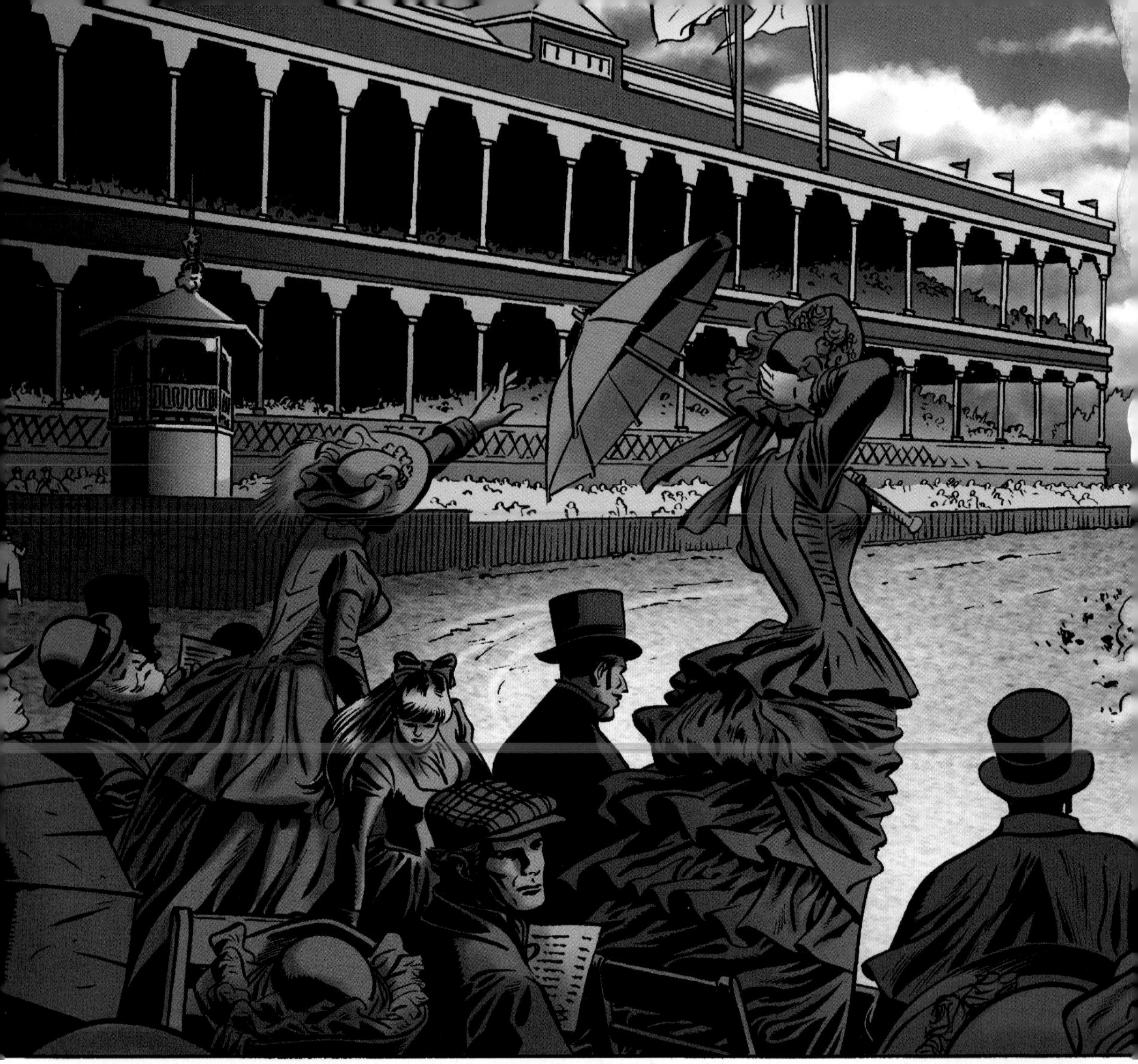

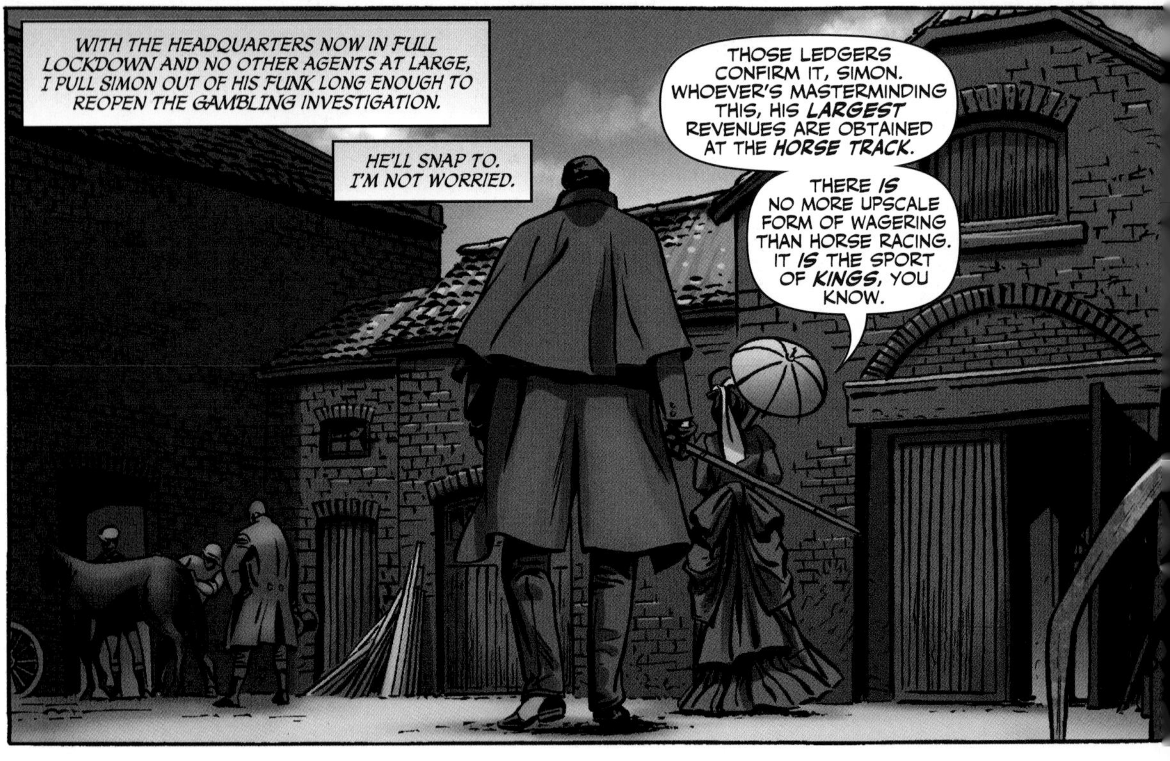
WITH THE HEADQUARTERS NOW IN FULL LOCKDOWN AND NO OTHER AGENTS AT LARGE, I PULL SIMON OUT OF HIS FUNK LONG ENOUGH TO REOPEN THE GAMBLING INVESTIGATION.
HE'LL SNAP TO. I'M NOT WORRIED.
THOSE LEDGERS CONFIRM IT, SIMON. WHOEVER'S MASTERMINDING THIS, HIS LARGEST REVENUES ARE OBTAINED AT THE HORSE TRACK.
THERE IS NO MORE UPSCALE FORM OF WAGERING THAN HORSE RACING. IT IS THE SPORT OF KINGS, YOU KNOW.

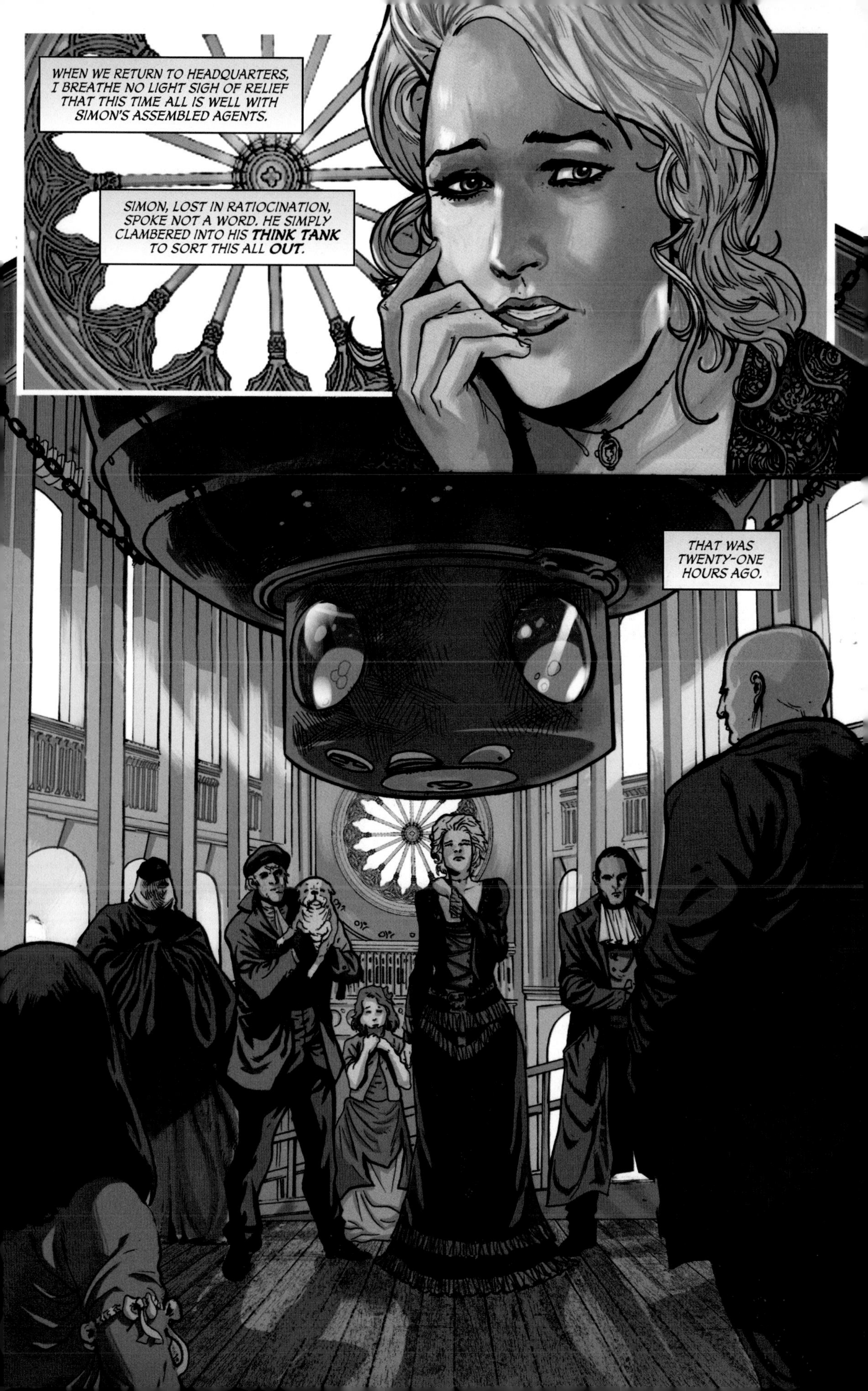
WHEN WE RETURN TO HEADQUARTERS, I BREATHE NO LIGHT SIGH OF RELIEF THAT THIS TIME ALL IS WELL WITH SIMON'S ASSEMBLED AGENTS.
SIMON, LOST IN RATIOCINATION, SPOKE NOT A WORD. HE SIMPLY CLAMBERED INTO HIS THINK TANK TO SORT THIS ALL OUT.
THAT WAS TWENTY-ONE HOURS AGO.

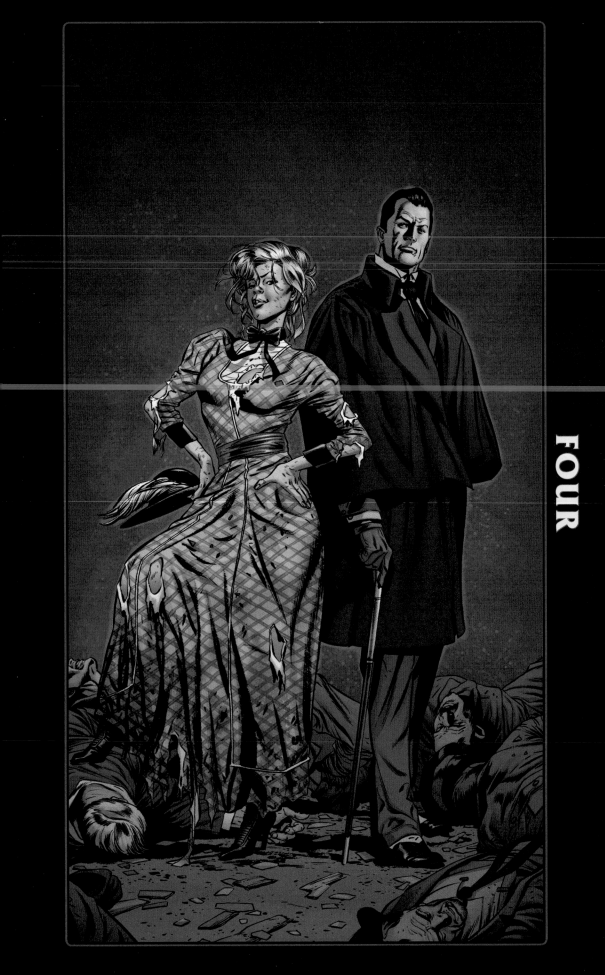

FOUR

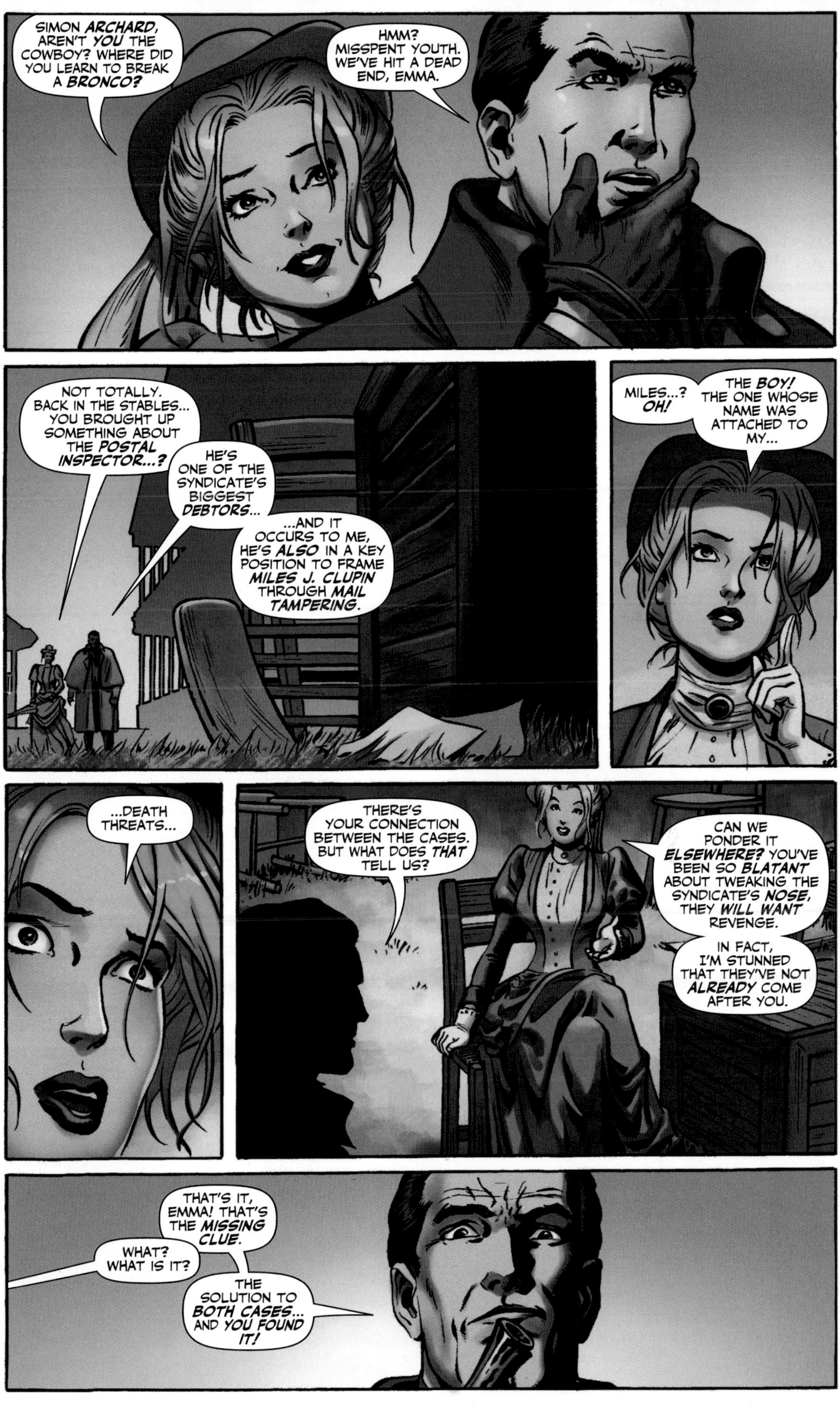
SIMON ARCHARD, AREN'T YOU THE COWBOY? WHERE DID YOU LEARN TO BREAK A BRONCO?
HMM? MISSPENT YOUTH. WE'VE HIT A DEAD END, EMMA.
NOT TOTALLY. BACK IN THE STABLES... YOU BROUGHT UP SOMETHING ABOUT THE POSTAL INSPECTOR...?
HE'S ONE OF THE SYNDICATE'S BIGGEST DEBTORS...
...AND IT OCCURS TO ME, HE'S ALSO IN A KEY POSITION TO FRAME MILES J. CLUPIN THROUGH MAIL TAMPERING.
MILES...? OH!
THE BOY! THE ONE WHOSE NAME WAS ATTACHED TO MY...
...DEATH THREATS...
THERE'S YOUR CONNECTION BETWEEN THE CASES. BUT WHAT DOES THAT TELL US?
CAN WE PONDER IT ELSEWHERE? YOU'VE BEEN SO BLATANT ABOUT TWEAKING THE SYNDICATE'S NOSE, THEY WILL WANT REVENGE.
IN FACT, I'M STUNNED THAT THEY'VE NOT ALREADY COME AFTER YOU.
THAT'S IT, EMMA! THAT'S THE MISSING CLUE.
WHAT? WHAT IS IT?
THE SOLUTION TO BOTH CASES... AND YOU FOUND IT!

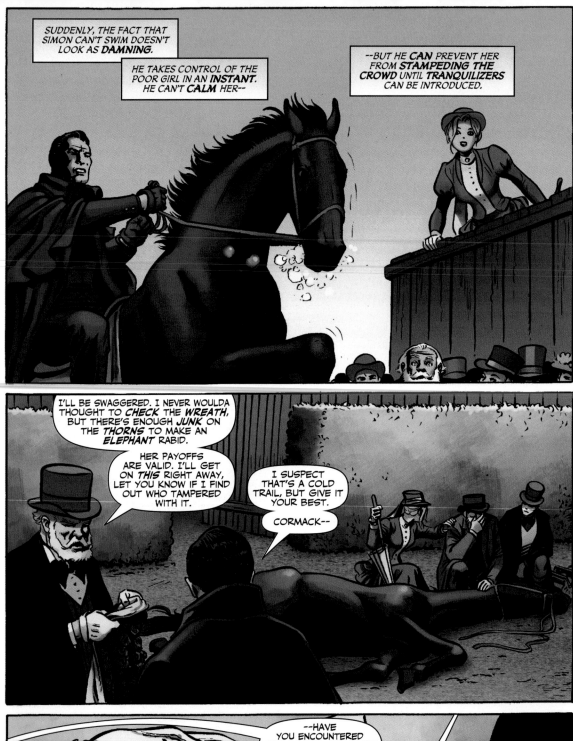

SUDDENLY, THE FACT THAT SIMON CAN'T SWIM DOESN'T LOOK AS *DAMNING*.

HE TAKES CONTROL OF THE POOR GIRL IN AN *INSTANT*. HE CAN'T *CALM* HER--

--BUT HE *CAN* PREVENT HER FROM *STAMPEDING THE CROWD* UNTIL *TRANQUILIZERS* CAN BE INTRODUCED.

I'LL BE SWAGGERED. I NEVER WOULDA THOUGHT TO *CHECK* THE *WREATH*, BUT THERE'S ENOUGH *JUNK* ON THE *THORNS* TO MAKE AN *ELEPHANT* RABID.

HER PAYOFFS ARE VALID. I'LL GET ON *THIS* RIGHT AWAY, LET YOU KNOW IF I FIND OUT WHO TAMPERED WITH IT.

I SUSPECT THAT'S A COLD TRAIL, BUT GIVE IT YOUR BEST.

CORMACK--

--HAVE YOU ENCOUNTERED THIS SYMBOL ANYWHERE IN YOUR DUTIES OF LATE? ANYWHERE AT ALL?

CAN'T SAY AS I HAVE. SORRY.

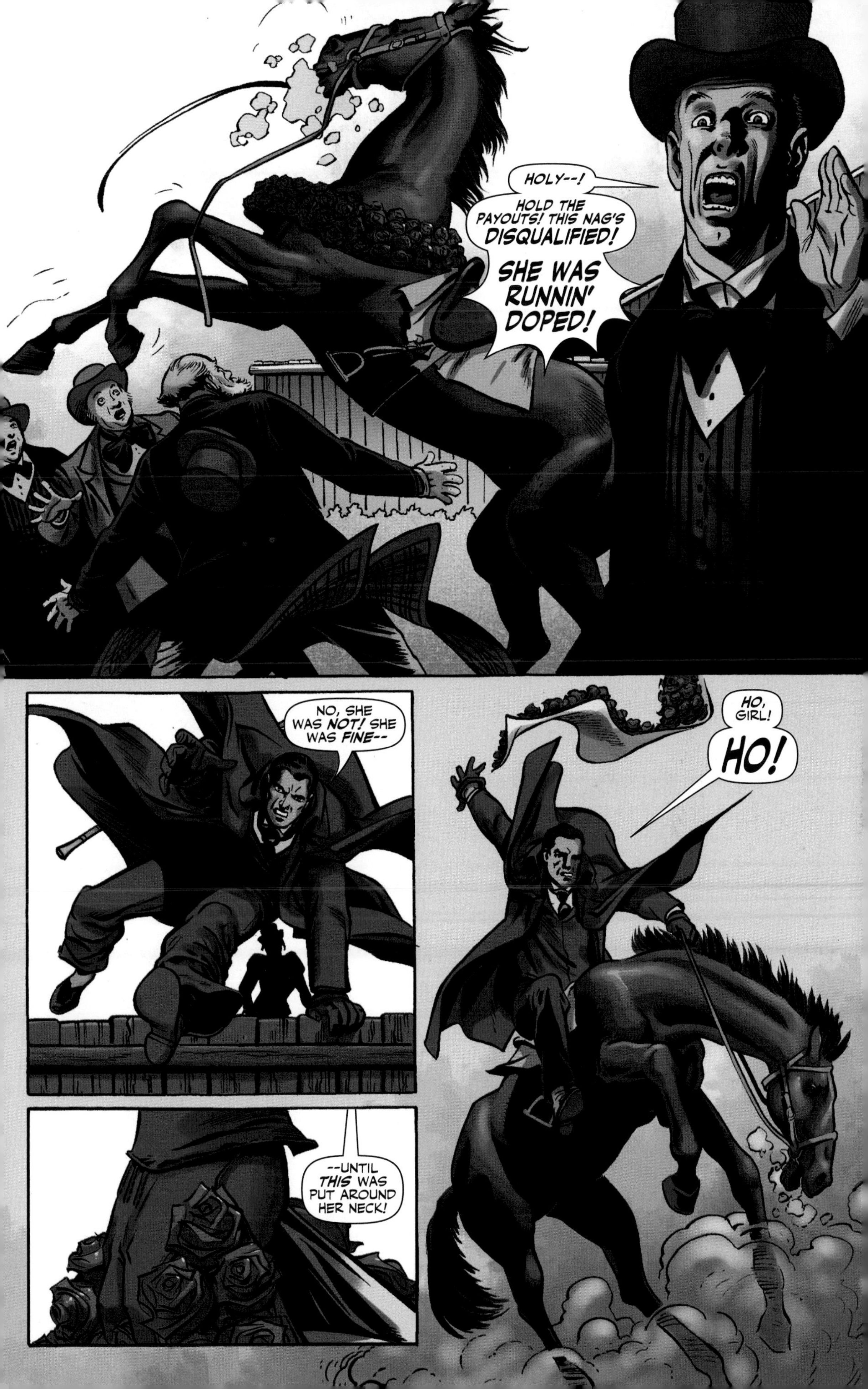
HOLY--!
HOLD THE PAYOUTS! THIS NAG'S DISQUALIFIED!
SHE WAS RUNNIN' DOPED!
NO, SHE WAS NOT! SHE WAS FINE--
--UNTIL THIS WAS PUT AROUND HER NECK!
HO, GIRL!
HO!

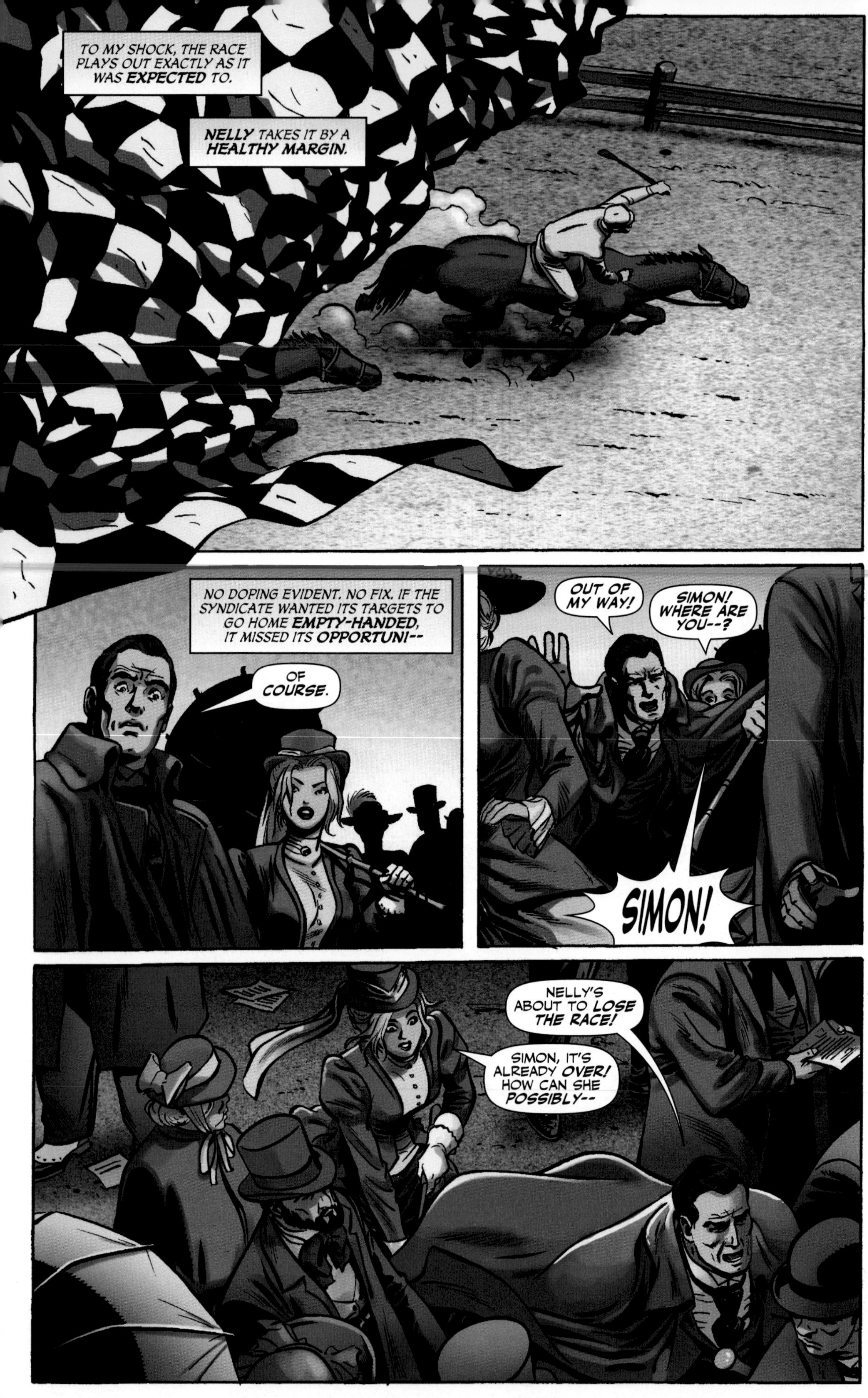
TO MY SHOCK, THE RACE PLAYS OUT EXACTLY AS IT WAS EXPECTED TO.
NELLY TAKES IT BY A HEALTHY MARGIN.
NO DOPING EVIDENT. NO FIX. IF THE SYNDICATE WANTED ITS TARGETS TO GO HOME EMPTY-HANDED, IT MISSED ITS OPPORTUNI--
OF COURSE.
OUT OF MY WAY!
SIMON! WHERE ARE YOU--?
SIMON!
NELLY'S ABOUT TO LOSE THE RACE!
SIMON, IT'S ALREADY OVER! HOW CAN SHE POSSIBLY--

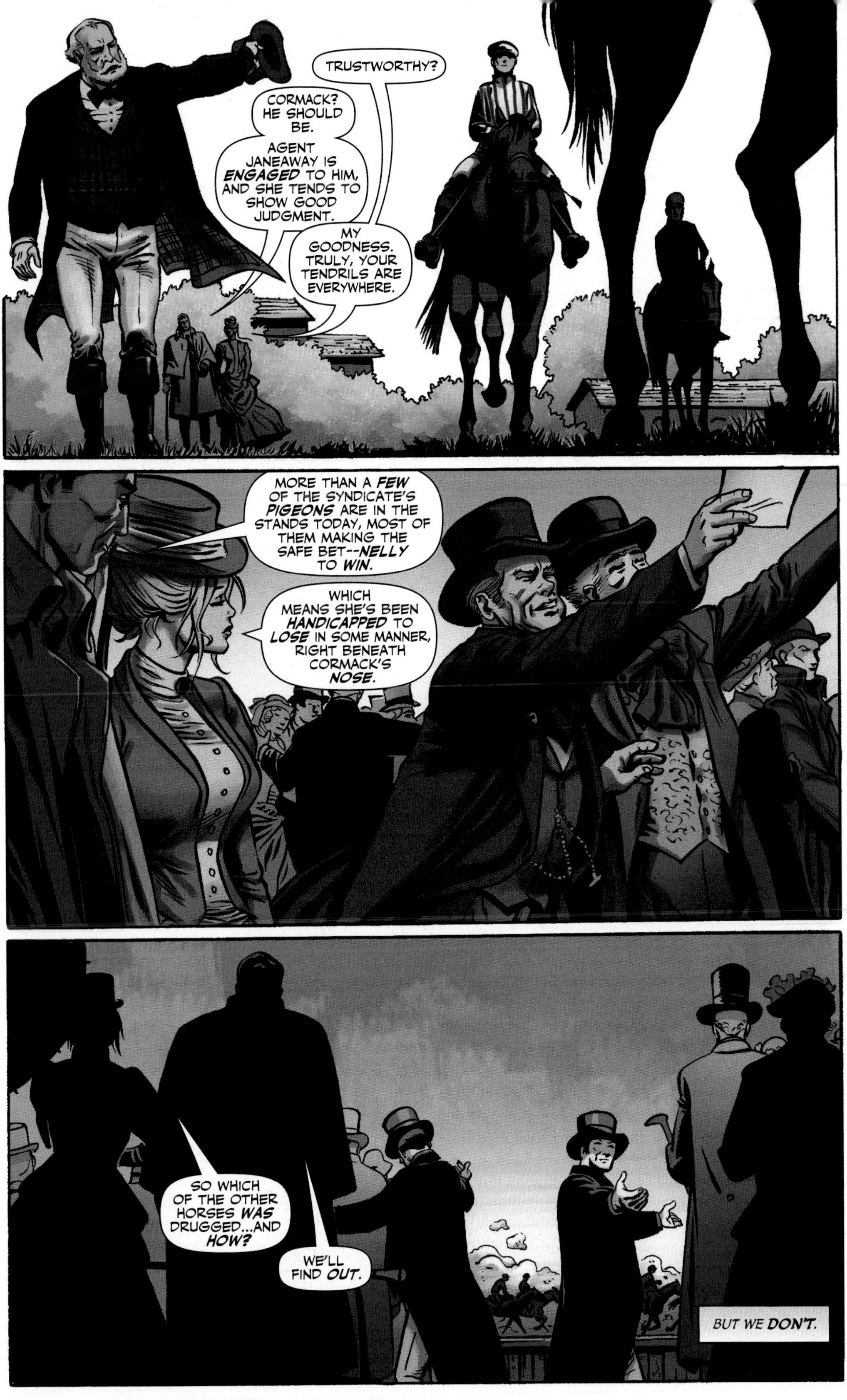
TRUSTWORTHY?
CORMACK? HE SHOULD BE.
AGENT JANEAWAY IS ENGAGED TO HIM, AND SHE TENDS TO SHOW GOOD JUDGMENT.
MY GOODNESS. TRULY, YOUR TENDRILS ARE EVERYWHERE.
MORE THAN A FEW OF THE SYNDICATE'S PIGEONS ARE IN THE STANDS TODAY, MOST OF THEM MAKING THE SAFE BET--NELLY TO WIN.
WHICH MEANS SHE'S BEEN HANDICAPPED TO LOSE IN SOME MANNER, RIGHT BENEATH CORMACK'S NOSE.
SO WHICH OF THE OTHER HORSES WAS DRUGGED...AND HOW?
WE'LL FIND OUT.
BUT WE DON'T.

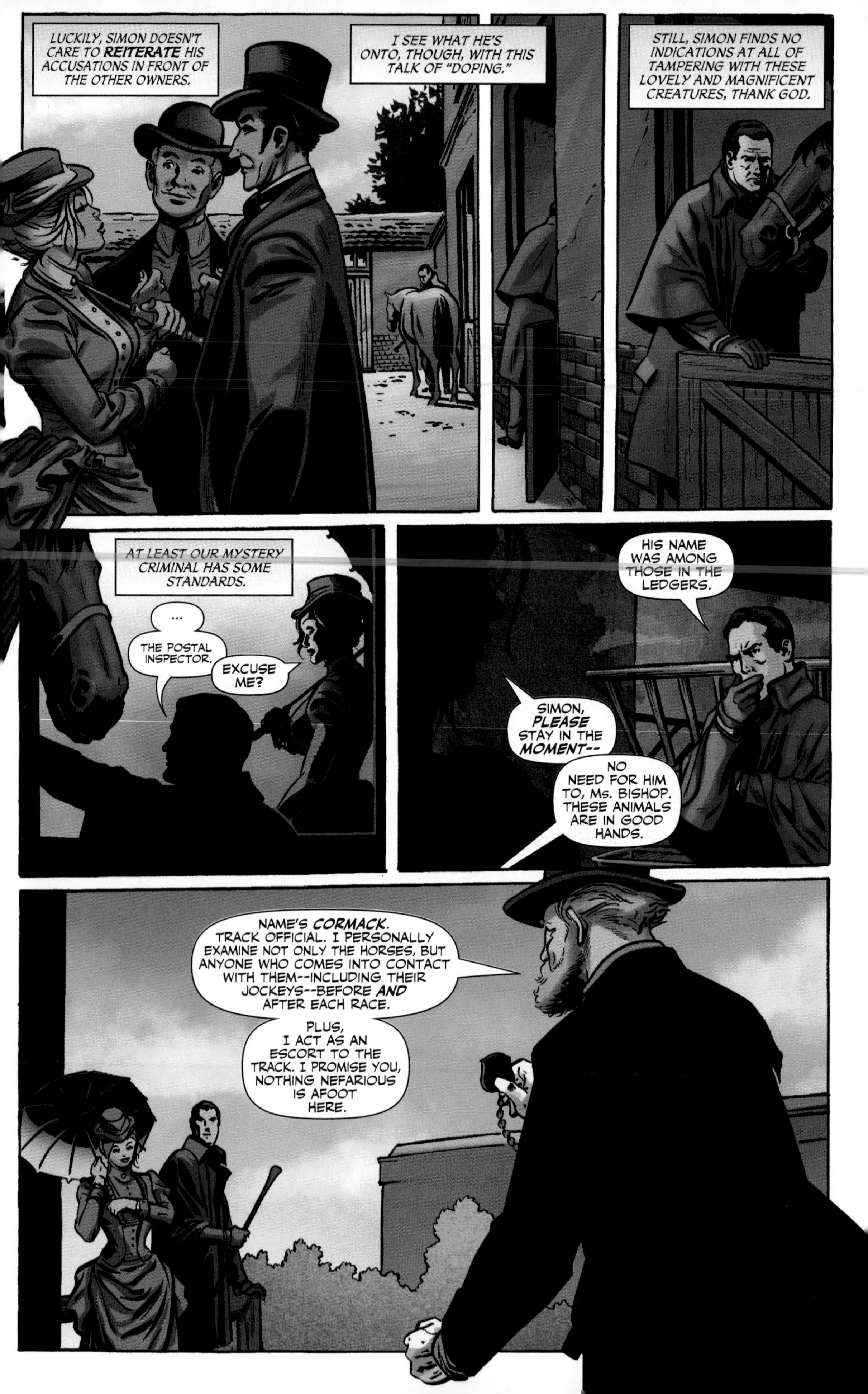
LUCKILY, SIMON DOESN'T CARE TO REITERATE HIS ACCUSATIONS IN FRONT OF THE OTHER OWNERS.
I SEE WHAT HE'S ONTO, THOUGH, WITH THIS TALK OF "DOPING."
STILL, SIMON FINDS NO INDICATIONS AT ALL OF TAMPERING WITH THESE LOVELY AND MAGNIFICENT CREATURES, THANK GOD.
AT LEAST OUR MYSTERY CRIMINAL HAS SOME STANDARDS.
...
THE POSTAL INSPECTOR.
EXCUSE ME?
HIS NAME WAS AMONG THOSE IN THE LEDGERS.
SIMON, PLEASE STAY IN THE MOMENT--
NO NEED FOR HIM TO, Ms. BISHOP. THESE ANIMALS ARE IN GOOD HANDS.
NAME'S CORMACK. TRACK OFFICIAL. I PERSONALLY EXAMINE NOT ONLY THE HORSES, BUT ANYONE WHO COMES INTO CONTACT WITH THEM--INCLUDING THEIR JOCKEYS--BEFORE AND AFTER EACH RACE.
PLUS, I ACT AS AN ESCORT TO THE TRACK. I PROMISE YOU, NOTHING NEFARIOUS IS AFOOT HERE.

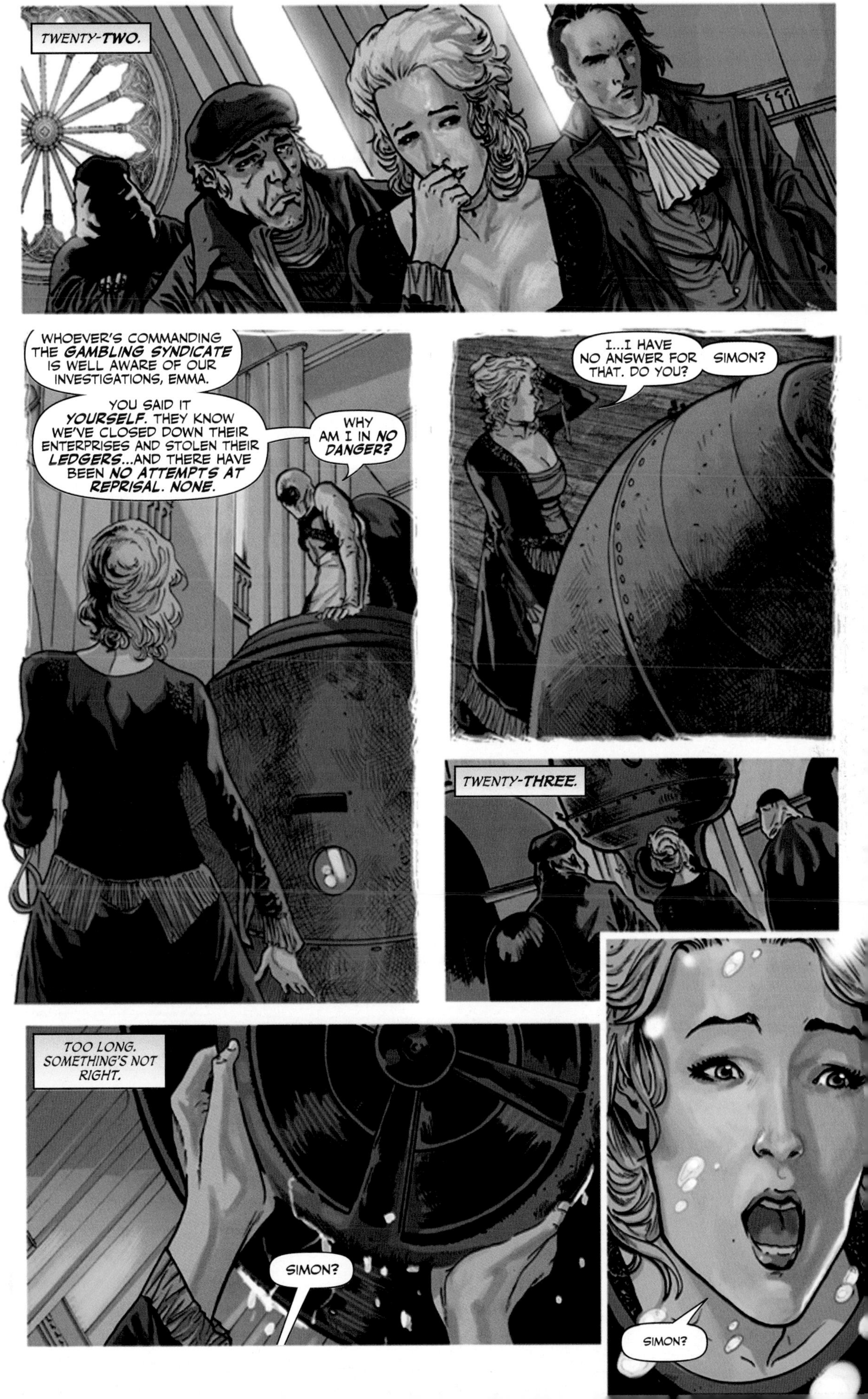
TWENTY-TWO.
WHOEVER'S COMMANDING THE GAMBLING SYNDICATE IS WELL AWARE OF OUR INVESTIGATIONS, EMMA.
YOU SAID IT YOURSELF. THEY KNOW WE'VE CLOSED DOWN THEIR ENTERPRISES AND STOLEN THEIR LEDGERS...AND THERE HAVE BEEN NO ATTEMPTS AT REPRISAL. NONE.
WHY AM I IN NO DANGER?
I...I HAVE NO ANSWER FOR THAT. DO YOU?
SIMON?
TWENTY-THREE.
TOO LONG. SOMETHING'S NOT RIGHT.
SIMON?
SIMON?

The PENNY ARCADIAN

Copiously Illustrated

Afternoon Edition, Price One Penny

SIMON ARCHARD DEAD

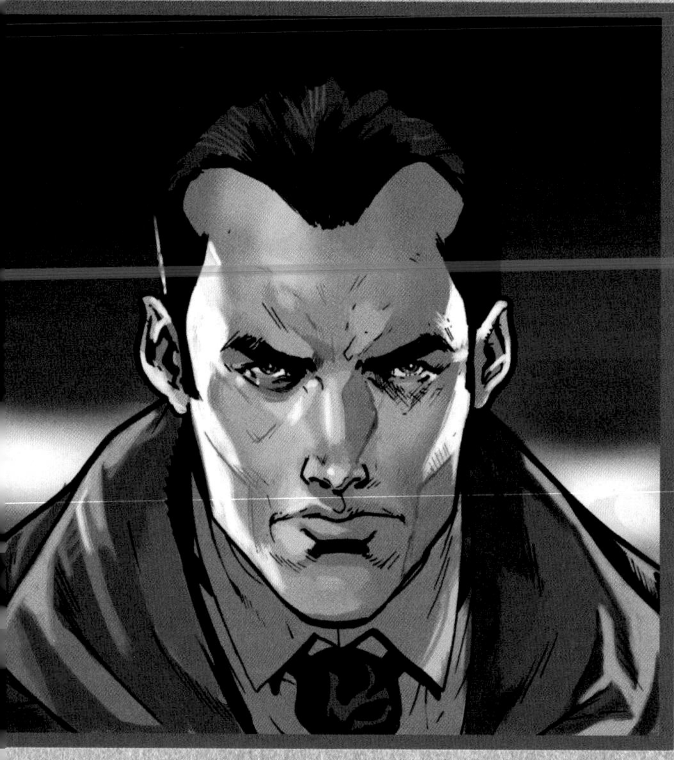

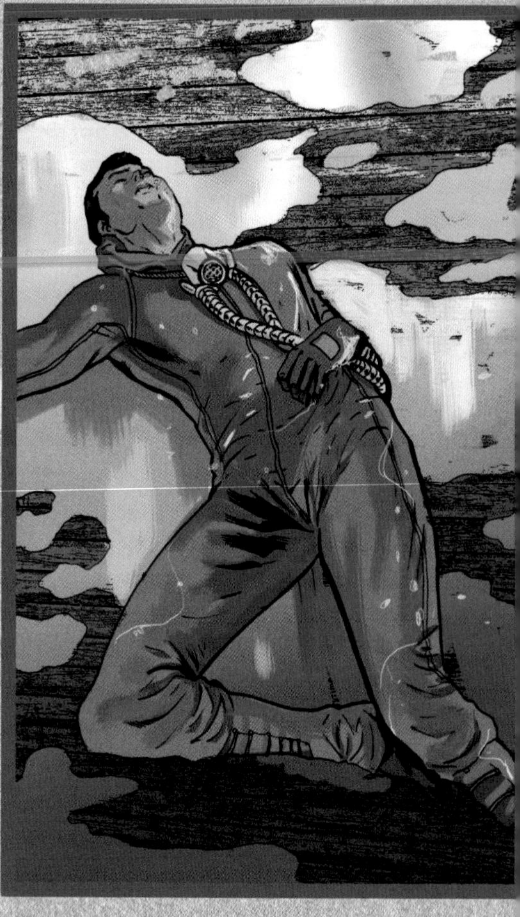

DETECTIVE ARCHARD SLAIN

In a tragic turn of events, the fabled sleuth Simon Archard, known in law-enforcement circles as "The Maestro," was found dead inside his own headquarters yesterday evening.

Ironically, he himself seems to have fallen victim to a "locked-room mystery" the type of which he himself was adept at unraveling. Self-immersed in his water-filled "deprivation tank" to ponder his most current case, Archard was found nearly twenty-four hours later by his assistant, name unknown, his lungs filled with water and no life remaining in his body.

While foul play is suspected, no evidence has yet been found supporting this hypothesis, as eyewitnesses attest no one could have at any time entered the tank with Archard and that he was alone inside its confines.

As for the witnesses to the fatality,
[STORY CONTINUES ON FOLLOWING PAGE]

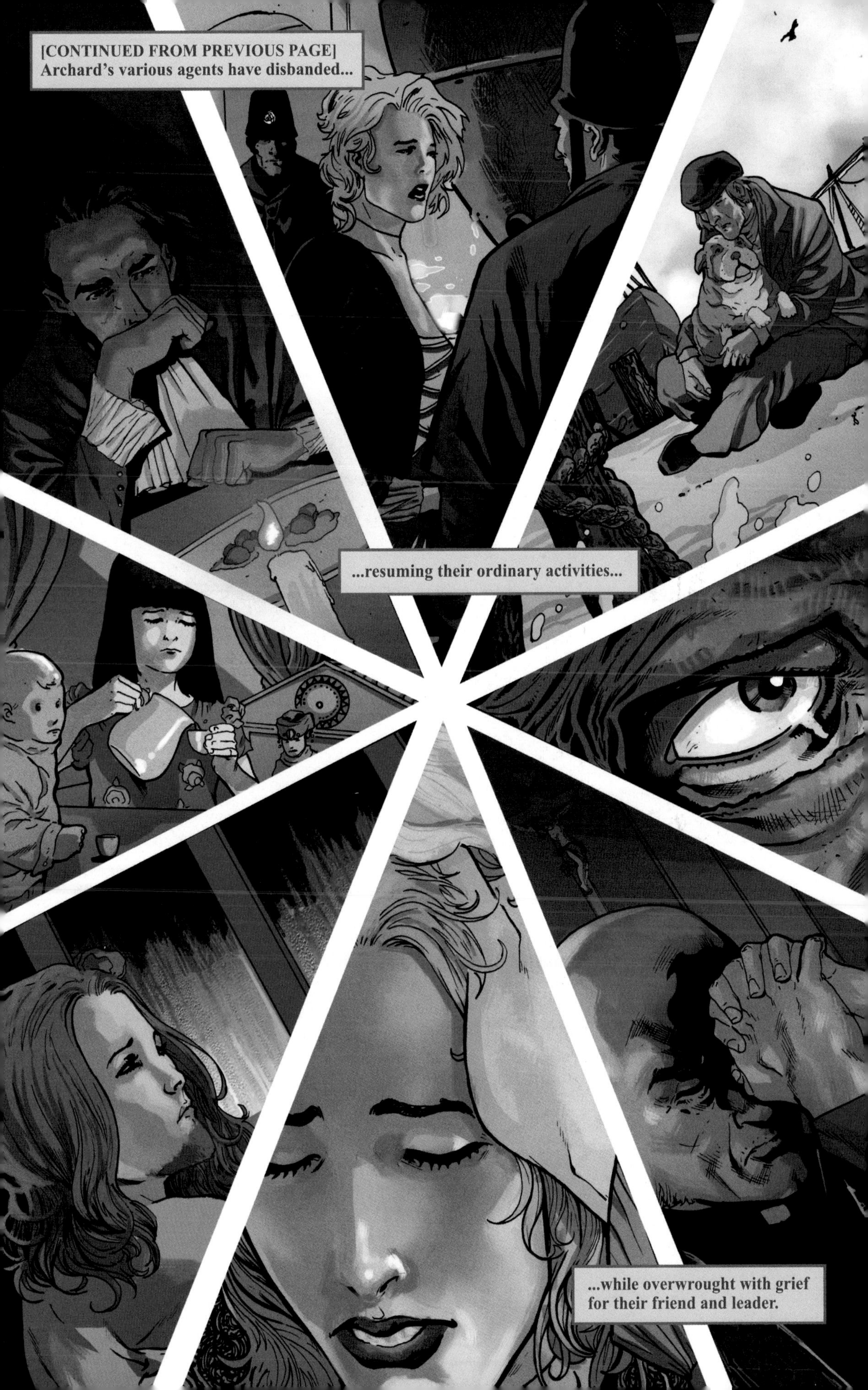
[CONTINUED FROM PREVIOUS PAGE]
Archard's various agents have disbanded...
...resuming their ordinary activities...
...while overwrought with grief for their friend and leader.

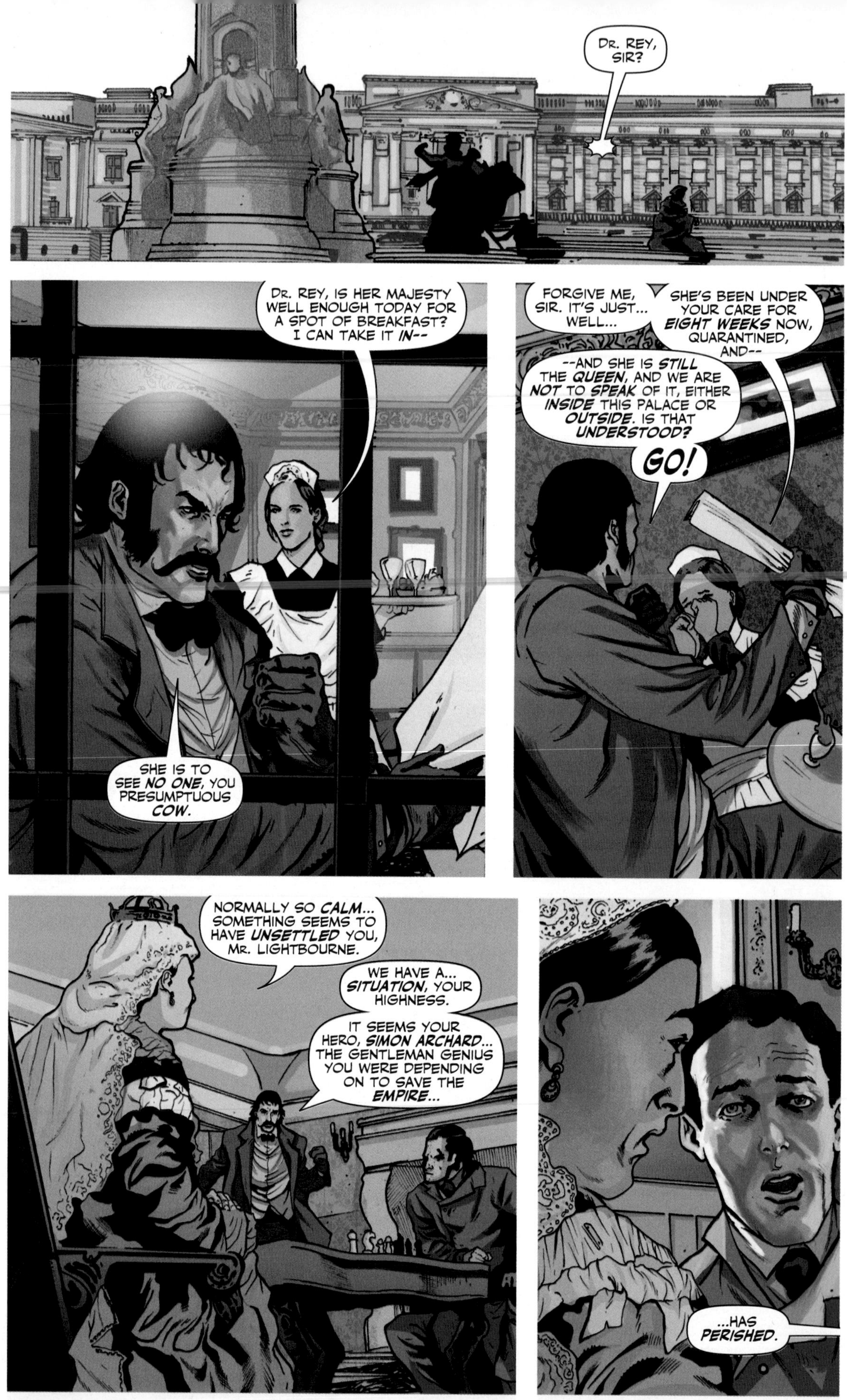
DR. REY, SIR?
DR. REY, IS HER MAJESTY WELL ENOUGH TODAY FOR A SPOT OF BREAKFAST? I CAN TAKE IT IN--
SHE IS TO SEE NO ONE, YOU PRESUMPTUOUS COW.
FORGIVE ME, SIR. IT'S JUST... WELL...
SHE'S BEEN UNDER YOUR CARE FOR EIGHT WEEKS NOW, QUARANTINED, AND--
--AND SHE IS STILL THE QUEEN, AND WE ARE NOT TO SPEAK OF IT, EITHER INSIDE THIS PALACE OR OUTSIDE. IS THAT UNDERSTOOD?
GO!
NORMALLY SO CALM... SOMETHING SEEMS TO HAVE UNSETTLED YOU, MR. LIGHTBOURNE.
WE HAVE A... SITUATION, YOUR HIGHNESS.
IT SEEMS YOUR HERO, SIMON ARCHARD... THE GENTLEMAN GENIUS YOU WERE DEPENDING ON TO SAVE THE EMPIRE...
...HAS PERISHED.

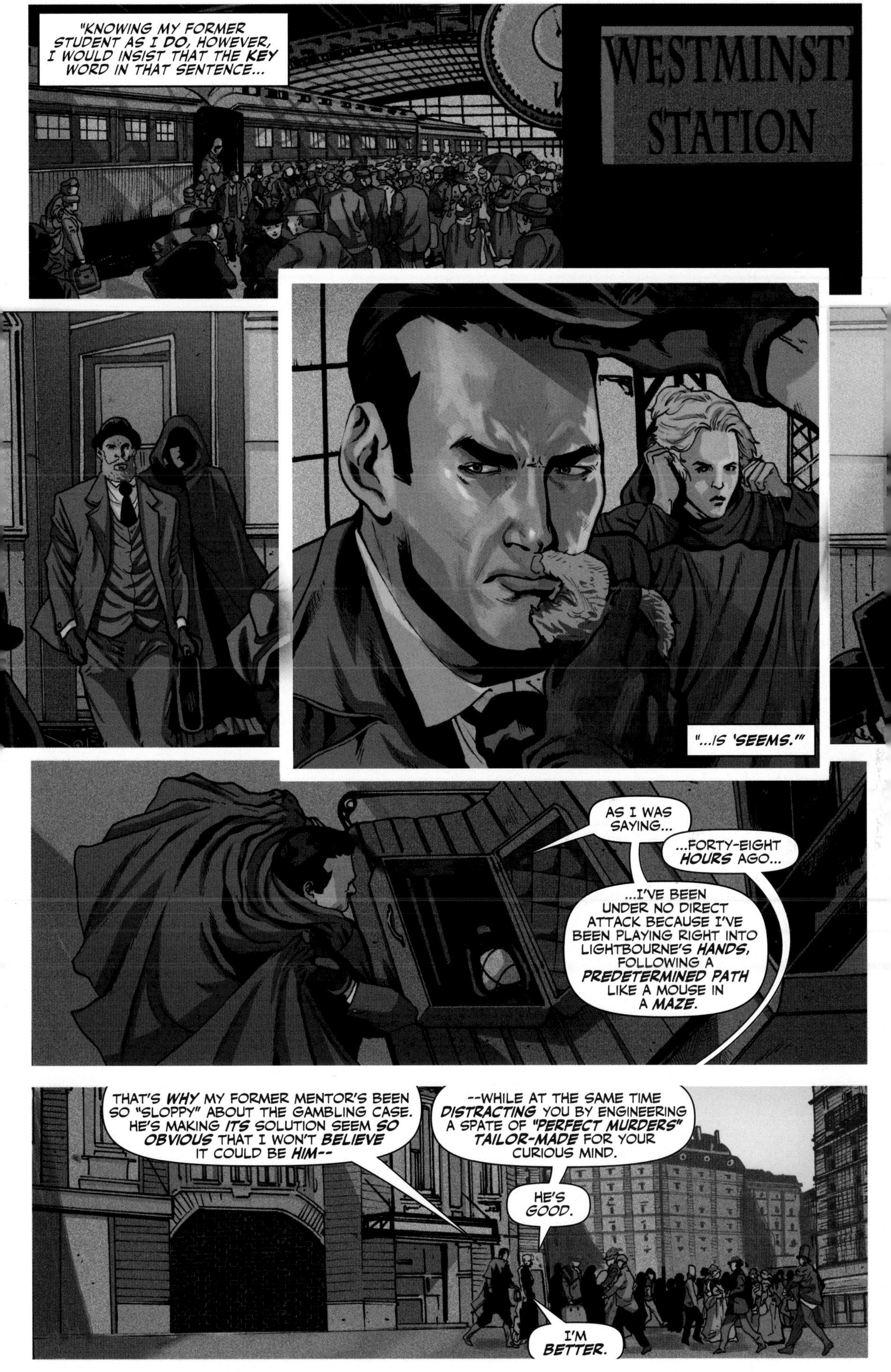
"KNOWING MY FORMER STUDENT AS I DO, HOWEVER, I WOULD INSIST THAT THE KEY WORD IN THAT SENTENCE...
WESTMINST
STATION
"...IS 'SEEMS.'"
AS I WAS SAYING...
...FORTY-EIGHT HOURS AGO...
...I'VE BEEN UNDER NO DIRECT ATTACK BECAUSE I'VE BEEN PLAYING RIGHT INTO LIGHTBOURNE'S HANDS, FOLLOWING A PREDETERMINED PATH LIKE A MOUSE IN A MAZE.
THAT'S WHY MY FORMER MENTOR'S BEEN SO "SLOPPY" ABOUT THE GAMBLING CASE. HE'S MAKING ITS SOLUTION SEEM SO OBVIOUS THAT I WON'T BELIEVE IT COULD BE HIM--
--WHILE AT THE SAME TIME DISTRACTING YOU BY ENGINEERING A SPATE OF "PERFECT MURDERS" TAILOR-MADE FOR YOUR CURIOUS MIND.
HE'S GOOD.
I'M BETTER.

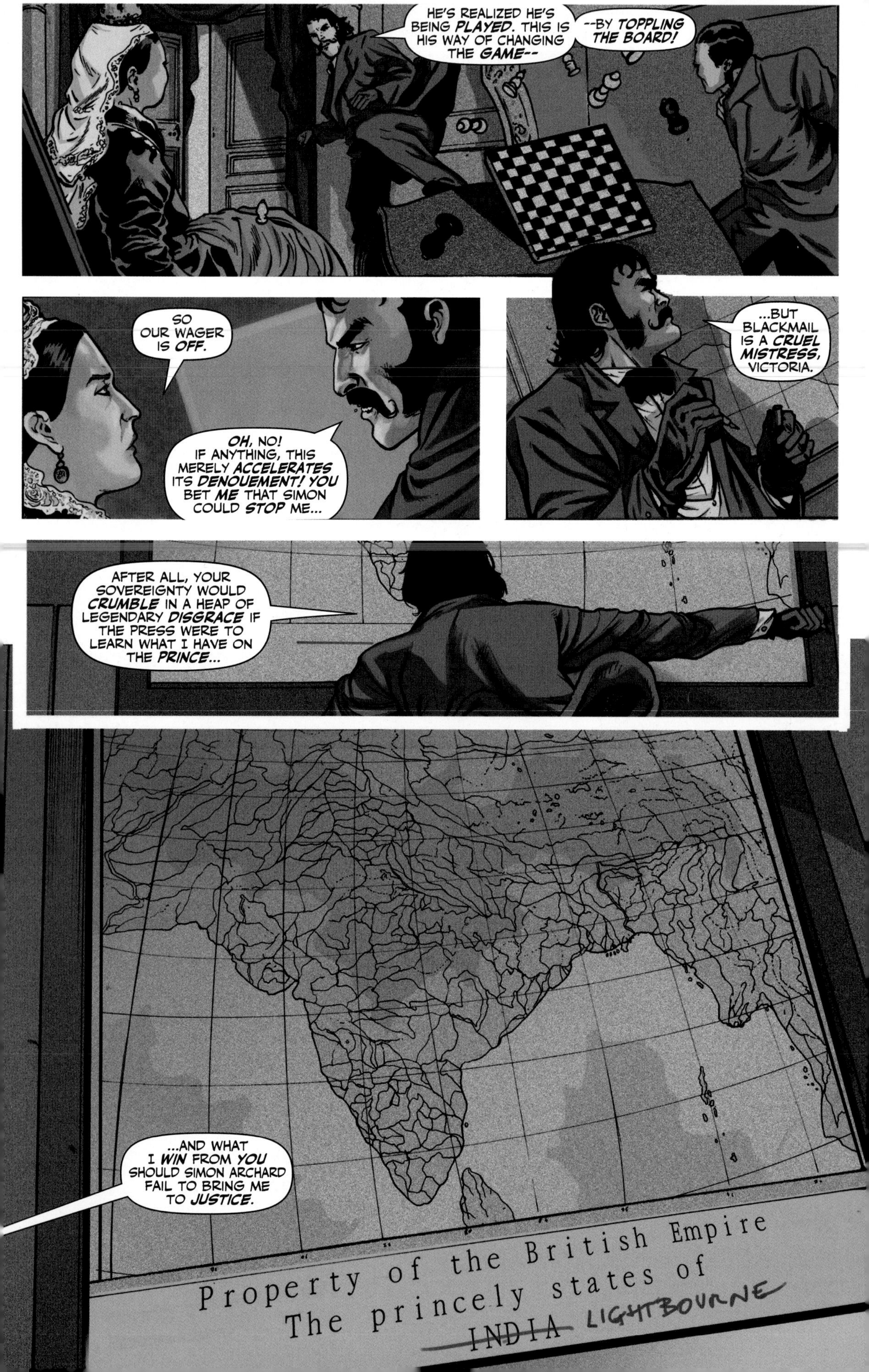

HE'S REALIZED HE'S BEING PLAYED. THIS IS HIS WAY OF CHANGING THE GAME--
--BY TOPPLING THE BOARD!
SO OUR WAGER IS OFF.
OH, NO! IF ANYTHING, THIS MERELY ACCELERATES ITS DENOUEMENT! YOU BET ME THAT SIMON COULD STOP ME...
...BUT BLACKMAIL IS A CRUEL MISTRESS, VICTORIA.
AFTER ALL, YOUR SOVEREIGNTY WOULD CRUMBLE IN A HEAP OF LEGENDARY DISGRACE IF THE PRESS WERE TO LEARN WHAT I HAVE ON THE PRINCE...
...AND WHAT I WIN FROM YOU SHOULD SIMON ARCHARD FAIL TO BRING ME TO JUSTICE.
Property of the British Empire
The princely states of
~~INDIA~~ LIGHTBOURNE

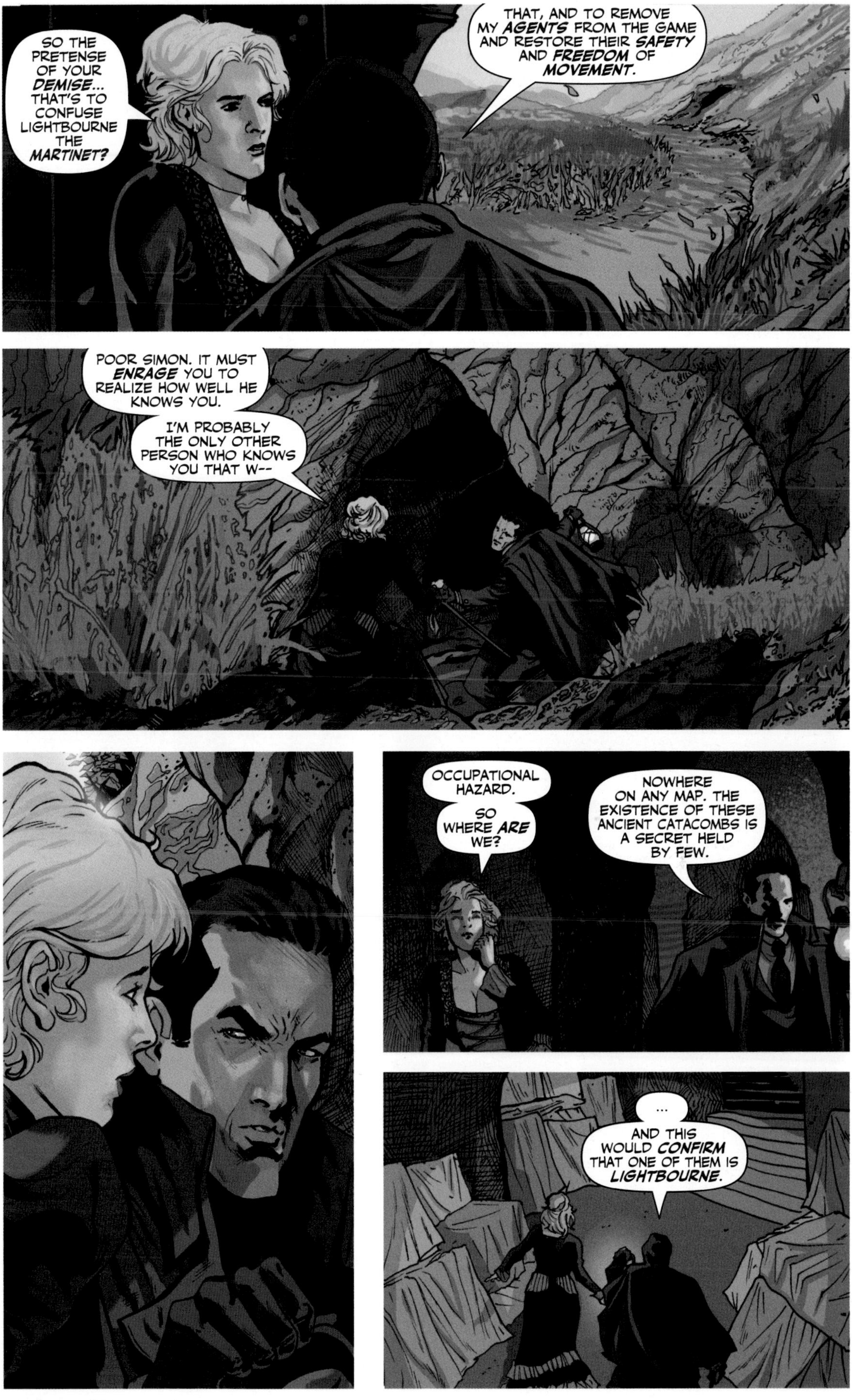
SO THE PRETENSE OF YOUR DEMISE... THAT'S TO CONFUSE LIGHTBOURNE THE MARTINET?
THAT, AND TO REMOVE MY AGENTS FROM THE GAME AND RESTORE THEIR SAFETY AND FREEDOM OF MOVEMENT.
POOR SIMON. IT MUST ENRAGE YOU TO REALIZE HOW WELL HE KNOWS YOU.
I'M PROBABLY THE ONLY OTHER PERSON WHO KNOWS YOU THAT W--
OCCUPATIONAL HAZARD.
SO WHERE ARE WE?
NOWHERE ON ANY MAP. THE EXISTENCE OF THESE ANCIENT CATACOMBS IS A SECRET HELD BY FEW.
...
AND THIS WOULD CONFIRM THAT ONE OF THEM IS LIGHTBOURNE.

MOREOVER, JUDGING BY THE LACK OF DUST AND OTHER CONTAMINANTS, HIS *TAKEAWAYS* HAVE ONLY JUST BEEN SECRETED HERE IN THE LAST *DAY* OR TWO.

THAT'S A VICTORY. MY *"DEATH"* HAS SUCCESSFULLY PRESSED LIGHTBOURNE INTO RUSHING HIS *ENDGAME.*

WHAT IS ALL THIS?

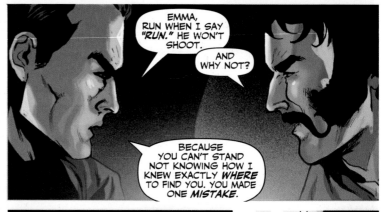

GIVEN ALL THOSE CLUES, AND YOU HAVEN'T YET *DEDUCED?*

NO *WONDER* SIMON CONSIDERS YOU A *SUBORDINATE,* MISS BISHOP.

THEN AGAIN, HE REALLY SHOULD START HIRING SOMEWHERE OTHER THAN THE *ZOO.*

EMMA, RUN WHEN I SAY *"RUN."* HE WON'T SHOOT.

AND WHY NOT?

BECAUSE YOU CAN'T STAND NOT KNOWING HOW I KNEW EXACTLY *WHERE* TO FIND YOU. YOU MADE ONE *MISTAKE.*

DOES *SHE* KNOW WHAT IT WAS?

ONLY ME.

THEN SHE'S *EXPENDABLE.*

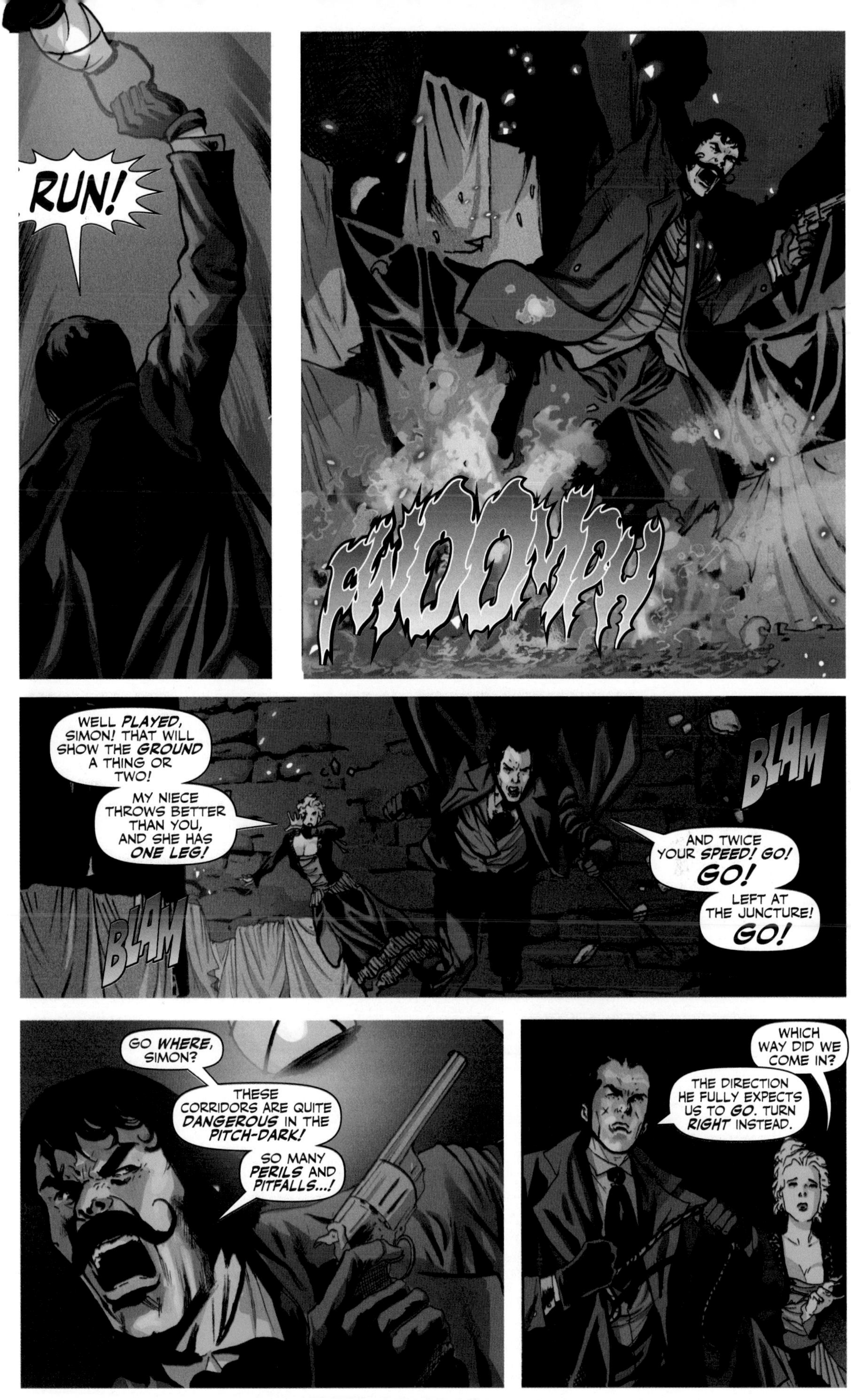
RUN!
FWOOMPH
WELL PLAYED, SIMON! THAT WILL SHOW THE GROUND A THING OR TWO!
MY NIECE THROWS BETTER THAN YOU, AND SHE HAS ONE LEG!
BLAM
BLAM
AND TWICE YOUR SPEED! GO! GO!
LEFT AT THE JUNCTURE! GO!
GO WHERE, SIMON?
THESE CORRIDORS ARE QUITE DANGEROUS IN THE PITCH-DARK!
SO MANY PERILS AND PITFALLS...!
WHICH WAY DID WE COME IN?
THE DIRECTION HE FULLY EXPECTS US TO GO. TURN RIGHT INSTEAD.

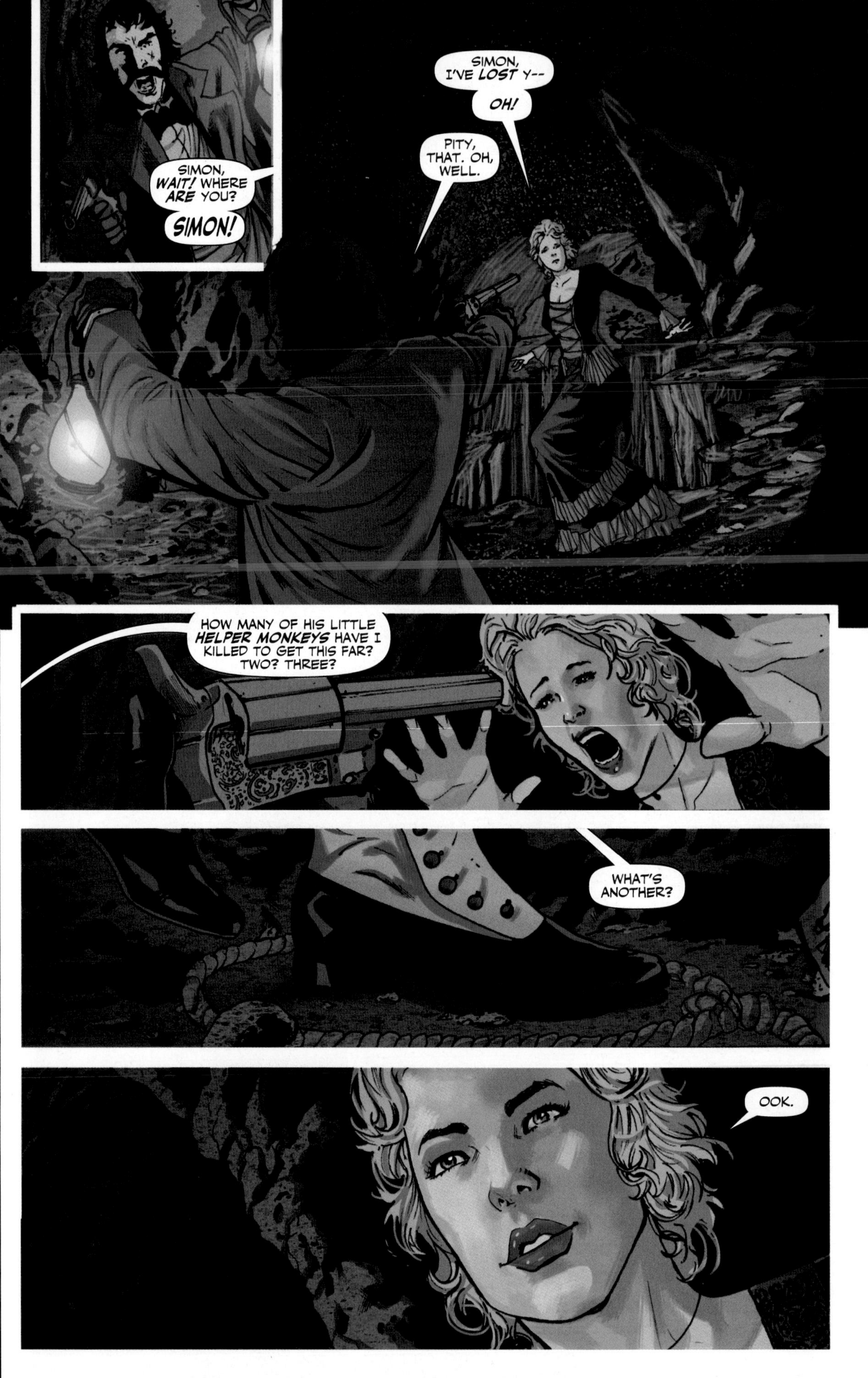
SIMON, WAIT! WHERE ARE YOU?
SIMON!
SIMON, I'VE LOST Y--
OH!
PITY, THAT. OH, WELL.
HOW MANY OF HIS LITTLE HELPER MONKEYS HAVE I KILLED TO GET THIS FAR? TWO? THREE?
WHAT'S ANOTHER?
OOK.

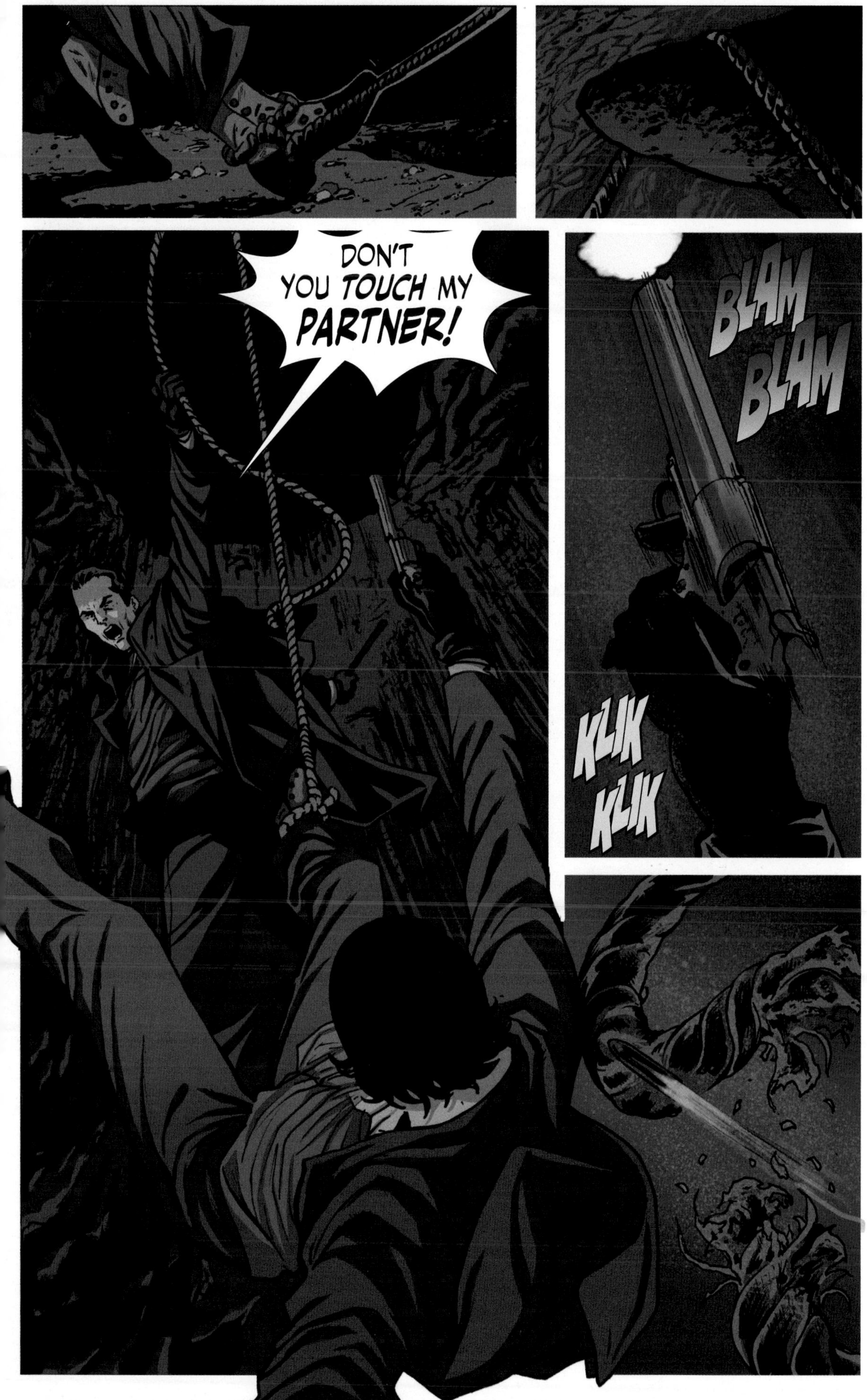
DON'T YOU TOUCH MY PARTNER!
BLAM BLAM
KLIK KLIK

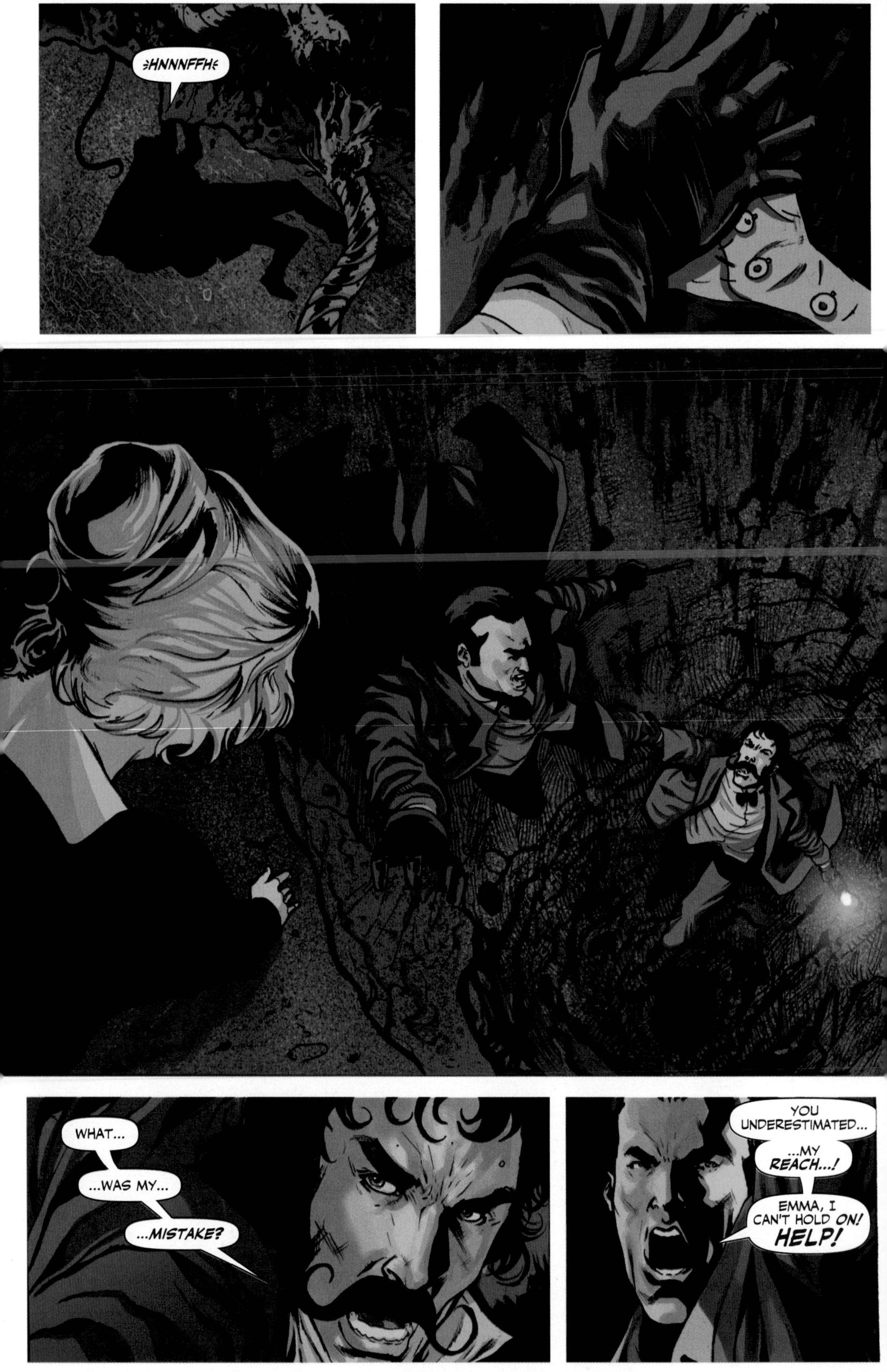
HNNNFFH
WHAT...
...WAS MY...
...MISTAKE?
YOU UNDERESTIMATED...
...MY REACH...!
EMMA, I CAN'T HOLD ON! HELP!

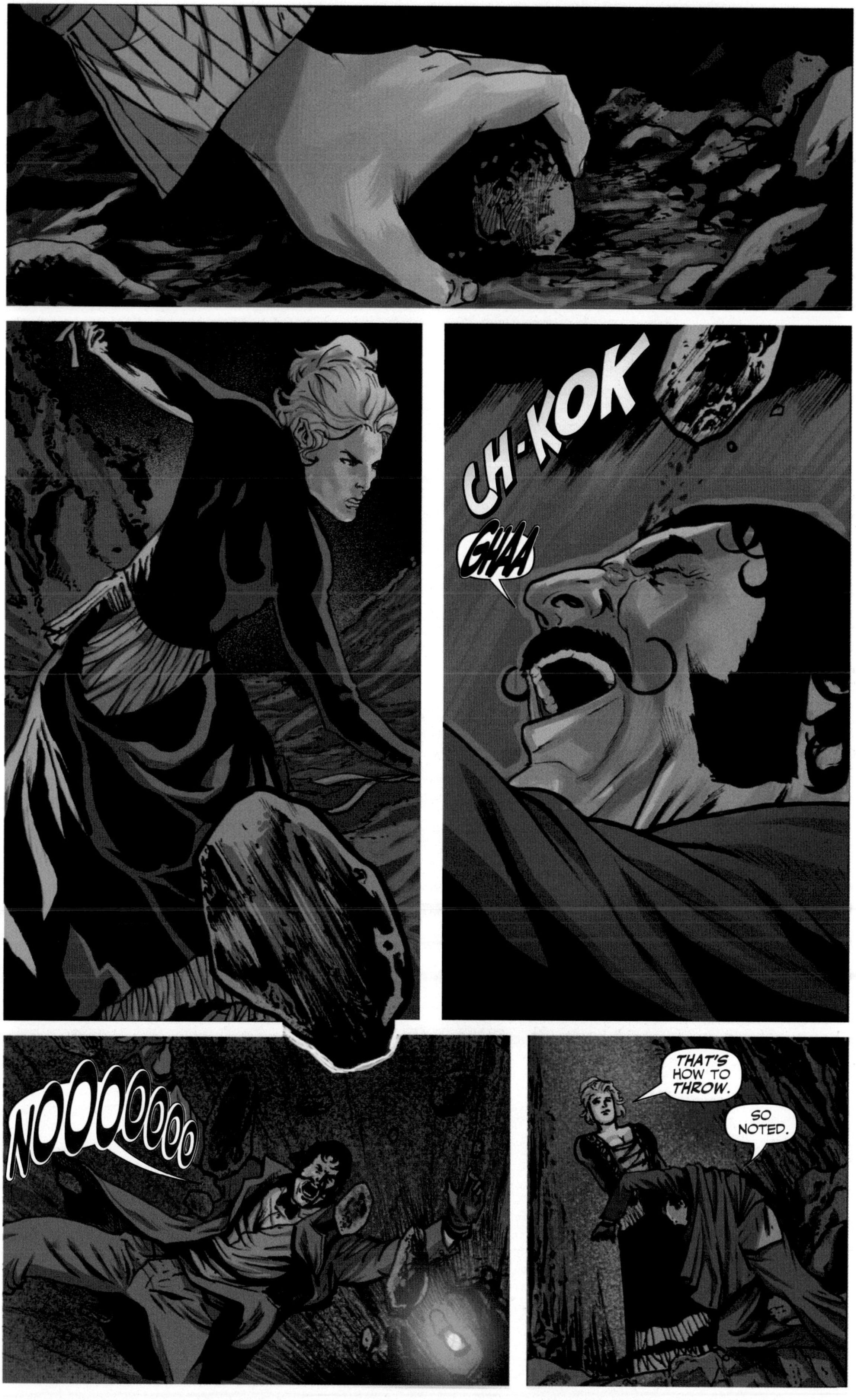
CH-KOK
GHAA
NOOOOOOO
THAT'S HOW TO THROW.
SO NOTED.

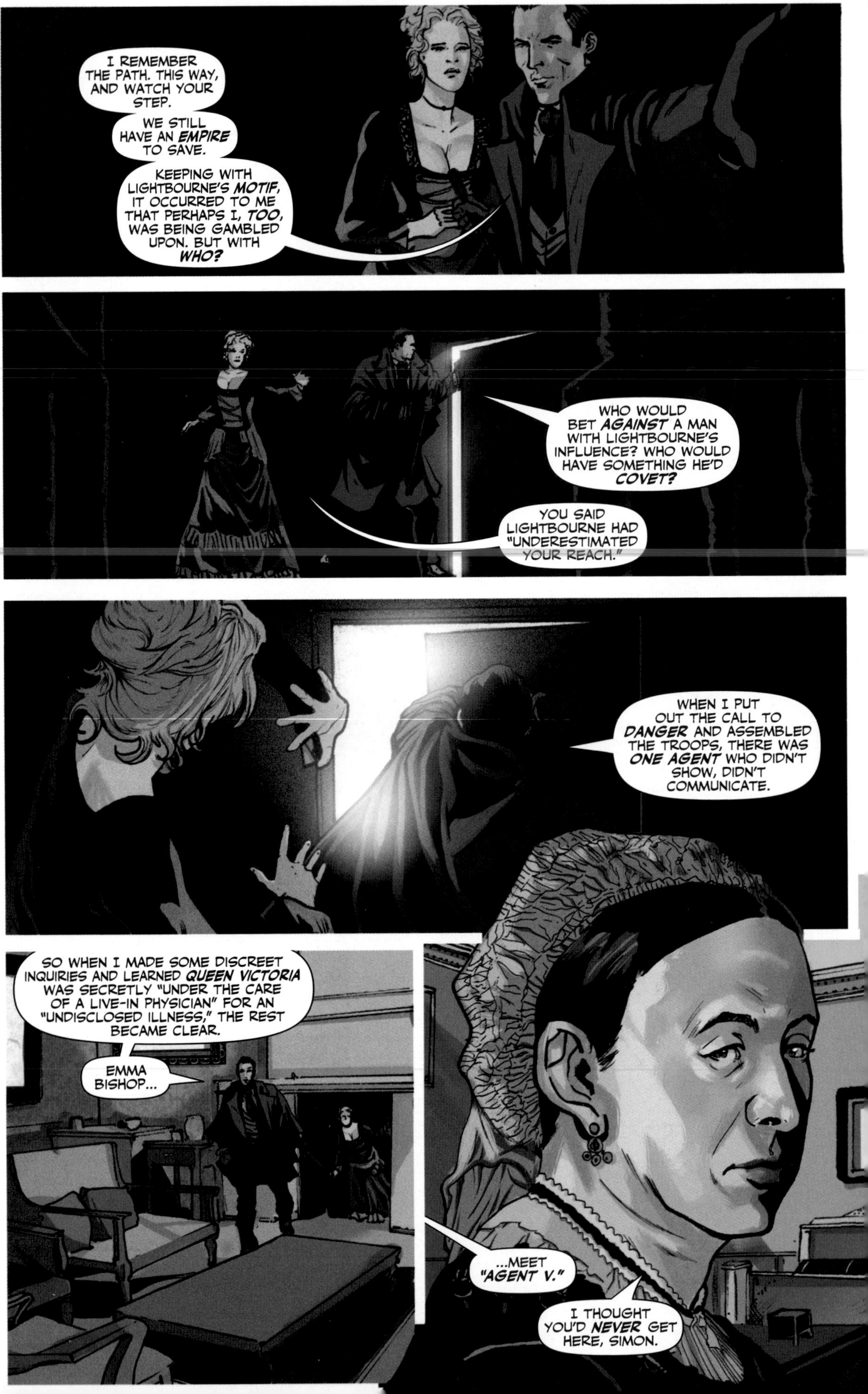
I REMEMBER THE PATH. THIS WAY, AND WATCH YOUR STEP.
WE STILL HAVE AN EMPIRE TO SAVE.
KEEPING WITH LIGHTBOURNE'S MOTIF, IT OCCURRED TO ME THAT PERHAPS I, TOO, WAS BEING GAMBLED UPON. BUT WITH WHO?
WHO WOULD BET AGAINST A MAN WITH LIGHTBOURNE'S INFLUENCE? WHO WOULD HAVE SOMETHING HE'D COVET?
YOU SAID LIGHTBOURNE HAD "UNDERESTIMATED YOUR REACH."
WHEN I PUT OUT THE CALL TO DANGER AND ASSEMBLED THE TROOPS, THERE WAS ONE AGENT WHO DIDN'T SHOW, DIDN'T COMMUNICATE.
SO WHEN I MADE SOME DISCREET INQUIRIES AND LEARNED QUEEN VICTORIA WAS SECRETLY "UNDER THE CARE OF A LIVE-IN PHYSICIAN" FOR AN "UNDISCLOSED ILLNESS," THE REST BECAME CLEAR.
EMMA BISHOP...
...MEET "AGENT V."
I THOUGHT YOU'D NEVER GET HERE, SIMON.

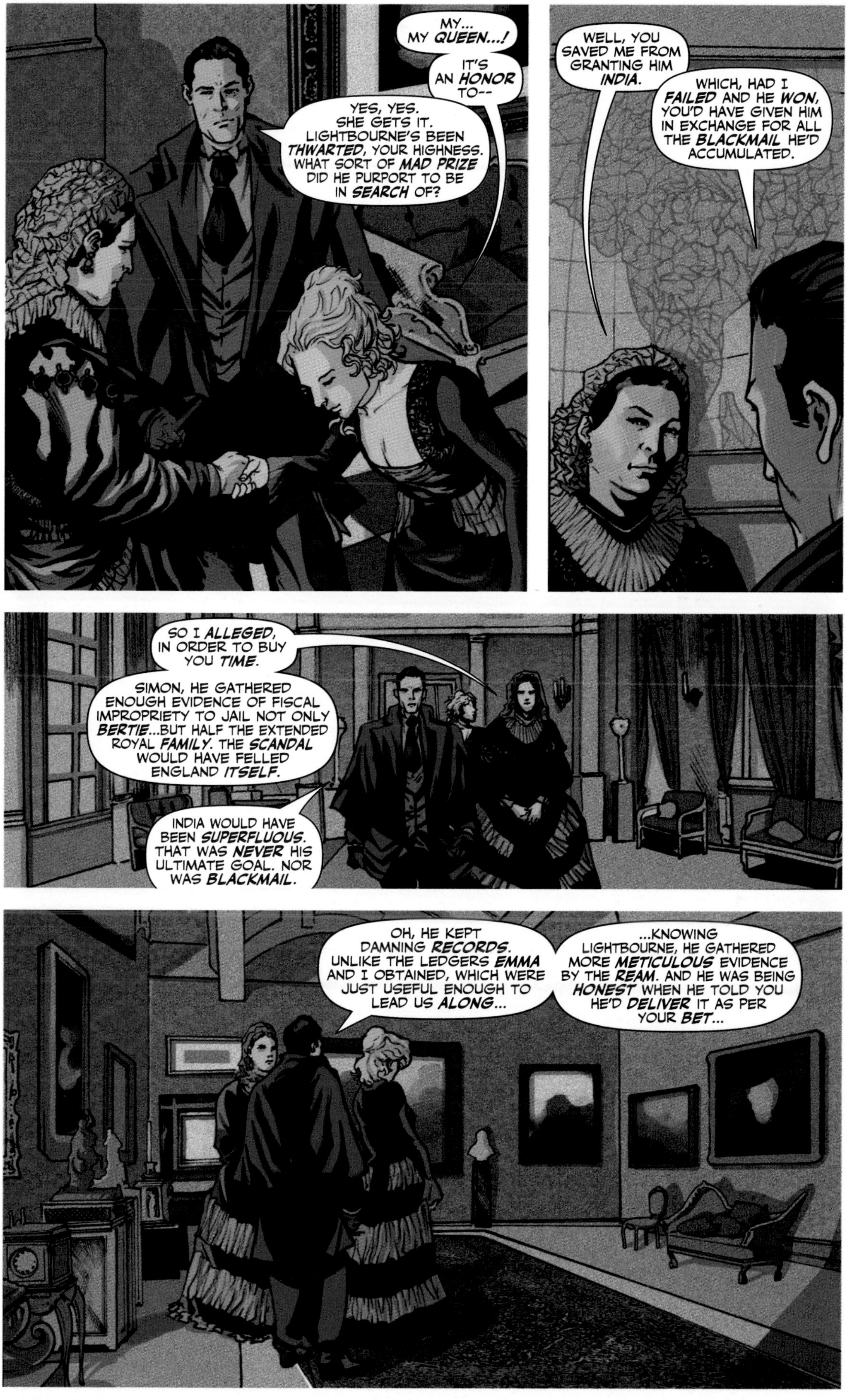

MY... MY QUEEN...!
IT'S AN HONOR TO--
YES, YES. SHE GETS IT. LIGHTBOURNE'S BEEN THWARTED, YOUR HIGHNESS. WHAT SORT OF MAD PRIZE DID HE PURPORT TO BE IN SEARCH OF?
WELL, YOU SAVED ME FROM GRANTING HIM INDIA.
WHICH, HAD I FAILED AND HE WON, YOU'D HAVE GIVEN HIM IN EXCHANGE FOR ALL THE BLACKMAIL HE'D ACCUMULATED.
SO I ALLEGED, IN ORDER TO BUY YOU TIME.
SIMON, HE GATHERED ENOUGH EVIDENCE OF FISCAL IMPROPRIETY TO JAIL NOT ONLY BERTIE...BUT HALF THE EXTENDED ROYAL FAMILY. THE SCANDAL WOULD HAVE FELLED ENGLAND ITSELF.
INDIA WOULD HAVE BEEN SUPERFLUOUS. THAT WAS NEVER HIS ULTIMATE GOAL. NOR WAS BLACKMAIL.
OH, HE KEPT DAMNING RECORDS. UNLIKE THE LEDGERS EMMA AND I OBTAINED, WHICH WERE JUST USEFUL ENOUGH TO LEAD US ALONG...
...KNOWING LIGHTBOURNE, HE GATHERED MORE METICULOUS EVIDENCE BY THE REAM. AND HE WAS BEING HONEST WHEN HE TOLD YOU HE'D DELIVER IT AS PER YOUR BET...

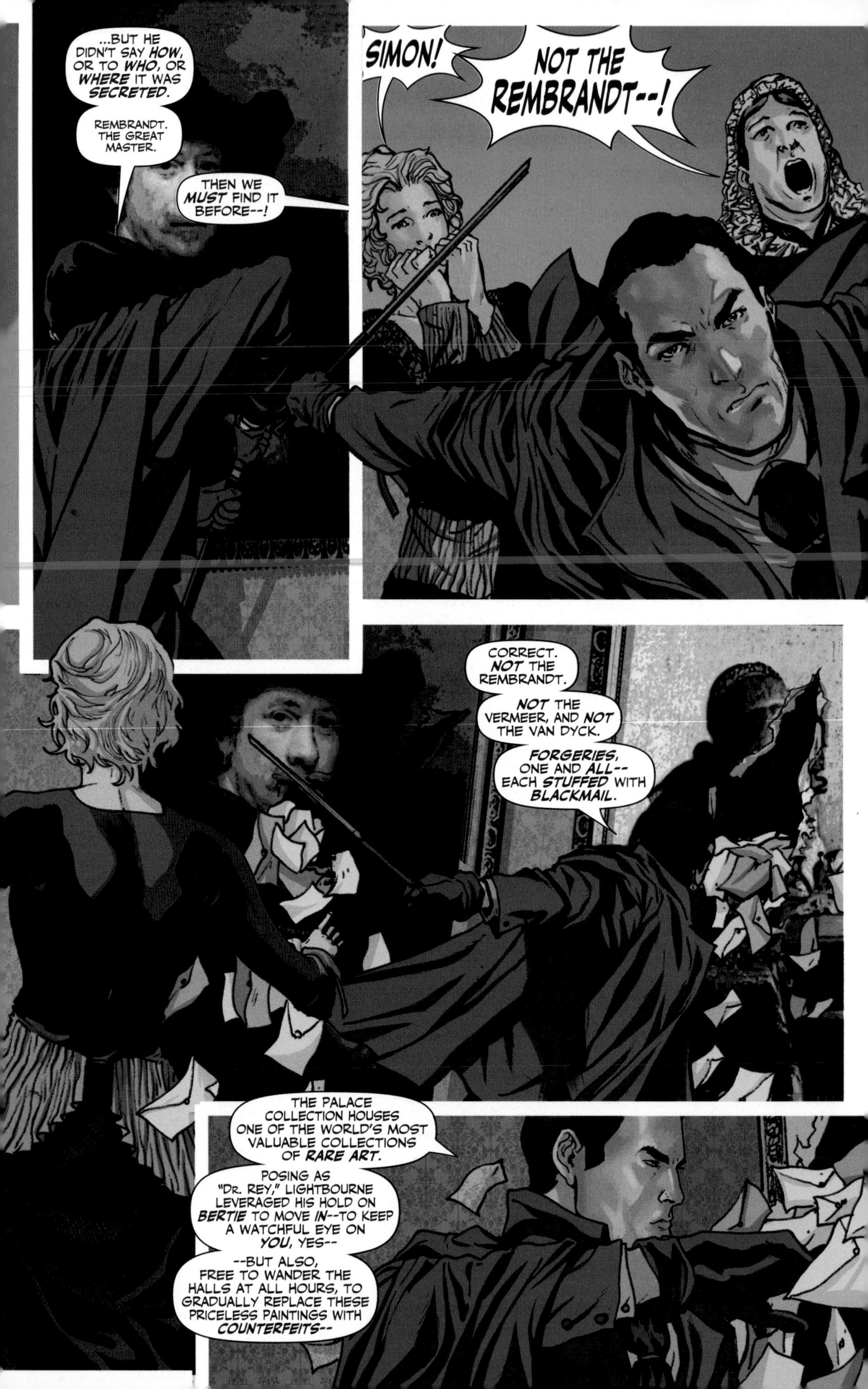
...BUT HE DIDN'T SAY HOW, OR TO WHO, OR WHERE IT WAS SECRETED.
REMBRANDT. THE GREAT MASTER.
THEN WE MUST FIND IT BEFORE--!
SIMON!
NOT THE REMBRANDT--!
CORRECT. NOT THE REMBRANDT.
NOT THE VERMEER, AND NOT THE VAN DYCK.
FORGERIES, ONE AND ALL-- EACH STUFFED WITH BLACKMAIL.
THE PALACE COLLECTION HOUSES ONE OF THE WORLD'S MOST VALUABLE COLLECTIONS OF RARE ART.
POSING AS "DR. REY," LIGHTBOURNE LEVERAGED HIS HOLD ON BERTIE TO MOVE IN--TO KEEP A WATCHFUL EYE ON YOU, YES--
--BUT ALSO, FREE TO WANDER THE HALLS AT ALL HOURS, TO GRADUALLY REPLACE THESE PRICELESS PAINTINGS WITH COUNTERFEITS--

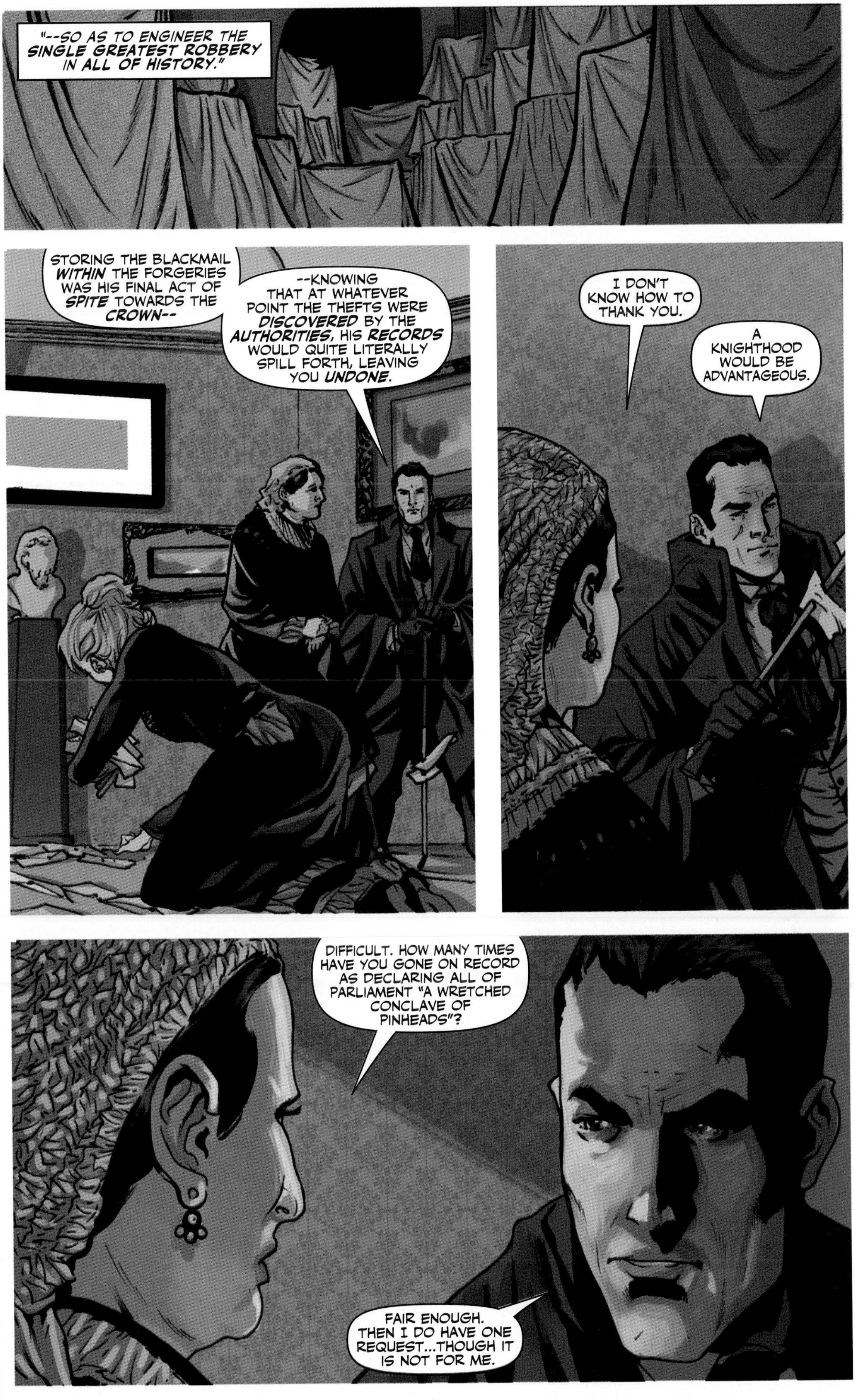
"--SO AS TO ENGINEER THE SINGLE GREATEST ROBBERY IN ALL OF HISTORY."
STORING THE BLACKMAIL WITHIN THE FORGERIES WAS HIS FINAL ACT OF SPITE TOWARDS THE CROWN--
--KNOWING THAT AT WHATEVER POINT THE THEFTS WERE DISCOVERED BY THE AUTHORITIES, HIS RECORDS WOULD QUITE LITERALLY SPILL FORTH, LEAVING YOU UNDONE.
I DON'T KNOW HOW TO THANK YOU.
A KNIGHTHOOD WOULD BE ADVANTAGEOUS.
DIFFICULT. HOW MANY TIMES HAVE YOU GONE ON RECORD AS DECLARING ALL OF PARLIAMENT "A WRETCHED CONCLAVE OF PINHEADS"?
FAIR ENOUGH. THEN I DO HAVE ONE REQUEST...THOUGH IT IS NOT FOR ME.

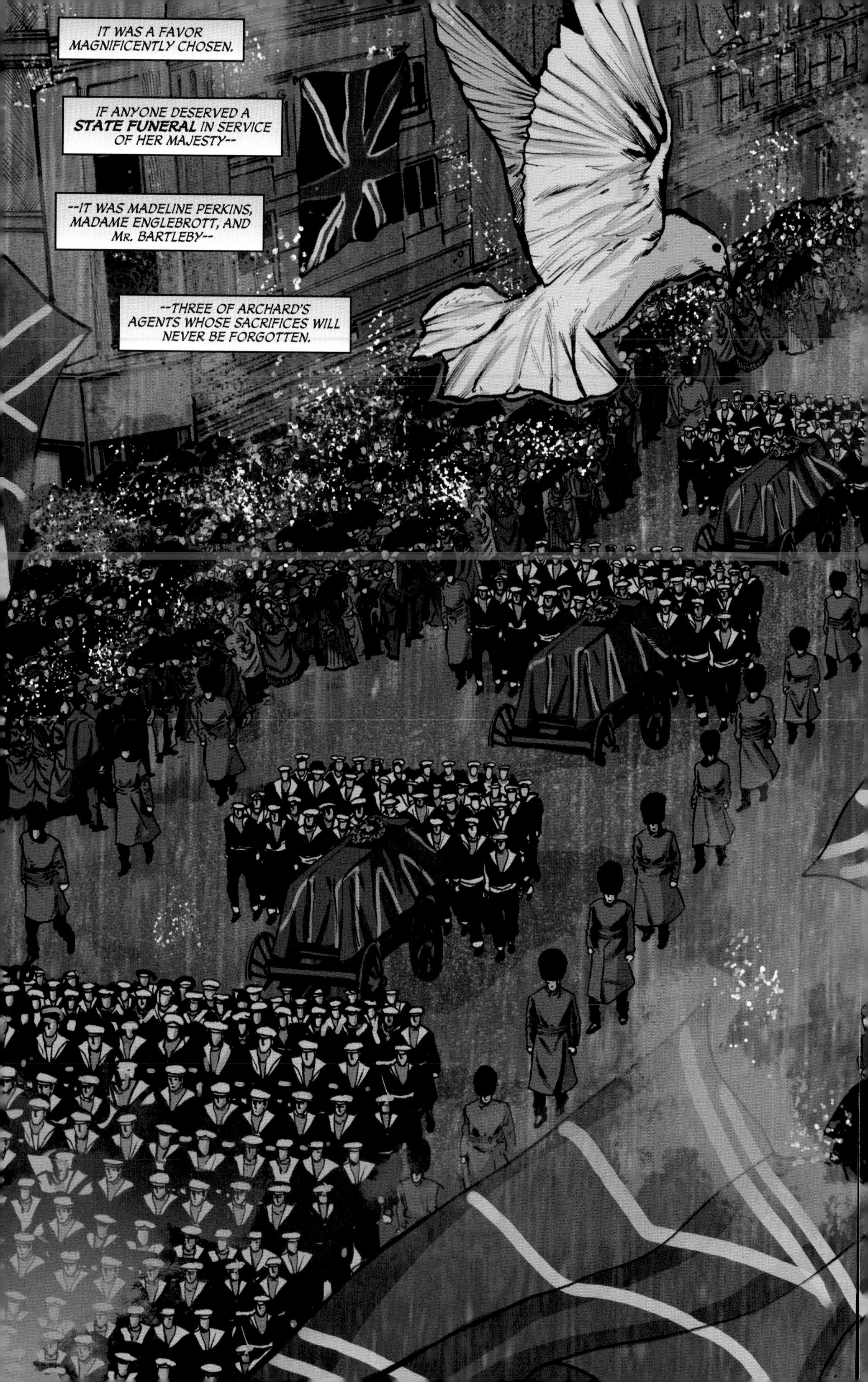
IT WAS A FAVOR MAGNIFICENTLY CHOSEN.
IF ANYONE DESERVED A STATE FUNERAL IN SERVICE OF HER MAJESTY--
--IT WAS MADELINE PERKINS, MADAME ENGLEBROTT, AND MR. BARTLEBY--
--THREE OF ARCHARD'S AGENTS WHOSE SACRIFICES WILL NEVER BE FORGOTTEN.

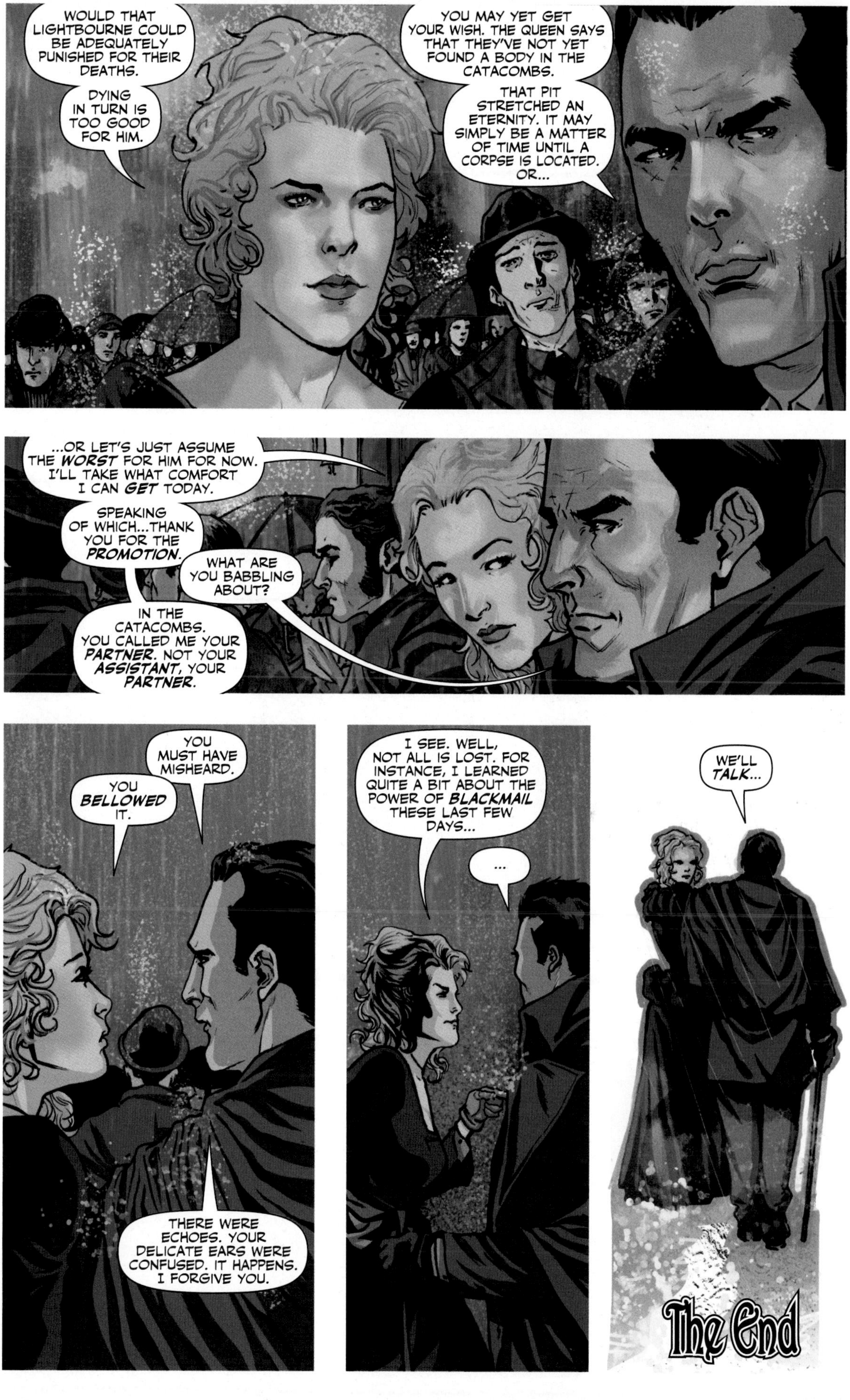
WOULD THAT LIGHTBOURNE COULD BE ADEQUATELY PUNISHED FOR THEIR DEATHS.
DYING IN TURN IS TOO GOOD FOR HIM.
YOU MAY YET GET YOUR WISH. THE QUEEN SAYS THAT THEY'VE NOT YET FOUND A BODY IN THE CATACOMBS.
THAT PIT STRETCHED AN ETERNITY. IT MAY SIMPLY BE A MATTER OF TIME UNTIL A CORPSE IS LOCATED. OR...
...OR LET'S JUST ASSUME THE *WORST* FOR HIM FOR NOW. I'LL TAKE WHAT COMFORT I CAN *GET* TODAY.
SPEAKING OF WHICH...THANK YOU FOR THE *PROMOTION*.
WHAT ARE YOU BABBLING ABOUT?
IN THE CATACOMBS. YOU CALLED ME YOUR *PARTNER*. NOT YOUR *ASSISTANT*, YOUR *PARTNER*.
YOU MUST HAVE MISHEARD.
YOU *BELLOWED* IT.
THERE WERE ECHOES. YOUR DELICATE EARS WERE CONFUSED. IT HAPPENS. I FORGIVE YOU.
I SEE. WELL, NOT ALL IS LOST. FOR INSTANCE, I LEARNED QUITE A BIT ABOUT THE POWER OF *BLACKMAIL* THESE LAST FEW DAYS...
...
WE'LL *TALK*...
The End

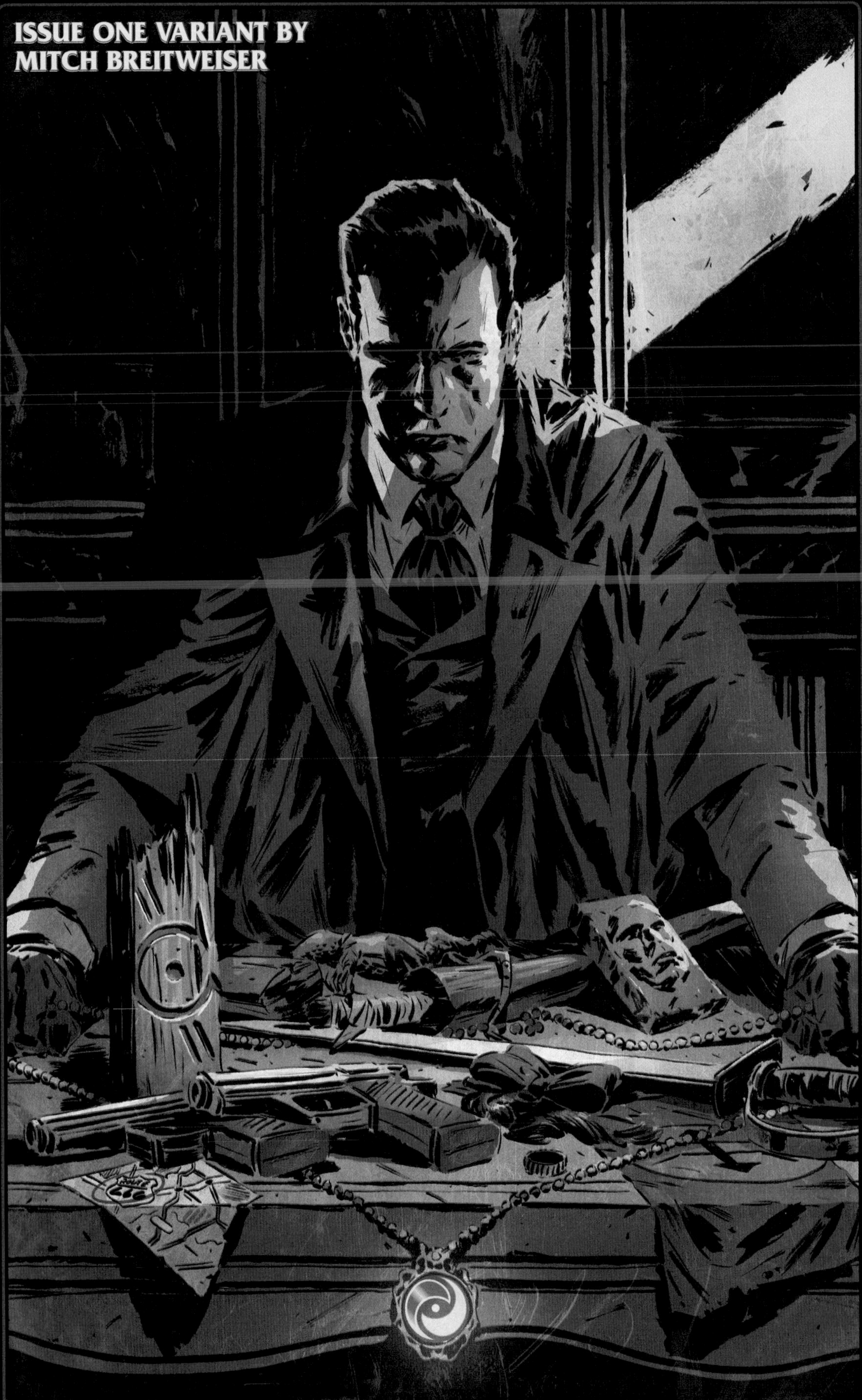

ISSUE ONE VARIANT BY
MITCH BREITWEISER

THE MYSTERY
WITH MARK WA

MARVEL: What kind of character is Simon Archard? What about him is going to appeal to fans?

MARK WAID: Simon is an effete, razor-tongued superdetective who does not suffer fools gladly. He has the mind of a computer and the social skills of a steak knife. I find him appealing because he's utterly unpredictable and will generally take the least expected option in any scenario – not because he's a master planner, but because he's so focused on what he can see and hear in the moment that he never ever wastes time and brainpower considering the consequences of his actions. That's Emma's job.

MARVEL: What sort of relationship does Emma Bishop have with Archard? Is it the classic hero/sidekick scenario or is Bishop on more of a level playing field?

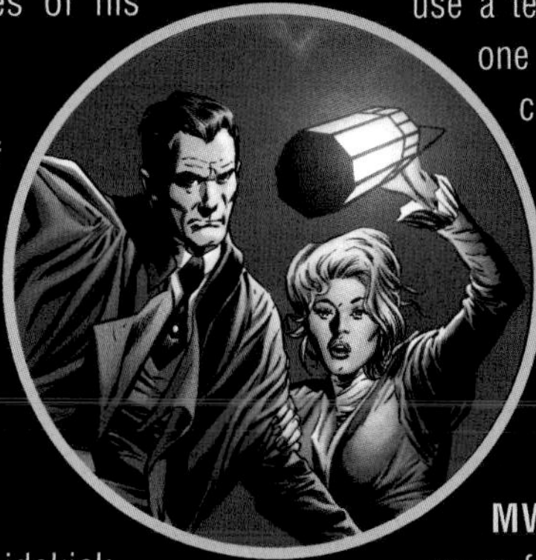

MW: Emma's a partner, not a sidekick (though Simon may disagree with this). She brings to the table the social graces that Simon lacks, and her charm opens up doors that would otherwise be closed to them as they investigate impossible crimes. She's not as smart as Simon – no one is – but she's far more world-wise and far more observant of things and events and people not immediately in her line of sight, unlike Simon, who thinks only about what's right in front of him.

MARVEL: Ruse plays with many element not usually employed in standard comic book fare – Victorian social mores, classic detective formulae and a pair of intelligent witty protagonists. Are there any unique challenges in writing it?

MW: The period language is a huge challenge but that's what *The Highly Selective Thesaurus For The Extraordinarily Literate* is for, thank you HarperCollins. It's tough enough remembering not to have the characters accidentally slip into modern turns of phrase, but it's even more difficult writing a character like Simon who won' use a ten-cent word when a ten-dolla one is available. Oh, yeah, and also concocting impossible crimes.

MARVEL: What is your favorite thing about working with characters in Ruse as opposed to traditional supe hero stories?

MW: Probably that there's more room for humor and less compulsion to have characters punching each other every few pages. That said, it's still a fantastica setting – Simon's headquarters alone is like a steampunk Baxter Building, and the villains our detectives go up against are often more than simple street-level thugs. They have access to weird magical artifacts and bizarre devices that make them the Victorian-era equivalent of super villains!

TALKING CROSSGEN

WITH DAVID GABRIEL, S.V.P. OF PUBLISHING SALES

MARVEL: What does Marvel hope to achieve with the CrossGen properties?

DAVID GABRIEL: We're looking to expand our universes a bit and add some fresh new genres to our mix. There are some great concepts that exist within the older CrossGen universe of characters and this is a great opportunity to reimagine these characters and stories with a Marvel sensibility.

MARVEL: What made Marvel decide to launch the CrossGen imprint with Sigil & Ruse?

DG: Honestly this was an editorial and creative decision. We cast the net wide to see what kinds of pitches we could get back using all the characters and titles that exist within this new universe and bringing in a range of new ideas from our extended creative pool. We had narrowed it down to five, and we thought that Sigil made the most sense to launch with because of its original importance to the CrossGen universe. And combining Mark Waid and Ruse seemed like a surefire win!

MARVEL: What future plans does Marvel have for CrossGen and what other titles will we see?

DG: We have a plan for which books we are going to release and when but we don't want to tip our hand just yet. There are a lot of titles to choose from so we're really taking our time and working on these books to make them the best possible stories we can.

MARVEL: Super hero stories are Marvel's bread and butter. What are fans going to be attracted to about the CrossGen properties and how does Marvel plan to make these non-super hero tales viable?

DG: I think a few years back we proved that Marvel isn't just about super hero stories anymore with books like Dark Tower, Halo, Wizard of Oz, Pride and Prejudice, Ender's Game, and even Zombies and now we see the CrossGen properties as another extension of our reaching out into new genres of mystery, fantasy, sci-fi, horror, sword and sorcery, and a whole slew of other untapped universes for us.

We'll be taking the same sensibilities that we use in our super hero storytelling and using those within this new universe. We'll be using the best talent Marvel has to offer to create stunning tales of these imaginative worlds. We'll be getting to the core elements that made these stories resonate with so many fans years ago and reignite those passions for these stories. I think we'll be finding the "super hero" in these concepts and really making them Marvel!

MARVEL: Does Marvel have any plans to reprint the old CrossGen material?

DG: Not at present. We've talked about it, perhaps launching some digitally later on. But in looking at everything we want to accomplish, we really want these new series to be seen as fresh new concepts. They're not continuations of the originals so we want to avoid any confusion. No one will need to read the old stories to know what's going on or who these characters and titles are. This is a brand new universe for Marvel to explore and reinvigorate. In a way it's like looking at the Ultimate Universe and trying to match those up with the Marvel U masterworks of similar titles. We may do it down the road for nostalgia, but for now, we want to let these new books stand on their own.

RUSE
SIGIL